The Perfect Business?

Southeast Asia

POLITICS, MEANING, AND MEMORY

David Chandler and Rita Smith Kipp

SERIES EDITORS

THE
PERFECT BUSINESS?

*Anti-trafficking and the Sex Trade
along the Mekong*

SVERRE MOLLAND

UNIVERSITY OF HAWAI'I PRESS   *Honolulu*

17 16 15 14 13 12   6 5 4 3 2 1

Library of Congress Cataloging-in-Publication Data

Molland, Sverre.

The perfect business? : anti-trafficking and the sex trade
along the Mekong / Sverre Molland.

  p. cm.—(Southeast Asia—politics, meaning, and memory)

Includes bibliographical references and index.

ISBN 978-0-8248-3610-8 (cloth : alk. paper)—
ISBN 978-0-8248-3653-5 (pbk. : alk. paper)

  1. Human trafficking—Laos—Prevention. 2. Human trafficking—
Thailand—Prevention. 3. Prostitution—Laos. 4. Prostitution—Thailand.
I. Title. II. Series: Southeast Asia—politics, meaning, memory.

HQ281.M63 2012

364.15'3409594—dc23

2012010485

University of Hawai'i Press books are printed on acid-free
paper and meet the guidelines for permanence and durability
of the Council on Library Resources.

Series designed by Richard Hendel

Printed by Sheridan Books, Inc.

Contents

Acknowledgments

THIS BOOK would never have materialized if it were not for the invaluable support from several individuals and institutions. First and foremost, I carry an eternal debt of gratitude to my dear wife, Samorn, and my two daughters, Stella and Astrid, for being extremely patient and supportive throughout this research project, which has not been the easiest to combine with family life. Samorn has also provided priceless feedback and criticisms on the book itself. I would like to express my sincere gratitude to Chris Lyttelton and Pál Nyiri for advice, support, and constructive criticisms throughout my research. I am also immensely grateful to Bridget Anderson, Marc Askew, Mary Beth Mills, David Chandler, Pamela Kelley, and one anonymous reviewer for their detailed criticisms of the manuscript. In the field, I would like to thank Manichan Keoviriyavong, Vilakhone Simahuck, and Prayoon Namprai for providing outstanding support in accomplishing what was very challenging and delicate fieldwork. Their help has enabled both access to and development of rapport with several informants who were not the easiest to come by. I would also like to thank Chulalongkorn University, the National Research Council of Thailand, and Norwegian Church Aid for facilitating various logistical arrangements relating to the execution of this research. On this note, I would in particular like to acknowledge Margrethe Volden as well as Supang Chantavanich and her staff for their generous support and willingness to take my project under their protective wings. I am also grateful to Grant Evans, who, besides providing intellectual inspiration in the field, encouraged me to pursue a "tandem ethnography" of both traffickers and anti-traffickers. A number of individuals provided helpful critical comments on early drafts and sections of the book: Greg Downey, Casimir Macgregor, Douangphet Sayanouso, Mukdawan Sakboon, Sumant Monty

Badami, Roy Juijsmans, Victoria Loblay, Guy Threlfo, Jessie Zhang, Robbie Peters, Anne Monchamp, and Rebecca Miller. Fragments of the book first appeared as parts of other publications (see the bibliography), and comments from anonymous readers of those portions have indirectly shaped this book. Special thanks go to Frances Happ, who kindly proofread large parts of the book. I would also like to thank Rosemary Wetherold, who has meticulously copyedited my manuscript, as well as Cheri Dunn for seeing through the final editorial stages of this book. Finally, I offer a big thank-you to all the anonymous individuals who volunteered their time to enlighten me on a topic I am still struggling to understand.

I Introduction
The Perfect Business?

First, we need to criminalize human trafficking. All countries
must ratify the United Nations anti-trafficking Protocol. Second, we must prevent victimization by teaching people about
their rights and protecting them. Third, we need to reduce
demand. Fourth, there must be an end to impunity. . . . Fifth
and lastly, we must protect the victims. If we think about it,
we understand that fighting human trafficking cuts across all
fundamental issues. It is about human rights, peace and security,
development and family health. In the most basic sense, it is
about preserving the fabric of society. That is why, to succeed,
we have to mainstream our fight against human trafficking
into broader programmes. From poverty reduction to reducing
gender discrimination.
> —Secretary-General Ban Ki-Moon's remarks to the
> General Assembly New York, 13 May 2009

IT IS EARLY MORNING. I am sitting with a group of project officers in a
small office in Vientiane. All the participants work in aid programs that
seek to combat trafficking in persons in the Lao Peoples' Democratic
Republic (PDR). I have previously proposed that one project manager,
Tom,[1] arrange an informal workshop where I could share some case studies from my own research. I explained that I was curious to learn how
anti-trafficking program workers would perceive these cases. Tom was
enthusiastic about the idea, suggesting not only that this could be an
opportunity for me to obtain data for my research but also that we could
treat the meeting as a training exercise for program officers. Hence the
purpose of this meeting is twofold: to strengthen project staff's skills

regarding victim identification and protection, and to allow me to gain insight into how anti-trafficking programs implement their victim support plans. I have brought along nine case studies to the meeting. We now read the fifth one:

> A bar owner tells a girl called Nok, who has been a sex worker in the bar for a while, that more girls are needed at the bar to sell sex. The owner promises to give Nok 10,000 baht if she can bring a girl from her village to sell sex. Nok goes back to her village, where she tells another girl that she can offer her a good job, but Nok does not tell her what the work is. When the new girl comes to the bar, the owner tells her that she has to sell sex and that she owes the owner 10,000 baht for the recruitment. The girl does not want to sell sex. The owner suggests that she can work in the bar, selling drinks but not selling sex. The girl agrees. After two months the girl sees how much money the other girls earn when they sell sex, and she decides she will do this too.

Silence. Then one meeting participant says, "The owner knows that with soft pressure she [the recruited girl] will do this." Tom adds, "It is trafficking because we have here displacement and indirect force, or pushing." Phetsamorn, a third participant, disagrees: she says this is mere prostitution and not trafficking. Tom objects, pointing out that this is trafficking for labor: "She arrives with debt. She has been displaced, lured, and exploited—it's trafficking." Phetsamorn responds, "But she can go home. Nothing holds her back!" Tom says, "No, she has debt to the bar."

So far a few participants have dominated the discussion, but now others are becoming involved. There is disagreement about how to "read" Nok. Is she a trafficker or not? And what should aid programs and the police do about cases like this? One informant recommends that we write down the "three elements of trafficking" on the whiteboard: movement, deception/force, and exploitation. As in so many other workshops, the definition from the United Nations protocol on human trafficking (UN 2000) is referenced when analyzing trafficking cases.

The discussion drifts into considerations of whether the girl in the case study can in any meaningful way leave the premises and to what extent the debt bonds her to the premises. And they discuss Nok. Is she a trafficker, given that she herself is subject to the same work conditions that might be seen as exploitative? In the end the discussion remains inconclusive, and most of the participants agree that "more information" is needed in order to judge whether this is a trafficking case.

Along the Mekong—Traffickers, Victims and Anti-traffickers

The preceding quotation from United Nations secretary-general Ban Ki-moon and account of the anti-trafficking group's discussion of Nok's case study foreshadow the three-layered composition of this book. Nok's story depicts the local context of recruitment and sex work along the Thai-Lao border. Ban Ki-moon's statement points to the international focus on human trafficking. And between the two are individuals like Tom and Phetsamorn, who work for anti-trafficking programs. Of course, trafficking activists—or anti-traffickers, as I refer to them in this book—are in many ways part of, and reproduce, conceptualizations of trafficking. Yet they also need to reconcile two worlds. They have to translate an international concern regarding human trafficking into programs and activities to be implemented on the ground. It is these three facets of trafficking—global trafficking discourse, anti-traffickers, and the local context of sex commerce—along the Thai-Lao border that this book seeks to illuminate.

The anti-traffickers' responses in the account above indicate the ambiguities inherent in marrying a legalistic definition of trafficking with on-the-ground realities—a challenge I have personally experienced, having previously worked as a project adviser for the Lao office of the UN Inter-Agency Project on Human Trafficking in the Greater Mekong Sub-Region (UNIAP). The hesitant responses also reflect the relative novelty of anti-trafficking programming. Far from being a well-established apparatus engaging in a straightforward combat against traffickers, such programming is precarious, as this book will elucidate.

It is only in the last few years that anti-trafficking has been on the agenda within the development aid industry in the Mekong region. I myself ended up working for UNIAP by happenstance. A friend of mine forwarded an advertisement from the Norwegian Ministry of Foreign Affairs website for a job with a regional anti-trafficking program in the Lao PDR. This position, which was fully funded by the Norwegian government, was restricted to Norwegian citizens, thereby limiting the number of qualified applicants. I had no previous experience in combating trafficking, but I did have some background in project management and an interest in the Southeast Asian region. Although I did not think I had the remotest chance of getting the job, I applied. To my surprise, I was offered the position. When I started working for UNIAP, I soon expressed my concern about my lack of experience related to anti-trafficking. My boss at the time responded half-jokingly, "Don't worry. In a few months everyone will see you as an expert." In this sense, anti-traffickers are pioneers, social agents who need to make sense of a frontier with which they are not necessarily familiar. Hence this book, in a general sense, is about what happens when development agencies become involved in fighting trafficking, and in particular, it describes how that process may unfold in a small Southeast Asian country such as Laos.

Translating an international discourse of trafficking into operational anti-trafficking programming, as evidenced in the previous vignette, tends to evoke idealized forms of knowledge that produce particular, yet uneven, effects on how local anti-trafficking strategies are shaped. That being said, the local sex industries along the Thai-Lao border not only differ from these idealized depictions but also remain in many respects untouched by them.

Although human trafficking has a long history and is often referred to as a "slave trade" (Bales 2005; Miller 2005), it nevertheless constitutes something new in contemporary globalized moral politics. Over the last few years, the world has witnessed a proliferation of media articles, international and national legislation, government action plans, and international aid programs, as well as action television series and movies, that in various ways address "trafficking in persons." As Ban Ki-moon's statement suggests, today human trafficking is not merely seen as a crime but is also caught up in notions of our global destiny. The phenomenon depicts struggles of life and death and speaks to what it means to be human, and the increasing use of the term "trafficking survivors" to refer to its victims is no coincidence (US State Department 2006, 2007). It is not only survival of victims but survival of a global morality that makes trafficking such a powerful trope. The increasing attention to trafficking raises questions of ontology: Does it reflect a real increase in global trafficking? Or are there other forces at play? It is not possible to separate these questions. The meaning of the term "human trafficking" is not self-evident. On the contrary, the term can take on a range of different meanings and can shape actions in various ways. Therefore it is crucial to explore both trafficking itself and the institutions and actors that use this concept in their everyday practice. Any meaningful study of trafficking must examine the interconnections between mobility and labor practices, on the one hand, and the organizations and actors that seek to combat trafficking, on the other.

There is an almost knee-jerk tendency to associate trafficking with commercial sex. This is particularly evident in the way the media report on the topic and, more recently, in how the film industry portrays the subject in movies and television shows on "sex trafficking." This book is limited to exploring the commercial sex industry along the Thai-Lao border, with a specific focus on the border towns of Vientiane and Nong Kai, and hence might be guilty of reinforcing stereotypical images of sex trafficking. The decision to take this approach was primarily a methodological one.

Clearly, trafficking may include forms of exploitation other than those related to sex. The existence of sweatshops and deplorable working conditions for migrant workers is well known in many parts of the world. In both Thailand and Laos, anti-trafficking programs have pointed to trafficking for domestic, factory, and construction work, as well as alleged trafficking of men and boys onto fishing boats (Pongkhao 2007; UNIAP et al. 2004). In fact, some of the best-known alleged cases of trafficking are unrelated to sex trafficking. In 2000 several Chinese labor migrants were found suffocated inside a container on a port in Dover, England, sparking considerable media attention (Pieke and Biao 2007). Eight years later, a chilling replay of those events unfolded in Thailand when fifty-four Burmese labor migrants suffocated in a truck heading for Phuket (Kongrut and Nukaew 2008). The Thai government was quick to discredit the idea that the incident constituted trafficking. A senior Thai police officer stated: "This initial finding may run counter to general sentiment and reports which labelled this as a case of human trafficking. But there is a difference between human smuggling and trafficking, it's a matter of degree" (ibid.). The Thai government argued that because both Thai and international law define trafficking as having the purpose of placing a migrant in an exploitative labor situation, this case should be treated as "people smuggling" because labor exploitation had not yet taken place, thereby justifying deportation (as opposed to legal protection) of the migrants. This claim was, however, a point of considerable contention. At around the same time, Chulalongkorn University professor, Supang Chantavanich (2008) wrote in the *Bangkok Post:*

> The anti–human trafficking law states clearly that migrants who have been cheated to come to work in Thailand and are being exploited, are victims of trafficking. The 67 survivors who paid 5,000 baht to brokers to come to Thailand are clearly those who have been exploited by illegal recruiters. Even though they have not started working yet, they must be considered victims and placed under custody at shelter homes, not in prisons.

That the transportation of the Burmese migrants in itself was exploitative—indeed fatal—undoubtedly blurred the boundaries between legislative definitions of people smuggling and human trafficking. At the same time, the incident highlights how the labeling of migrants can be used strategically. Such ambiguities become particularly pronounced when a government, academics, international organizations, and nongovernmental organizations (NGOs) contest a dramatic case like this in the media. But the implications here are far wider. Migration trajectories do not come neatly prepackaged for anti-traffickers to respond to; each carries its own particularities and ambiguities, that must be dealt with on the microsocial level of anti-trafficking program activities. This raises a larger question of how anti-trafficking programs deal with a social reality that might not fit their own models and definitions. Such ambiguities are further reinforced when it comes to sex commerce, since the question of consent is subject to considerable contestation.

Hence the point of departure for this book consists of straightforward questions: Who is a victim and who is a trafficker? And according to whom? How does recruitment into the sex industry in Laos and Thailand unfold? And how does it compare with representations in aid reports? What is the relationship between life experience within an oscillatory sex industry along the Thai-Lao border and aid programs that combat trafficking? What does it mean to assert that trafficking in persons is demand driven? How does such a proposition reflect on how both mobility and sex commerce unfold? What makes it possible to ask such questions, and what effects does asking them produce? And how do such questions frame how anti-traffickers understand their subject matter?

In 2000 the first international legal definition of trafficking emerged in the United Nations' *Protocol to Prevent, Suppress and Punish Trafficking in Persons, Especially Women and Children* (2000, 2). Article 3 of the protocol states:

(a) "Trafficking in persons" shall mean the recruitment, transportation, transfer, harbouring or receipt of persons, by means of the threat or use of force or other forms of coercion, of abduction, of fraud, of deception, of the abuse of power or of a position of vulnerability or of the giving or receiving of payments or benefits to achieve the consent of a person having control over another person, for the purpose of exploitation. Exploitation shall include, at a minimum, the exploitation of the prostitution of others or other forms of sexual exploitation, forced labour or services, slavery or practices similar to slavery, servitude or the removal of organs;

(b) The consent of a victim of trafficking in persons to the intended exploitation set forth in subparagraph (a) of this article shall be irrelevant where any of the means set forth in subparagraph (a) have been used;

(c) The recruitment, transportation, transfer, harbouring or receipt of a child for the purpose of exploitation shall be considered "trafficking in persons" even if this does not involve any of the means set forth in subparagraph (a) of this article;

(d) "Child" shall mean any person under eighteen years of age.

At this stage, I will address only four aspects of this definition. First, the definition is made up of (1) movement of a migrant, (2) facilitated by certain means (threats, coercion, deception, etc.), for (3) a specific purpose—that is, exploitation. These are "the three elements of trafficking" to which Tom, Phetsamorn, and the other anti-traffickers referred in the story recounted above. Second, the definition makes a distinction in cases of children, where the "means" is deemed irrelevant. Thus any movement of a person under the age of eighteen for the purpose of exploitation is defined as a case of trafficking, regardless of that person's consent. Third, focusing on the prelude to labor exploitation (i.e., the nonconsensual recruitment and transport of migrants) allows considerable leverage for governments (and others) to selectively emphasize migration rather than labor exploitation. Fourth, agency is doubly enacted as a yardstick for determining a trafficking case, as the definition refers both to various means of manipulating consent and to the ability to place a person into what is deemed an exploitative situation. Consequently the trafficking definition evokes a dyadic conception of agency. By this I mean that the definition focuses on whether a third party (an individual or a group) deceives or coerces a migrant into an exploitative labor situation. The determination of trafficking becomes primarily a question of a relationship between a deemed victim and a deemed trafficker or traffickers and ignores circumstantial reasons as to why a migrant ends up in a given labor situation.

The UN trafficking protocol has become immensely influential. It has been ratified by many countries and affected national legislation, and it is widely used by anti-trafficking programs. As will become clear, however, the protocol's definition contains a range of contradictions and ambiguities that have multiple effects.

Perfections and Imperfections

For those who stand to benefit from this crime, human trafficking remains almost the perfect business. Supply is constant, with large numbers of people crossing countries and borders in search of better opportunities, and intermediaries along the way willing to deliver them to factories, brothels, fishing boats and private homes, or onto the streets to beg. Costs are low, and mostly include an initial one-off investment to "buy" the victim, or a loan to pay back the debt they have incurred in transit, to be recovered at extortionist rates—plus perhaps a small, regular "tax" to law enforcement authorities. For those at the end of the trafficking chain, human trafficking is almost the perfect business. (UNIAP 2006)

To date the academic literature on human trafficking is limited, and most discussions have focused on questions of migrants' agency with reference to social control and human rights concerns. Such endeavors are welcome and have underscored much commentary within the global prostitution debate (Doezema 2000; Kempadoo 2005) and in critiques of various governments' migration regimes (Berman 2003; Shangera 2005). Anti-trafficking programs themselves have also come under scrutiny, with some people viewing them as contributing to the betterment of humankind (Bales 2005), while others take a far more skeptical stance (Agustín 2007). However, the trafficking literature to date has tended to confine its discussion to debates regarding prostitution policy and migration control. What has thus far been almost totally overlooked is the simple fact that in regions where trafficking is deemed rife—such as the Mekong region—anti-trafficking activities are usually implemented by development aid programs, often in collaboration with government and local partners.

To suggest that trafficking is primarily a Trojan horse of anti-immigration and anti-prostitution agendas is too simplistic and misses the important point that individuals and organizations that take part in combating human trafficking straddle moral-political controversies over border control and prostitution. Hence, this book offers an analysis of the interrelation between global attention to trafficking, localized unfolding of labor migration, and anti-trafficking programming. Whereas much research has explored how both immigration and prostitution policy intersect with public concerns regarding human trafficking, few studies have provided a detailed account of how the anti-trafficking sector makes tacit assumptions regarding where and how trafficking takes place, who is trafficked, and by whom. The quotation above highlights this trend, by portraying trafficking as a "perfect business" governed by the laws of supply and demand and operating as a seamless organic whole. This book is concerned with operationalization. It considers the way anti-traffickers imagine trafficking to "function" and how these ideas compare with recruitment practices within the sex industry along the Thai-Lao border, as well as how anti-traffickers' own programmatic activities shape these same notions. Hence, a central argument of this book is that, rather than being a "perfect business," human trafficking is characterized by imperfections that are not easily grasped through policy directives and bureaucratic maneuvers.

Ideal forms of knowledge are often espoused by trafficking reports, media, legislation, UN agencies, NGOs, and governments. Allow me to foreshadow this imagery in the form of three concentric circles. At the center, we have the victim and the trafficker, an asymmetrical dyad with an imagined clear-cut boundary between them. Surrounding this dyad, we have the all-knowing gaze of organized crime. Traffickers and their entourages are commonly imagined to be the most extreme expression of contemporary forms of global capitalism gone wrong—a kind of hedonistic and dark maximizing agent, gone off the rails. In turn, the traffickers and victims who are embedded in organized crime networks are imagined to act in a marketplace that straddles international borders and operates according to the mechanical laws of supply and demand. There is one underlying common denominator among these concentric circles: perfections. The victim is the perfect pawn representing total innocence and a total deprivation of agency. The traffickers are perfect villains, a pure form of evil with total control and the ability to adapt to market opportunities. And the marketplace where all this takes place is perfect—a classical liberal economic marketplace subject to only a handful of simple and predictable laws of cause and effect. It is this formulaic and quintessential imagery that this book critiques. That being said, the anti-trafficking sector is far from being a homogenous group. There is a great deal of variety in the way trafficking is understood among aid programs, government officials, and NGOs. Yet the somewhat burlesque depiction of ideal types I give here is commonplace, and it has real consequences for how human trafficking is dealt with in practice. International trafficking discourse and the move toward perfections in the form of a market metaphor constitute Part I of this book.

Perhaps unsurprisingly, migration and the commercial sex industry in the Mekong towns of Vientiane and Nong Kai are rather different from the idealized depiction of trafficking. Sex commerce and recruitment along the Thai-Lao border are characterized by paradox and contradiction, and Part II therefore explores these imperfections. It

critiques the assumption that there are neat distinctions between victim and perpetrator, underpinned by organized crime, which in turn is
taking place in a mechanical cross-border marketplace. Part II points
to differences between the map (trafficking discourse) and the terrain
(commercial sex and recruitment along the Thai-Lao border), raising
the question of how anti-traffickers along the Thai-Lao border navigate
between these two poles of perfections and imperfections.

Indeed, anti-traffickers are unable to reconcile the disjuncture
between imperfections and perfections. They are, as elaborated in Part
III, "betwixt and between" (Turner 1967). More often than not, simplistic models of trafficking take precedence over the imperfect realities. In fact, anti-traffickers depend in several ways on such models in
their everyday work as they become meaning-making entities. The
effect is that human trafficking discourse reproduces atomized and
decontextualized imageries of migration and sex commerce within the
local trafficking sector. This diverts attention away from what is essential to understanding migration and sex commerce along the Lao-Thai
border—that is, careful attention to social relationships. But trafficking
discourse is not reproduced in a straightforward manner. Although trafficking discourse shapes (but does not determine) the practices of anti-
traffickers, the local sex industry itself remains remarkably detached. In
several respects the social worlds of victims and traffickers on the one
hand, and anti-traffickers on the other, pushes and pulls in many directions, making them strangely separate, yet interconnected in subtle
and surprising ways. In fact, traffickers and anti-traffickers are in some
ways similar, as they both externalize their complicity in events through
plays of selective ignorance and willed forgetting.

Laos and Thailand

Trafficking in persons is commonly embedded in understandings of
modernization and development, particularly the way trafficking is
parasitic on labor migration, which is understood to flow from poorer
areas to destination points that promise opportunity and income. Thailand and Laos reflect this view. Laos is categorized as a least developed
country by the United Nations (UNDP and NSC 2006) and has only
recently opened its borders after several years of isolationist socialist

policies (Evans 1998). By international and even regional standards, Laos is characterized as a landlocked boondocks that is making careful and anxious steps into the "dangerous adventure" (Giddens 1994, 59) of modernity. The Lao population of only 5.6 million is primarily agrarian (UNDP and NSC 2006). It is governed by the Pathet Lao, a one-party authoritarian regime that came to power in 1975 after the turmoil of the Vietnam War. Like its political mentors—Vietnam and (increasingly) China—the Lao People's Democratic Republic maintains a nominal status as a communist country despite significant changes in its economic sphere. Since the late 1980s, market reforms have been introduced, and there has been a halting liberalization of social controls. Although Laos has had strong political ties with Vietnam, economic liberalization since 1975 has resulted in increasing interactions with some of its neighbors, particularly Thailand. Laos joined the Association of Southeast Asian Nations (ASEAN) in the early 1990s within the rubric of regional market integration (Rigg 2005; Walker 1999). In policy terms, the Lao government sees itself as transforming from landlocked to land-linked, as exemplified by numerous road projects and border crossings. However, this regional reengagement has made socioeconomic disparities across its border more apparent, particularly in comparison with Thailand.

Thailand and Laos are culturally, socially, and linguistically very close, and although cross-border movement has a long history, out-migration from Laos to Thailand appears to have increased considerably since the early 1990s. In contrast to Laos, Thailand is in many respects a regional vanguard, with a population of 64 million, developed export industries, and superior economic opportunities and standards of living. Thailand also provides public spaces and infrastructure (such as shopping malls) that enable modern forms of leisure experiences. Data on migration remain scarce, but several aid reports, the majority produced by anti-trafficking programs in Laos and Thailand, draw attention to considerable cross-border migration to Thailand (UNDP and NSC 2006). Recent data (UNIAP 2008a) point to there being almost two hundred thousand registered Lao migrants in Thailand, and the actual number is likely to be much higher than this, considering that many migrants cross the border without official papers. Several studies document Lao villages in which migration to Thailand appears to be institutionalized and is simply part of what young villagers aspire to do—that is, go to Thailand to "see the world" and earn money. One study from southern Laos depicts this trend:

> Migration to Thailand for work is a fact of life in many Lao villages, especially those close to the border. . . . In Nong Snow, a village bordering the Mekong in Lakhonephieng District, Salavan Province, villagers seem to not even make a distinction between the two sides of the border, going back and forth as if it did not exist, for example to buy goods in Thailand every Saturday at the Pakseng village Flea Market. Villagers here migrate in great numbers: in 2003, 15% of all Nong Snow inhabitants migrated for work in Thailand at one point or another. . . . In Xox (Khanthabouri District, Savannakhet Province) researchers struggled to find a single household without a member working in Thailand. (UNIAP et al. 2004, 23–24)

It is noteworthy that United Nations Development Programme's national human development report on Laos for 2006 estimates that the total amount of remittances from Lao migrants in Thailand might exceed US$100 million, making migrant labor one of the largest export industries of Laos (UNDP and NSC 2006).

Thailand and Laos also contrast with regard to commercial sex. Thailand's sex industry is sizeable and well known internationally. In contrast, few would associate Laos with commercial sex. Although rarely reported in the media, Laos, with its limited population and widespread poverty, has a growing sex industry within its borders (Lyttleton 1999a; UNICEF and Ministry of Labour and Social Welfare 2001). Furthermore, both Thailand and Laos are associated with "hot spots" of human trafficking. In 2006 the United Nations Office for Drugs and Crime ranked Thailand in the top ten worst countries where twenty-first-century slavery occurs (UNODC 2006c), and the US State Department in its controversial annual *Trafficking in Persons Report* (2006) ranked Laos in its tier three, which in principle can result in bilateral sanctions and unfavorable voting in bodies such as the World Bank. Simultaneously, and partly in response, both the Thai and Lao governments (as well as organizations and development projects) have paid considerable attention to efforts to combat human trafficking, as evident in a steady increase in trafficking projects as well as bilateral and multilateral agreements.

Human Trafficking and the Question of Power

Human trafficking ultimately raises questions of power and agency. On the one hand, we have a dyad of traffickers and victims in the former controls the latter—a question of domination. On the other, we have anti-traffickers who attempt to alter this very same dyad of victims and traffickers—a question of transformation. Thus we are dealing with interpersonal relationships, but at the same time we must also examine how institutions shape practices and vice versa. Throughout this book, I explore traffickers, victims, and anti-traffickers in light of three theoretical approaches to power. First, a focus on discourse brings to light how institutional practices do not merely respond to an external world but also take part in shaping it. Second, practice theory allows us to consider how individuals and groups employ a range of strategies and maneuvers to achieve certain ends but, in doing so, internalize these very same ends. Third, Jean-Paul Sartre's (1957) analysis of bad faith brings to light how individuals who in principle can pursue different courses of action come to terms with their own conduct by attempting to distance themselves from their complicity in events. These three echelons of power are useful to contemplate when analyzing human trafficking, for they allow us to appreciate both limits and excesses of power in terms of interpersonal relationships as well as interactions between institutions, the individuals who occupy positions within them, and the peoples presumably touched by them.

"Discourse analysis" draws its legacy from the works of Foucault, which examine the ways in which complex relations of institutions, practices, and technologies shape individuals' perceptions of themselves and their surroundings.[2] A particular focus is placed on how issues related to government increasingly involve techniques for the optimization of life (such as health and productivity) where individuals internalize discursive knowledge through modes of self-regulation ("the conduct of conduct"). A key question is how these techniques shape populations in ways that allow for their easier control and regulation. Foucault has called this type of power "governmentality."

This view of power has been influential in anthropological analyses of development aid, as reflected in the writings of Arturo Escobar (1994) and James Ferguson (1990). Both scholars draw explicitly from Foucault's concept of discourse and governmentality, arguing that although development aid does not necessarily result in intended outcomes, it does produce certain, often unintended, effects. They both argue that in the postwar years poverty and "the poor" have been increasingly perceived as a problem that requires legitimate intervention by development institutions. Escobar (1994) argues that developmental discourse enables new ways of both acting and being, where most people of the third world come to define themselves by what they lack, thus paving the way for a range of normalizing interventions (such as health care, sanitation, and nutrition). Similarly, James Ferguson in his *Anti-Politics Machine* (1990) shows that although development institutions tend to be technocratic in character, they may have political effects. Focusing on Lesotho, Ferguson demonstrates that development programs are always apolitical in the sense that they perpetually articulate development in managerial terms as opposed to recognizing local political asymmetries. Because of this discrepancy between local realities and instrumental (and apolitical) depictions by aid programs, development projects rarely succeed, according to Ferguson. Yet the failure to achieve intended results does not equate to benign results. Pointing to the side effects of development practice, Ferguson asserts that the machinery of development results in increased (yet unintended) bureaucratic power and control. Hence one of the essential points of both Ferguson's and Escobar's arguments is that development discourse enables an aid apparatus that exercises increasing control and regulation of the third world.

Such arguments have been influential and deserve attention in this study of trafficking, because they deal directly with power relations between development aid institutions, the practices that unfold from them, and the social arena in which aid programs seek to intervene. However, discourse analysis has become subject to considerable criticisms, including the charge that it implies a monolithic and deterministic view of power (Brigg 2002; Mosse 2005). Consequently, this form of analysis has a tendency to come uncomfortably close to presuming that discourse is what creates and causes social action.[3] Although development programs may be driven by their internal bureaucratic logics as opposed to the social arena in which they seek to develop (Ferguson 1990), how discourse translates into social practice—whether it produces "docile" self-governing subjects, is reappropriated, is resisted, or something else—cannot be axiomatically presumed. Rather, it must be subject to careful study of social actors, which is to say that it must explore both the social world of sex work, migration, and recruitment on one hand, and the everyday life practices of individuals who work for anti-trafficking programs on the other.

Trafficking raises questions of the intentional subject. As we will see in later chapters, agency is commonly understood in a utilitarian fashion. The notion of maximization of profit is strong in trafficking literature, not only in its conception of "traffickers" but also in the way the larger "trafficking economy" functions where rational choice models are ubiquitously implied. An obvious problem with a utilitarian view of agency is that it tends to treat agents in a mechanistic fashion, portraying reason as being outside, and prior to, social interaction (Emirbayer and Mische 1998). In contrast, praxis theory has drawn attention to the embodied social agent, where practical, as opposed to discursive, knowledge is emphasized (Bourdieu 1977 [1972]; Giddens 1984; Ortner 1984). Similarly to utilitarianism, praxis theory stresses that practice is always in part governed by agency. Social agents are capable of comprehending their own actions and adopting a range of strategies in their lives to achieve certain ends. That is, they seek to acquire different forms of capital. Simultaneously, such strategies are shaped by social, political, and cultural structures, or fields (Bourdieu 1977 [1972]). Through the course of life, social actors internalize such fields as sets of dispositions, which Bourdieu calls the habitus (ibid.). Consequently, social actors seek to gain forms of capital that are valued within a given field. Hence praxis theory is what we might call "an economy of the proper place" (de Certeau 1988, 55), which draws attention to the interrelation of how social actors strategically seek resources and positions (capital) yet by doing so internalize dispositions (the habitus) that shape (but do not determine) action (practice). Praxis theory thus allows us to illuminate ways in which traffickers, victims, and anti-traffickers seek various ends (i.e., capital) but at the same time are influenced by the surroundings of these pursuits (the habitus).

Such processes raise a broader question of the relationship between agency and structure. As will become evident, trafficking literature sees agency not with reference to structure but primarily in terms of a dyad—that is, whether a third party has actively manipulated a migrant's consent for the purpose of labor exploitation. In this way agency is understood neither as embedded in the subject nor in relation to a constellation of structural forces. Trafficking discourse perceives agency primarily in intersubjective terms, privileging a focus on the relationship between a trafficker and a victim. Yet it sees this relationship as resembling a zero-sum game. Traffickers and exploiters have a totalized form of agency. Victims have none. Paradoxically, although trafficking definitions presume a dyadic conception of agency, trafficking discourse has in fact a tendency to draw attention away from social relationships. This has in part to do with its insistence on ideal models, which has the effect of producing totalizing caricatures.

Intention and agency lead us back to the question of power and domination. Trafficking literature has a tendency to compartmentalize certain "yardsticks" to determine what may or may not compromise agency; as a result certain forms of domination are privileged while others are ignored. In contrast, academic literature relating to agency is full of examples where social agents do not overtly resist but internalize and participate in their own domination. Drawing on Sartre's existential analysis of bad faith, Nancy Scheper-Hughes (1992a) has shown in her study of hunger among squatters in Brazil that social actors—the poor and medical practitioners alike—act in an economy of bad faith. That is, they deny themselves as subjects by externalizing their own complicity in events. This does not mean that the unconscious, or a highly calculating purposive form of consciousness, governs social action. As Sartre himself pointed out, bad faith is still faith (Sartre 1957, 67). It is a process through which social agents are able to engage in an act of self-deception[4] by externalizing their own complicity. Whereas discourse analysis places emphasis on what limits and enables agency, an analysis of bad faith considers agency itself a problem.[5] Hence bad faith is particularly useful in coming to terms with individuals who have the upper hand in asymmetrical relations of power. Yet the way individuals come to terms with their own conduct does not take place in a vacuum. As Arthur Kleinman and Erin Fitz-Henry (2007) have pointed out, acts of bad faith must be understood in their social, economic, and political context. Even in the case where social agents are authors of extreme violence, "our affect is always both internal and external to us—located as much within the contours of our bodies as within the shifting parameters of our sociopolitical worlds" (ibid., 64).

In contrast to the anti-trafficking community's portrayal of trafficking as a highly conscious coercive or deceptive process, the deceptive recruitment that at times takes place along the Thai-Lao border can best be understood as a form of bad faith on the part of both recruiters and recruits, as it (for reasons to be explored) takes on a trope of helping, which allows subjective actions to be externalized and complicity thereby denied. Furthermore, I suggest that to understand how one individual comes to take an active part in placing another person in a situation against his or her will, one needs to emphasize "the shifting parameters of our sociopolitical worlds." As we will see, at play is a range of processes that allow social actors to rationalize their actions, and the social environment in which social agents find themselves is a key to this.

When I draw attention to bad faith, I am referring not only to victims and traffickers but also to anti-traffickers. Just as Derrida (2001), with reference to contemporary immigration policies in Europe, has demonstrated the simultaneous universal yet conditional imperative of hospitality within the concept of cosmopolitanism, human trafficking produces a peculiarly inherent polarity. Trafficking appears to enable, protect, and advocate for marginalized migrants' agency, yet by doing so, it constrains what it attempts to enable by projecting a particular framework onto this effect. Both a technocratic developmental apparatus and a legalistic framework regarding trafficking in persons shape development programs that combat trafficking, thereby projecting certain parameters for how categorization of victimhood is understood by development practitioners.

However, formulaic views within the anti-trafficking sector do not necessarily fit neatly with the social world of migration and sex commerce. We must take note that the relationship between traffickers, victims, and anti-traffickers is a two-way street. Without denying that many anti-trafficking programs provide real and meaningful support for individuals who have been subject to deplorable treatment, we must also note that, as Montgomery (2001b) has pointed out in regard to the iconic nature of "child prostitution," anti-traffickers depend on the imagery of the trafficked victim to give legitimacy to the very existence of anti-trafficking programs. Hence it is perfectly reasonable to ask who needs whom.

Trafficking discourse tacitly distinguishes between overt and covert forms of domination, with human trafficking programs focusing on the latter and tending to either ignore or be at the very least ambivalent about the former. When domination is discursively framed using overt and covert categories, it becomes notoriously difficult to apply such frameworks to the social field of recruitment within the Thai and Lao sex industries. The important point is that anti-trafficking programs find themselves in a process whereby they attempt to make a fluid, contradictory, and ambivalent social reality fit ideal types of knowledge in order to make it legible (Scott 1998b) and receptive to anti-trafficking interventions. This raises a broader question of how this process is negotiated, and we will later see that this negotiation allows for deliberate ignorance—that is, bad faith.

Approaches to Research

A central approach in this book is the drifting between me as an anthropologist investigating sex work and recruitment along the Thai-Lao border and my own previous status as a project adviser for an anti-trafficking program. My own movement between the worlds of traffickers, victims, and anti-traffickers means that this study is of necessity multisited both socially and spatially. George Marcus has pointed out that one of the strengths of multisited research is its "capacity to make connections through translations and tracings among distinctive discourses from site to site" (1995, 100–101). The concept of trafficking is so closely linked with the spatial imagery of borders that it became somewhat of an imperative to research both sides of the Thai-Lao border. This aspect of the research implies not only making comparisons of the two sides but also exploring translocal linkages (Hannerz 2003).

More specifically, this book places its main focus on a border zone between Laos and Thailand where Vientiane and Nong Kai are located. Vientiane is the Lao capital and is situated on the northeastern side of the Mekong River. Nong Kai is a Thai town located approximately forty kilometers downstream from Vientiane. Although the total population of Vientiane Province is approximately 700,000, the urban population is less than 300,000 (State Planning Committee 1997; Vallee et al. 2007). Conversely, the population of Nong Khai Province is approximately 800,000, with 20 percent living in Nong Khai municipality (UNESCAP 2001). The two cities are physically proximate and are connected by the Friendship Bridge, which is the main land crossing between Thailand and Laos.

There are several reasons why this book places its focus on this border zone. During my time working for the UN anti-trafficking project in Laos, I saw the limitations of conducting research in village communities where migrants come from. In trying to understand not only migratory practices but also the nature of migrants' labor situations, being in a village community carries with it a challenge: one finds oneself in the village, yet the object of research remains far away. This is precisely the problem with many of the "rapid assessment" studies on trafficking in Laos that are carried out among aid organizations; they are all attempts to understand outcomes of migration trajectories through after-the-fact interviews[6] with returning migrants and family members (Doussantousse and Keovonghit 2006; Phetsiriseng 2001). This approach is taken partly because of the political constraints faced by anti-trafficking programs, as well as the familiarity of development aid programs with rural development in specific geographic areas (a development project always has a project site). Governments are far more accommodating when research can serve socioeconomic development in rural village communities, rather than having aid organizations uncover abuse and exploitation within various labor sectors. This is partly why anti-trafficking programs attempt to emphasize the "demand" side of trafficking, which shifts focus from source communities toward where the "exploitative situation" is taking place. Hence, I decided to carry out research, not where migrants come from, but where they end up. And for pragmatic reasons, I decided to focus solely on the commercial sex industry. Although prostitution is surrounded by much sensationalism and is commonly associated with "clandestine economies," it is nonetheless easier for a male researcher to access establishments that cater to sex commerce than to access private households (to research domestic labor), factories, or fishing boats. Of all semilegal segments of labor markets, commercial sex is after all one of the very few in which work is conducted in a semipublic space, depending as it does on customers' transitory visits.

So where are Lao women trafficked into the sex industry? Ironically, even after working with anti-trafficking in Laos for about three years, I was incapable of accounting for any specific places where Lao women were trafficked, let alone voluntarily migrated into the sex industry. Within the Lao anti-trafficking sector it is fairly well documented that migrants—whether trafficked or voluntary—go to Thailand, and some attention has also been paid to internal trafficking (UNICEF and Ministry of Labour and Social Welfare 2004). However, when it comes to more specific data, the picture is contradictory and sketchy. To date, few of the identified victims who have come through the official repatriation program between Laos and Thailand are known to have worked in the sex industry (IOM 2004a). Some reports note the presence of Lao women and girls working in the commercial sex industry in various places in Thailand, including Nong Kai, but are silent on more specific whereabouts (UNICEF and Ministry of Labour and Social Welfare 2004; Wille 2001).

Furthermore, a report by UNIAP et al. (2004), which is to date the most detailed and in-depth study on Lao trafficking,[7] did not encounter clear evidence of Lao women being trafficked into the sex industry, although there were signs of women working voluntarily in the "entertainment" sector. This contrasts with the aforementioned UNICEF report, which claims that 35 percent of trafficking victims from Laos are delivered into the sex industry (UNICEF and Ministry of Labour and Social Welfare 2004). However, despite claims of considerable amounts of "sex trafficking," the UNICEF report offers little detail as to where this form of exploitation is taking place. Provinces and sometimes cities (such as Bangkok) are mentioned, but to conduct my research, I needed to know the names of streets and venues so that I could identify specific locales where trafficking was assumed to be taking place. Before commencing my research in 2005, I discussed possible research sites with colleagues and individuals from other anti-trafficking programs. I soon came to realize that nobody had specific knowledge of the whereabouts of Lao trafficked victims. Nor was anyone capable of suggesting actual places where Lao women worked in the Thai sex industry voluntarily.

I would get responses such as "Perhaps somewhere in Bangkok" or "I think you should look along the border." The fact that, despite the presence of twelve anti-trafficking programs in Laos, nobody had clear and specific information of the whereabouts of Lao women who worked in the sex industry is intriguing. This lack of information is partly due to the difficulties of researching trafficking from a source community.[8]

For this reason I carried out initial research in four sites, all differing as gravity points for migration: Bangkok, Houaxay (northwestern Laos), Vientiane, and Nong Kai. In Vientiane and Nong Kai, I had the most success making logistical arrangements (research assistance, access to sites, etc.), and because of the proximity of the cities, they proved the most promising for comparative and analytical purposes. Although I will make some reference to both Bangkok and Houaxay, the crux of this research concerns the border zone of Nong Kai and Vientiane: its traffickers, its victims, and the local anti-trafficking community. It is important to emphasize that my focus on Vientiane and Nong Kai does not mean that the anti-trafficking community had singled out these localities as hot spots, and neither do I intend to. As has already been noted, the anti-trafficking community has great difficulty in pinpointing exactly where trafficking is taking place.

The main reason for including different types of venues where sex commerce is obtainable has to do with assumptions within the anti-trafficking sector, where attention is sometimes paid to different segments of the sex industry. Data on a sensitive topic such as the organization of sex commerce (and the recruitment within it) are not easily captured by survey methods, because the researcher must make a substantial investment in building rapport with informants. Hence this research used the method of participant observation, which requires the researcher to spend considerable time within the social world studied in order to develop relationships and trust. A crucial aspect of participant observation—in addition to interviews, informal conversations, and observations—is interaction with informants over time, as it allows dissonances between what people say, do, and believe to come to light. Furthermore, it enables an approximation of how informants themselves understand their own life worlds. The way individuals within the local sex industry perceive recruitment is very different from what is assumed by anti-trafficking programs. In both Vientiane and Nong Kai, I built relationships with informants by visiting the same venues repeatedly throughout the duration of research. Although I visited a range of venues, the Vientiane research focused in particular on three beer shops and two high-end venues, whereas research in Nong Kai primarily explored three restaurant/karaoke venues and a handful of brothels and escort-style venues. On both sides of the border, informants included sex workers, recruiters, venue managers, and, to a lesser extent, clients.[9]

My own position as a Western male researcher obviously affects my interactions with informants. It is not uncommon for individuals who are associated with the sex industry to present different identities and narratives, as do people in any walk of life. This raises a question of the credibility of informants. The way my informants perceived me varied throughout the course of my research but can be summed up as "potential patron." On initial visits, informants not surprisingly perceived me as a client seeking remunerated sex. However, after I had visited these venues repeatedly and introduced myself as a student (and not a customer) who was researching such venues on both sides of the border, my identity as a "client" gradually faded and changed. It was commonplace for informants to associate me with health programs, and I often experienced both venue owners and sex workers initiating discussions regarding health checks and condom use. The reason for this, no doubt, is that many entertainment venues have regular contact with health programs. Hence "client" and "health worker" share one thing in common in the Thai-Lao context; they are both potential sources of material support. It was therefore not uncommon for informants to stress their poverty, understate their income, and posture "newness" to the industry. These identity formations and nuances of interactions can be difficult to grasp in short visits. By revisiting the same venues and becoming acquainted with several informants over long periods, it became possible to double-check information, at times cross-check claims with other informants, and observe social interactions in these venues over time.

In many respects my interactions with anti-trafficking informants were similar to those within the sex industry: sitting around a table and sharing a few drinks (beers in entertainment venues, coffee in anti-traffickers' offices) while discussing the mysterious workings of migration and sex commerce. Because I had previously worked for a UN anti-trafficking program, I knew most of my anti-trafficking informants in this context, many of them being friends and colleagues. I was also able to attend some workshops and meetings with organizations that combat trafficking. Anti-traffickers are peculiar informants, as they are "subject-object" informants. I was interested not merely in understanding them but also in knowing how they understood my other set of informants—traffickers, victims, and venue managers.

I conducted fieldwork from August 2005 to October 2006, with the help of a research assistant. Three individuals assisted in this capacity. Two of the research assistants were male and one female, and all had previous and/or current experience working for development programs, including anti-trafficking and health projects involved with the entertainment industry. There were several reasons for hiring a research assistant. I was operating in a bilingual environment (Thai and Lao), and with my limited language abilities it was unrealistic to carry out this research without local research assistance. All of the research assistants were trilingual (speaking Thai, Lao, and English) and knew the research sites very well. Their knowledge of the area helped me identify venues to visit and aided tremendously in developing rapport with informants. I carried out all research among anti-traffickers myself, however, as all of them were competent in English.

Researching human trafficking evokes several connotations in terms of risk. The methodology for this research was approved by my university's ethics committee, thus allowing me to contextualize specific problems in terms of both ethics and access. Many anti-trafficking organizations associate trafficking with the "low end" of the sex industry, and one UN official told me when I was planning my research that such venues were out of bounds for Western researchers. "*Farangs* [Westerners] will not be allowed in!" he said. Contrary to this assertion, I was able to access a range of venue types, from high-end venues to low-end ones in the slums of Bangkok, including brothels, escort networks, restaurants, karaoke clubs, and bars of various sorts. Generally, I found that commercial sex venues, whether I went with a male or female research assistant, were remarkably accommodating in both Laos and Thailand. My presence was rarely questioned, and I was even able to live for a while in one brothel masquerading as a hotel, which was the closest I got to the classical anthropological achievement of "when the natives build you a hut." This is not to say that access was a smooth process. For instance, in some venues in Nong Kai, sex workers were subject to partial confinement. It would have been possible to access sex workers in these places by "buying their time" and exchanging money for conversation (and not sex) in the bedroom. I am aware that both investigative journalists and some anti-trafficking projects have done this, but I chose not to do so, as I believed this would cross the boundary of informed consent. I do not think a sex worker can meaningfully consent to a conversation after the manager has been paid for the worker's time under such restrictive conditions. Instead, in these venues I was able—through informal friendships and connections—to gain access to the individuals who operate these venues.

The venues I researched were all in contact with health programs. Hence my research sites were in this sense not different from those of studies focusing on HIV/AIDS. Although prostitution is nominally illegal in both Thailand and Laos, it operates in a social and cultural environment where commercial sex does not receive strong moral sanctioning (Lyttleton 1994; Van Esterik 2000), and venues are generally allowed to operate undisturbed, despite official policy. What I wish to emphasize is that when the word "trafficking" is used, a particular sordid and mythical image is evoked that does not necessarily reflect field realities.

Another serious consideration is maintaining informants' anonymity and obtaining informed consent. In most venues, socializing and drinking commonly precede commercial sex. Indeed, conversation is an essential part of this form of interaction. In most settings sex workers have a fair amount of autonomy regarding the types of interactions and conversations they have with customers. From the point of view of research, this means that it is possible, with some skill, to engage in discreet conversation with women who work there, as well as managers and customers, without compromising their anonymity. At times informants were reluctant to engage in conversation, but in most cases this had more to do with the realization by the potential informant that little economic benefit would follow, as our intention was not to purchase sex. Discussing the ways sex workers debut in the industry can be difficult. Throughout the research such information usually came indirectly, either through women who knew of others, or informants who had been subject to such recruitment in the past but had since adapted to working in the sex industry and did so without the direct coercion of third parties. I observed the arrival of newcomers to venues but was always careful when choosing conversation topics in such situations. A typical "trafficker" is often herself a sex worker, so identities such as "sex worker," "victim," and "trafficker" are fluid. Although some informants happily admit to "helping" others, no informants admitted to deceptive recruitment tactics. However, information is more forthcoming when talking about others, and here revisiting the same venue repeatedly was a fruitful way of unraveling these complexities.

Throughout my research, I never directly observed anyone being physically abused or arrested. Several informants had experienced very difficult situations, however, including health problems, theft, and violent customers. From the outset I decided to be very careful about attempting to assist anyone. I had three reasons for this. First, there is always the risk of giving unrealistic impressions of what one could realistically do. Second, attempting to help could compromise my position as a researcher in the field. Third, there may be a very short step from "helping" to perpetuating, and even worsening, conditions of abuse. Ethics committees in Western countries might require researchers to report to the police when they encounter illegal activities and abuse, particularly of children. However, such an ethical guideline can have its own mixed ethical implications. It presumes an unquestioned and positive view of law enforcement authorities. When it comes to commercial sex and migration, the police in most parts of the world take an active part in maintaining the sex industry, and their attitudes toward migrants—as marginal groups—are usually negative and can be punitive. Indeed, as Julia O'Connell Davidson (2003, 61) has noted:

> Another reason to question the idea that governments will prove useful allies in any struggle to protect women from sexual exploitation concerns the fact that the civil and human rights of females who work in prostitution in the contemporary world are routinely, and often grossly, violated by state actors. Prostitutes variously face arbitrary detention, deportation, forcible eviction from their dwellings, enforced health checks—including HIV testing—forcible "rehabilitation," corporal

punishment, even execution; few states offer prostitutes adequate protection from violent crime or abusive employers, and prostitutes are often victims of crimes perpetrated by corrupt law enforcement agents, including rape, beatings and extortion.

When I worked for UNIAP and during my fieldwork, a continuous problem was that officially identified Lao trafficked victims were being held in shelters in Thailand for very long periods, in some cases more than one year (Huguet and Ramangkura 2007; Gallagher and Pearson 2010). I cannot recall many trafficking cases from Laos where a trafficker confined an individual for so long. It is therefore not unreasonable to speculate on the possibility that actions of governments and organizations to "help" sex workers have done more damage to, and violation of, their human rights than the misdeeds of traffickers (Davidson 2004). In the context of Laos and Thailand, any researcher worth his or her grant money would know that unconditionally committing oneself to reporting, say, the presence of underage girls in a brothel to the police would most likely result in entrenchment of exploitation ("rehabilitation," deportation, imprisonment, abuse, confiscation of earnings, and so on) of the girls themselves and not many consequences for those who operate such establishments.

A Note on Terminology and Disclaimers

I have already used various terms that require explanation. Thus far I have only briefly commented on the terms "human trafficking" and "trafficking in persons," and I will return to these. Throughout this book I will primarily refer to the United Nations' *Protocol to Prevent, Suppress and Punish Trafficking in Persons, Especially Women and Children* (also known as the Palermo Protocol) (UN 2000), but I will also make reference to Thai and Lao legislation. My use of the terms "human trafficking" and "trafficking in persons" does not imply that they carry particularly illuminating analytical properties or that these concepts are devoid of contradictions and ambiguities. I use these terms because most organizations and individuals who work to combat trafficking use these definitions.

Throughout this book I offer a critique of how trafficking is articulated, and several times I question how categories, such as "victim" and "trafficker," are used. This does not mean that I am trying to trivialize the abuse and exploitation of women and girls. Similarly, when I draw attention to the discursive and constructed nature of trafficking, this does not imply that I am advocating postmodern nihilism or that trafficking is merely a fantasy of cynical governments and UN bureaucrats. Conversely, neither am I suggesting an essentialist reading of trafficking in persons. As will become apparent, some young Lao women in the sex industry end up in very difficult circumstances, and at the same time there are certain ways in which trafficking tends to be articulated among development programs and governments, and it is with regard to these two processes that I seek to engage in analysis. I do argue that the forms of exploitation and domination that are taking place do not fit neatly with discursive models produced by anti-trafficking programs. This does not mean that I seek to trivialize darker aspects of the sex industry. On the contrary, I am attempting to identify blind spots.

I use the term "anti-traffickers" to refer to individuals, institutions, and groups who are in one way or another involved in combating trafficking in persons. Although I point to similarities among anti-traffickers, it is important to note that this is a highly varied cohort of people. It includes government officials, police officers, aid workers, lawyers, journalists, UN agency staff, bilateral aid donors, and community group members who might all differ in their moral-political views of both migration and prostitution. I specifically reference groups, individuals, and organizations when this is necessary in the text.

In terms of scale, I might thus far seem to imply that I am talking about neatly separated universes of global trafficking discourse and a subordinate group of local anti-traffickers who merely adopt a discourse from above. Although that does take place in some cases, it is of course a simplification. To give one example, two senior management consultants for two regional anti-trafficking projects in the Mekong region have done extensive work in Laos (trainings, workshops, negotiations, meetings, research, village consultations) and are in regular formal and informal contact with other anti-trafficking experts in South Asia, Europe, and elsewhere. Regionally, they have been central to the development of bilateral and multilateral governmental agreements on trafficking among the Mekong countries. They also take part in shaping trafficking response globally. One of them was a central person (in a technical capacity) in the development of the UN trafficking protocol, and both were key in the development of arguably the best-known text (after the protocol itself) on trafficking: the United Nations' *Recommended Principles and Guidelines on Human Rights and Human Trafficking* (ECOSOC 2002). So when I make distinctions between a global discourse of trafficking and local anti-traffickers, this is merely a heuristic device to discuss different aspects of how anti-traffickers engage in the practice of articulating trafficking and implementing programs.

When discussing individuals who work in the sex industry, I use various words and phrases, such as "prostitute," "sex worker," "woman," "young woman," and "girl." Legal age does not translate easily from Lao and Thai. The commonly used word is *phusaw*, which translates roughly as "young unmarried lady" or "female coming of age." Indeed, sometimes venue owners use the English word "lady." I am explicit, however, when I discuss cases of underage prostitution. I also use the politically sanctioned term *sao borigan*, which directly translates as "service woman" and is a euphemism for a woman working in the sex industry.

This book points to shortcomings of development programs. I do not, however, intend ridicule aid workers. On the contrary, I seek to illuminate the extremely difficult work they confront in their everyday assignments. Finally, this book points to the lack of the empirical data that could demonstrate the claim that human trafficking is a problem of massive proportions, underpinned by transnational organized crime and adapted to the laws of a globalized marketplace. Let me make it clear that this book does not suggest that the ethnographic material it presents falsifies such claims, even though the material might question some of the underlying assumptions. What I seek to do is to point out (1) moral-political reasons why trafficking in persons takes on a certain formulaic character; (2) how such fashioning of categories intersects with local realities of sex commerce and migration along the Thai-Lao border; and (3) what effects these processes have on local anti-trafficking programming.

PART I

GLOBAL PERFECTIONS

The Idealized Discourse of Trafficking

2 Do Traffickers Have Navels?

> It may well be, of course, that no general theory of slavery is possible given that the core of the phenomena to which we attach the term—the transfer of full rights in a person—is so simple that the idea can arise again and again in quite disparate cultural and structural contexts.
> —Igor Kopytoff, "Slavery," *Annual Review of Anthropology* 11 (1982, 224)

THE TERM "HUMAN TRAFFICKING" appeared in the *New York Times* for the first time in 1976, in an article regarding trafficking in persons out of East Germany.[1] The same topic resurfaced in a 1978 story. Not before 1999 did the term "human trafficking" reappear in *Times'* pages. Since then, reporting on the topic has increased steadily. In 2010, no fewer than 118 *Times* articles mentioned the term (table 1). In other words, by 2010 the *New York Times* on average was reporting on human trafficking more than twice a week, whereas about a decade earlier the term was not mentioned at all. Use of the term "sex trafficking" has followed a similar trend.

This acceleration in attention to human trafficking reflects a general shift in focus with regard to cross-border migration. Over the past few years, it is not only the Western media that has increasingly reported on human trafficking. Since the 1990s, governments and international organizations have given it more attention. Within the development aid sector, trafficking projects have mushroomed in numerous countries. The United Nations has defined trafficking as one of its key priority areas of concern for the new millennium, launching several regional and country-based programs as well as establishing in 2004 a special

Table 1 Use of the terms "human trafficking" and "sex trafficking" in the *New York Times*, 1997–2010

Year	Number of articles in which the term appears	
	"Human trafficking"	"Sex trafficking"
1997	0	0
1998	0	0
1999	1	0
2000	7	3
2001	6	0
2002	7	3
2003	11	8
2004	27	22
2005	22	25
2006	42	23
2007	54	27
2008	59	36
2009	73	31
2010	118	45

Source: New York Times

rapporteur on trafficking in persons, especially women and children. This growing attention is perhaps most pronounced in the legal sector, spearheaded by the United Nations' *Protocol to Prevent, Suppress and Punish Trafficking in Persons, Especially Women and Children* (UN 2000), which supplements the Transnational Organized Crime (TOC) Convention (UN 2001). Reflecting on this shift, Anne Gallagher (2006a, 163) notes:

> Just a decade ago the international legal framework consisted of a single, long-forgotten treaty dating back to 1949 and a few vague provisions in a couple of human rights treaties. Today, trafficking is the subject of a vast array of international legal rules and national laws and a plethora of "soft" standards ranging from policy directives to regional commitments. The breadth and depth of this legal shift is

truly remarkable. It took just two short years for the international community to negotiate a global agreement on fighting trafficking and only a further three years for that treaty to gain enough ratifications for it to enter into force.

Does this increase in attention to human trafficking reflect a response to a recent global crisis of migration and labor exploitation? Consulting both academic literature and development reports, one quickly realizes that the state of knowledge production surrounding trafficking is highly contentious. Depending on which report one reads, global estimates of annual trafficking cases range from fewer than five hundred thousand to several millions.[2] To give just one example, the estimates of annual trafficking cases in Australia vary from fewer than ten to more than a thousand, depending on which organization you consult (Parliament of the Commonwealth of Australia 2004). The spurious nature of trafficking statistics has already been a subject of commentary among both academics and development practitioners, pointing to the methodological difficulty of researching a phenom- enon that is clandestine in nature, as well as the lack of consensus with regard to conceptualizing agency (Anderson and Davidson 2004; Kempadoo 2005). However, such critiques often use trafficking as both an instrument and an object of research. They have a tendency to rein- force essentialist forms of knowledge as they seek to unravel underly- ing ontological "truths" about trafficking in their evaluations of the moral-political agendas of state parties and other interest groups. In this vein, it becomes possible for Thomas Steinfatt et al. (2002, 2) to note political reasons why organizations quote unsubstantiated traf- ficking numbers and yet claim that "hard numbers on sexual traffick- ing can . . . be obtained." In a similar fashion, Gallagher (2006a, 187) assesses the "correctness" of the recent European Trafficking Conven- tion by measuring it "against the gold standard, set by the 2002 U.N. Principles and Guidelines on Human Rights and Human Trafficking." In other words, much literature on trafficking aims to be corrective in its critiques of the anti-trafficking sector, while at the same time implying underlying truths regarding trafficking (see also Tyldum and Brunovskis 2005).

But if the purported increase in human trafficking is not backed up with clear and solid data, then what explains this recent attention to the issue? We will begin exploring this question by considering the claim that trafficking is the new slave trade.

Human Trafficking—A Modern Form of Slavery?

Do traffickers have navels?[3] In other words, do traffickers engage in a form of egregious conduct that has a long historical legacy, or are traffickers a "first of their kind"—navel-less creatures committing unprecedented horrendous deeds never before witnessed? Human trafficking is, after all, commonly assumed to be a new and increasing problem. At the same time, human trafficking is also referred to as a modern slave trade. It is thus appropriate to consider precisely what human trafficking shares with its historical antecedents.

We saw in chapter 1 that the Palermo Protocol defines trafficking with reference to an action (recruitment, movement, etc.), its means (deception, coercion, etc.), and its purpose (exploitation). These three elements, understood in broad terms, can be found in many societies throughout human history. For example, the ancient civilization of Egypt is well known for its slavery population, and Scandinavian Vikings took slaves in the aftermath of plundering sprees around continental Europe. And little more than a hundred years ago the slave trade between Africa and America constituted the backbone of one of the new emerging global economies (Bhattacharyya 2005). Within small-scale societies, anthropologists have documented various forms of domination and abuse, and in this context it is interesting to consider Pierre Bourdieu's observation that debt bondage is—in addition to the gift—a common means of domination in precapitalist societies (1977 [1972], 191–192).

Slavery, in its classical sense, commonly fell under the hierarchy of state administration, or serfdoms (Brown 2006; David Brion Davis 1966; Patterson 1982). The best-articulated example of this type of polity is probably found in Plato's *Republic*. Today there are few states where such projects are officially sponsored or explicitly underpin social systems.[4] Although there may be contemporary examples of "classic slavery," human trafficking—as we understand the term today—is not primarily organized as such. This difference has in part to do with how morality in reference to commodification takes on new meanings under conditions of modernity. Igor Kopytoff (1986, 84) writes:

The separation [between persons and things], though intellectually rooted in classical antiquity and Christianity, becomes culturally salient with the onset of European modernity. Its most glaring denial lay, of course, in the practice of slavery. Yet its cultural significance can be gauged precisely by the fact that slavery did present an intellectual and moral problem in the West . . . , but almost nowhere else.

Slavery was officially abolished in several European countries in the 1830s (Britain in 1833; France, 1835) and the United States in 1865. Other countries followed suit in the late nineteenth century onward (Brazil in 1888; Laos, 1893; Thailand, 1905; China, 1906). It is within this period that we see the ascendance of a concern with a "white slave trade" and the "traffic" of Western women into prostitution in several colonies (Outshoorn 2005, 142). As Jo Doezema (2000, 2007) has shown, the public anxiety regarding the "white slave trade" reflects ambiguous conceptions of womanhood, in terms of female sexuality and mobility, both of which resonate with contemporary concerns surrounding prostitution and trafficking (discussed below). Hence, in the early twentieth century the term "trafficking" became a commonplace association with the mobility of Western women into prostitution. International legislation emerged in 1904 that culminated in the UN Convention for the Suppression of the Traffic in Persons and of the Exploitation of the Prostitution of Others (1949). These legal instruments did not define trafficking and made no explicit distinction between consensual and nonconsensual sex work, and few states ratified them. It is in this context that we see the contours developing of a controversy surrounding how one ought to define the relationship between trafficking and prostitution. This contention remains with us today and has played—and continues to play—an important part in both bringing attention to and shaping understandings about trafficking in persons.

In the aftermath of the Second World War and the subsequent civil rights movement and expansion of universities in Western countries, we see a proliferation of feminist literature. Prostitution, and to a lesser extent trafficking, became a fashionable topic among academics as well as organizations that dealt with gender issues in one form or another. In the 1980s the HIV/AIDS epidemic became apparent. Sex commerce became associated with tourism, and a focus on transnational sex reemerged (Outshoorn 2005). Just as had happened a century earlier, controversies regarding the relationship between prostitution and trafficking became subjects of contentious discussion and marked lobbying efforts in various international forums. As other authors have examined this controversy in detail (Doezema 2000; Sullivan 2003), I present only a brief summary here.

In this context, we have what Barbara Sullivan (2003) has termed "radical feminists" and "sex work feminists." Radical feminists see prostitution as a product of masculine domination and female oppression. They argue that it is, by definition, not possible to consent to sell sex. Therefore all movement of women into sex commerce should be considered as the trafficking of victims. Sex work feminists argue that there is a distinction between voluntary and nonvoluntary sex work. They see radical feminists' abolitionist agenda as underpinning a totalizing and deterministic view of sex work. Such an agenda, in their opinion, allows for only monolithic narratives of prostitution and fails to take into account the tremendous diversity within the sex industry, as well as the numerous differences in subjective experience and agency among sex workers themselves.

Furthermore, sex work feminists argue that it is unrealistic to attempt to abolish all sex work. Many also hold the view that it is undesirable and counterproductive to do so. Consensual sex work should be considered "real work," they say, and doing so would in practical ways support the status and well-being of sex workers. Most sex work feminists support either the legalization or the decriminalization of sex workers. Regarding trafficking, they believe that only women who are moved into the sex industry without consent should be categorized as "trafficked persons." Radical feminists, on the other hand, argue that legalizing commercial sex would legitimize prostitution, trafficking, and a system that oppresses women.

At the 1995 Women's Conference in Beijing the Coalition against Trafficking in Women lobbied for a new international legal instrument named the Convention against Sexual Exploitation. The draft convention sought to criminalize all forms of prostitution, and no distinctions were made between voluntary and nonvoluntary prostitution. There was considerable counterlobbying against this draft convention by other feminist groups. Some, such as the Network of Sex Worker Projects, maintained that sex workers would be best served by moving the focus away from trafficking, because anti-trafficking measures have tended to police and punish migrant sex workers instead of protecting them. Others, such as Global Alliance against Traffic in Women, believed that it was worthwhile to advocate against trafficking albeit with a clear distinction between voluntary and nonvoluntary sex work (Sullivan 2003). This draft convention failed to materialize because it was unable to gain support from many state parties.

Important historical continuities are worth noting here. The ascendance of international legal instruments to combat trafficking dates back more than one hundred years and overlaps with the demise of classic slavery of the colonial era. At the same time, trafficking has been strongly associated with prostitution and female mobility. It is precisely this focus on trafficking in relation to prostitution that has been given the most attention within both policy and academic circles. However, during the early 1990s two other concerns started to dominate the international policy agenda: larger irregular migration flows and transnational organized crime.

Levels of migration, as well as the way in which mobility is understood, have changed historically (Derrida 2001; Löfgren 2002). The world has seen an unprecedented acceleration in people movements during the past two decades, and there has been an expansion of trade and an opening up of markets (Appadurai 1996; Featherstone 1990). The fall of the Soviet Union was the main precursor for the global liberalization of trade. The deregulation of markets, however, has not always been followed by an erosion of boundaries for people movements (Kwong 1997; Löfgren 2002). Such situations create an incentive for people to move into affluent labor markets (often across borders), yet few measures exist to legalize such movements. In general terms, the relative discrepancy between incentives and the legality of labor migration has created considerable risks for migrant populations and led to labor practices that exploit migrant workers, as well as third-party involvement in facilitating people movements (Gallagher 2001;

Schloenhardt 1999). Several academics, some influenced by world system and dependency theory, see trafficking in this light—as merely a symptom of capitalist hegemony (Bhattacharyya 2005; Graycar 1999). Whereas slavery underpinned hierarchical polities, "trafficking in persons" appears to be parasitic on disparities between liberalized trade regimes and stringent migration controls.

This disparity must be understood in the context of how security—and more specifically, transnational organized crime—became a policy concern throughout the world in the 1990s (Eriksen et al. 2010; Duffield 2001). There is no doubt that the end of the cold war saw not only the beginning of increased people movements but also the absence of traditional enemy images defined by capitalist and communist blocs. Perhaps the most prominent concern of the decade was illegal drugs. South America, and to a lesser extent Asia, served as examples of how organized crime had the potential to seriously undermine nation-states (Dupont 1999). However, such concerns expanded to other forms of trade, and some scholars have argued that the formal globalized economy is in a symbiotic relationship with organized crime and extralegal trade (Bhattacharyya 2005; Nordstrom 2007).

It is in this context that development organizations have increasingly targeted "law and order" concerns in their international aid programs (Gould 2005; Mosse 2005). In 1997 the United Nations gave organized crime a higher profile in its policy agenda by merging the United Nations International Drug Control Programme and the Centre for International Crime Prevention to form the United Nations Office on Drugs and Crime. Paralleling this shift in focus is a growing concern for "failed states" and efforts to stamp out corruption, lawlessness, and illegal transnational activity through development programming. Needless to say, the September 11 attack on New York in 2001 reinforced the association of transnational organized crime and security.

At the same time, development aid gradually became a global project characterized by a postnational logic of transnational responsibility (Hettne 2009), where security takes on multiple meanings ranging from humanitarian relief efforts to sustainable development. This has opened up opportunities for nongovernmental organizations to play a far wider role in third world countries than before. In addition, security also became individuated, as exemplified by the United Nations

Development Programme's emphasis on "human security" in the context of its human development reports. I stress the emergence of concerns about transnational crime and its relation to development aid, because this trend helps us understand how development aid programs became involved in combating human trafficking and why humanitarian concerns have been increasingly merged with attempts to fight crime. However, the merging of criminality, security, and humanitarian concerns is best expressed within the context of the ascendance of the United Nations Convention against Transnational Organized Crime and its underlying protocol on trafficking in persons.

Ascendance of the Protocol:
The Convergence of Three Policy Concerns

In the early 1990s three policy concerns intersected in powerful ways: a century-old unease about prostitution and female mobility, mass migration in a globalized world, and transnational crime. At the same time, development aid was becoming intertwined with concerns about mobility and security. A focus on organized crime prompted increased security regarding international migration, and cross-border mobility has deterritorialized security concerns. This has allowed for the possibility—unthinkable only a few years ago—that migrants and people movers pose a security threat to nation-states. Furthermore, as this alleged threat transcends international borders, governments have sought solutions through bilateral and multilateral cooperation. In addition, directing attention to prostitution has given migration and transnational organized crime, quite literally, a sexual appeal. These policy concerns are reflected in how the Palermo Protocol was developed.

The trafficking protocol is of crucial importance to any study on trafficking, as it is the first international instrument that offers a definition of trafficking. It has also been extremely influential in the development of legislation in various nations, and governments, NGOs, and UN agencies commonly refer to it. The idea of a separate protocol dealing with human trafficking under a legal framework for addressing transnational organized crime stems from an intergovernmental meeting arranged by the UN General Assembly in 1998 and mandated to develop a draft convention to combat transnational organized crime

(Gallagher 2001). At the time, Argentina expressed frustration with the slow process of developing protocols for dealing with pornography and child prostitution under the Convention on the Rights of the Child (Argentina had proposed a convention on trafficking in minors the previous year). Other governments also showed growing concern regarding transnational sex commerce and irregular migration. Italy, worried about a growing influx of illegal migrants, approached the International Maritime Organization to push for stronger international cooperation on border protection prior to the trafficking protocol negotiations. But along with other governments, Italy subsequently decided to lobby its anti-immigration agenda under the auspices of a legal instrument for combating transnational organized crime (Gallagher 2001).

It has often been asserted that the trafficking protocol is an anti-immigration agenda in disguise (Berman 2003; Gallagher 2001). This viewpoint was reflected during sessions leading up to the UN protocol on trafficking. Some argued that stricter migration controls would actually necessitate third-party involvement in cross-border migration and fuel trafficking because it would go underground, whereas others argued that lax migration controls would encourage risky migration practices (see Ditmore 2005; and Kempadoo 2005).

Notably, the trafficking protocol does not directly criminalize labor exploitation; rather, it criminalizes the migratory prelude to it. The distinction becomes a question of whether third parties have applied some form of manipulation of consent (deception, coercion) in order to intentionally move a person into an exploitative situation. The reason the convention does not address labor exploitation in itself is obvious, as this would require governments that are primarily receiving countries for migrants to commit to provide services and legal rights to large numbers of migrants. In this way, trafficking is retrospectively defined; trafficking becomes manifest after someone has been subject to a nonconsensual recruitment process that—with the intent of the recruiter—leads to an exploitative situation. A migrant's consent as well as the recruiter's intent are crucial parameters for determining trafficking cases. This requirement allows for considerable entrepreneurship among receiving countries (Anderson 2007b). Governments can treat trafficking as a "migration issue" while at the same time turning a blind eye to working conditions of migrant labor, a point missed by neither academics (Gallagher 2001) nor organizations (IOM 2004b) in their critiques of the trafficking protocol. Ultimately, how a migrant is defined has considerable bearing on a state's responsibilities. Labeling someone as an "illegal migrant" justifies deportation with little regard to the migrant's circumstances, whereas identifying someone as a victim of trafficking places far more pressure on a government to provide assistance, such as legal support, shelter, and counseling (Anderson 2007b). Conversely, "rescues" and "repatriation" can euphemistically serve anti-immigration agendas under the auspices of a moral-public campaign to combat trafficking in persons.

Although the trafficking protocol gives the impression that its main purpose is to protect and assist trafficked victims, its predominant concerns with organized crime and controlling migration mean that national security takes precedence over the individual (i.e., the migrant). In other words, its overall objective is to protect states (through controlling migration), not individuals (protecting migrant laborers' working rights). The subtle difference between the two comes to light most clearly with the recognition that the protocol does not provide any clarity as to how to identify a victim. Gallagher (2001, 994) writes:

> One major weakness of the law enforcement/border control provisions of the protocol is their failure to address the issue of how victims of trafficking are to be identified. The obvious question has been asked by the Canadian Refugee Council: "If authorities have no means of determining among the intercepted or arrested who is being trafficked, how do they propose to grant them the measures of protection they are committing themselves to?"

From the point of view of a trafficked victim, the way human trafficking is defined in the UN protocol takes on the form of a lottery: one can potentially be protected if one is found to be a trafficked victim, or potentially be subject to legal action if one is treated as an illegal migrant. Hence the state paradoxically becomes both protector *and* threat, so that a trafficked victim needs to seek simultaneous protection by and against the state.

It is a mistake, however, to argue that claims about the increase in

trafficking are merely ploys by governments to legitimize antiprostitution and anti-immigration agendas. A range of organizations and interest
groups rightly point out the possibility of horrendous abuse of migrants in
a political and legal environment that is predominantly hostile to undoc-
umented migrants (Kempadoo 2005; Agustín 2007). Yet such critiques
can have the ironic effect of reinforcing the very notion that human trafficking is of an enormous, albeit unproven scale (see Bales 2005).

Besides the policy agendas of a range of state parties, the negotiations of the protocol on trafficking in persons were unique in that they
included considerable lobbying and participation of NGOs and other
interest groups. This was particularly pertinent in regard to the question of how the protocol relates to prostitution. During the negotiations of the protocol, organizations that lobbied both for and against
abolition participated in several sessions (Gallagher 2001). At times
the moral panic was unmistakable, as exemplified by the Philippine
delegation, who at one point solemnly suggested that trafficking should
be defined as "with or without consent of the victim by legal or illegal
means, for all purposes of sexual exploitation including prostitution,
marriage, employment" (Ditmore 2005, 115). The ad hoc committee
moved beyond discussions about prostitution early on and included
other forms of exploitation (Gallagher 2001). Nevertheless the negotiations did not resolve the prostitution debate, as is highlighted by the
partial tautology of the trafficking definition and by the failure of the
protocol to define terms such as "the exploitation of prostitution of others" (Anderson and Davidson 2004; Gallagher 2001). It is widely recognized that with regard to prostitution the Palermo Protocol's definition
of trafficking is a compromise.

That the definition includes "consent" as a yardstick can be seen
to support the view that a meaningful distinction can be made between
voluntary and nonvoluntary prostitution, suggesting a degree of success for the lobbying efforts of the sex worker feminists. However, the
inclusion of "consent" in the definition most likely stems from another
policy consideration—that is, the concern with controlling illegal
migration. If the Palermo Protocol had defined all migratory sex work
as trafficking and if it was understood that trafficked victims are just
that—victims—then the protocol would have considerably widened
the number of potentially trafficked victims within receiving coun-

tries and consequently placed substantial responsibility on receiving countries to provide services. In other words, the issue of "consent" and "agency" is a question not only of how sex work is viewed but also of how governments and other involved parties choose to treat migrants. This brings us to a broader point about the relationships between prostitution, mobility, and security. To suggest, as many authors have done (e.g., Agustín 2007), that human trafficking is primarily an expression of an antiprostitution agenda is too simplistic and overstates the lobbying power of the abolitionist movement. Although sex trafficking is frequently profiled in debates and media, the ratification of the trafficking protocol by so many governments can be explained, not by a sudden panic about transnational prostitution, but rather by nation-states' broader migration and security concerns.[5]

The Elasticity of Human Trafficking Discourse

I have mentioned that several academics and aid practitioners see trafficking policies merely as a Trojan horse of either antiprostitution or anti-immigration agendas. This view is limited, however, and fails to account for the myriad of different forms of interest groups involved in discursively shaping trafficking. One would perhaps think that the competing views on trafficking, which are so clearly delineated in debates about both prostitution and irregular migration, would weaken trafficking in persons as a focal point for policy and action. However, it is precisely because of, and not in spite of, this fragmentary nature that trafficking discourse has its mobilizing qualities. It is remarkable how different and even competing political and moral interests are served under the auspices of "combating trafficking in persons." A government (or a multilateral agency, an NGO, a donor, a lobby group, and so on) can simultaneously pursue the following alternative aims.

Border control. A government can demonstrate state autonomy and tap into nationalist sentiment in its own jurisdiction by performing border control to keep "aliens" out, by arguing that stopping movements of people prevents trafficking. Collapsing the distinction between trafficking and "illegal migration" makes it possible for nation-states to deny legal assistance to a trafficked victim by labeling the person an illegal migrant[6] or to "repatriate" illegal migrants under the auspices of the morally acclaimed international fight against trafficking (Ginzburg 2002a).

Naturalized exploitation. The ex post facto nature of trafficking allows a government to remain uncommitted to improving working conditions and social and legal services for migrants and, in some cases, even to deliberately profit from underpaid migrant workers. Because the exploitation happens to the "other," it is easier for governments to naturalize a benign-neglect approach to migrant workers. A focus on "trafficking in persons" allows for a narrative that redefines rights and responsibilities. The onus is placed on the communities where migrants come from as opposed to destination points of migrants. It is not a coincidence that the majority of policy programming and literature on trafficking tends to place an overwhelming emphasis on "source communities" and the conditions that engender out-migration (Caouette 1998; Wille 2001).

Promotion of labor exports (sending countries). A government can promote labor exports by lobbying receiving countries for better working conditions and by articulating its argument in relation to trafficking in persons. By referring to trafficking, a government gives an additional urgency to the need for such new policies.

State as "protector". Combating trafficking can be used as a vehicle to demonstrate that a government is in charge (Berman 2003)—in both a political and a moral sense. The notion of the state as the protector is a contradictory one, as it refers to simultaneously "protecting" national borders and "vulnerable" migrants. In pursuing the former, the latter objective is nullified, for policing borders has a tendency to produce vulnerable migrant populations (Anderson and Davidson 2004; Marshall and Thatun 2005). This contradiction is intensified when trafficking is rhetorically linked to organized crime, as it can humanize restrictive migration policies implemented in the name of security (Anderson and Davidson 2004). Indeed, when linked to security, fighting trafficking can make increased border control appear righteous, and the repatriation of illegal migrants under the label of "trafficked victims" sounds almost heartwarming.

Suppression of prostitution. Governments and interest groups can argue that prostitution is inherently exploitative and that hence all prostitution is a form of trafficking. By suppressing prostitution, trafficking in persons is also suppressed, or vice versa. Such a position draws supporters from very different quarters, such as radical Marxist feminists and Christian Right/"family values"–oriented interest groups. We see here an added religious element to the human rights discourse, which as such makes trafficking uncontroversial in a superficial sense in that everyone across the political spectrum in one way or another "agrees" to fight trafficking.

Legalization of prostitution. Governments and other interest groups can argue that legalizing prostitution will allow sex workers better access to protection from serious forms of abuse. Hence there will be a reduction in exploitation, the argument goes, which in turn means a reduction of trafficking. Both feminist groups and religious groups are among those who support this position.

Poverty reduction. Aid programs have been proven to play an important catalytic role in debates about poverty reduction by focusing on trafficking in relation to development. In recent years donors have reduced their contributions for "traditional" aid programs geared toward meeting basic minimum needs, shifting their support toward fashionable "global development challenges" such as the Millennium Development Goals, often in the name of security and governance (Mosse 2005). Many aid programs have responded to this by simply continuing what they have done in the past, but under a different name. By highlighting the assumption that people move because of lack of opportunities, development agencies have managed to direct donor attention—through the back door, so to speak—to more conventional poverty reduction programs with a stated objective of combating trafficking in persons (Ginzburg 2002a).

Instruments of discipline and social control. Governments can use trafficking programs as instruments to control subjects. Some countries, such as Laos and Vietnam, fine and "reeducate" returning migrants (Ginzburg 2002a, 2004). Although neither country explicitly justifies these actions under an anti-trafficking policy, this approach does raise questions regarding the ideological underpinnings of repatriation programs. This logic of "staying in place" can also be applied to trafficking prevention strategies. Aid donors have naively suggested setting up "early warning systems"[7] despite examples of "trafficking prevention programs" that have led to the policing of young women in village communities, compromising their freedom of movement (Doezema 2007; Shangera 2005).

Empowerment of migrants. Interest groups and organizations that seek to empower migrants can use trafficking as a vehicle to highlight negative aspects of strict migration policies. More generally, human trafficking can be used as an arena in which broader concerns regarding treatment of migrant workers can be raised. Referring to trafficking may make it easier to evoke emotion and sympathy surrounding a topic that otherwise is commonly perceived in negative terms.

Narration. Stories of trafficking—both real and imagined—have proven to be a fertile ground for populist narratives communicated through mass media, which appear to consider "rescues" a fashionable topic to cover (Feingold 1997; Shangera 2002). Human trafficking has an important psychological dimension and metaphorically has one thing in common with terrorism: its deterritoriality. In contrast to such third world problems as natural disasters, hunger, disease, and other forms of misery, human trafficking is not anchored to a specific locality. Whereas a civil war in Africa may be far away, human trafficking can in principle happen "at home," as people are—against their will—presumably transported to richer countries. Just like terrorism, trafficking is simultaneously nowhere and everywhere. And just as it is possible to imagine a trafficked victim being in one's own neighborhood, it becomes possible to reflect on and connect with a trafficking story in a personal way. It is therefore not a coincidence that when the media cover trafficking cases, they tend to show close-up portraits of young innocent victims who are enslaved in brothels. The disembedded quality of trafficking enables this form of intimate and personal association between the reader and the story. In contrast, we rarely see media stories that include close-up portraits of poverty-stricken chil-

dren narrated through the discourse of, say, immunization, opium rehabilitation, victims of civil war, and so on. That "trafficking in persons"
is a theme now taken up by Western crime investigation series and the
film industry reinforces that trafficking has proven itself to be particularly useful for storytelling.[8]

What we are left with is a myriad of different political interests that
can be pursued in the name of combating trafficking in persons. The
elastic quality of trafficking discourse has also led to some rather exotic
alliances, such as radical feminists arguing alongside Christian organizations for more powers to be given to police officers (Davidson 2003)
and immigration officers joining in workshops with health workers and
representatives from community-based microcredit lending institutions.
   The multiple conceptualizations of trafficking are simultaneously
a result of different contested political agendas that underpin its discursive power, and the reason why trafficking serves so many different
objectives. On the one hand, trafficking is the contested outcome of
how government and other interests groups respond to migration, economic development, and prostitution. On the other hand, trafficking is
the product of various forms of discursive instruments applied by these
same actors and institutions. The anti-trafficking sector is not merely
a passive audience responding to a preexisting world. It is engaged in
constructing, defining, and shaping meaning surrounding both migration and commercial sex.

3 The Market Metaphor

An international mechanism to monitor trends and patterns
of trafficking in persons needs to be established with the object
of continuing data collection of the sort gathered in the
present survey (data on legal and institutional frameworks;
criminal justice statistics; and victim service information).
Such a mechanism also could work toward gathering more
information on the market context for these crimes, including
data on price and demand. Coordinated efforts require
collective information systems, and the global struggle against
trafficking in persons needs knowledge to inform strategic
interventions.
     —United Nations Office on Drugs and Crime,
     Global Report on Trafficking in Persons (2009, 12)

THE ANTI-TRAFFICKING sector represents a tremendously diverse constellation of actors that include Christians and feminist groups who seek
to abolish prostitution, state officials who are concerned with controlling borders, activists who seek to legalize migration and sex work, and
aid workers who frame trafficking in terms of development and human
rights. This heterogeneity is truly remarkable yet often remains unacknowledged. Underlying this diversity are several common denomina-
tors that are expressed through legal binaries and a market metaphor. I
described these commonalities in chapter 1 as three concentric circles,
consisting of a dyadic power relationship between a victim and a perpetrator at the center, organized crime as the middle circle, and a cross-
border marketplace as the outer circle. This chapter deals with each in
turn.

Dyadic Power Relationships—Victim and Perpetrator

In an important study on law enforcement and social control in Western societies, David Garland (2001, 11) draws attention to how the victim has become a central trope in public policy:

> The victim is no longer an unfortunate citizen who has been on the receiving end of a criminal harm, and whose concerns are subsumed within the "public interest" that guides the prosecution and penal decisions of the state. The victim is now, in a certain sense, a much more representative character, whose experience is taken to be common and collective, rather than individual and atypical. Whoever speaks on behalf of victims speaks on behalf of us all—or so declares the new political wisdom of high crime societies. Publicized images of actual victims serve as the personalized, real-life, it-could-be-you metonym for a problem of security that has become a defining feature of contemporary culture.

This explains in part why media stories on human trafficking focus on victims. This tendency has come under criticism, and several commentators (e.g., Agustín 2007; and Frederick 2005) are correct in highlighting the well-meant but unfortunate tendency to assume migrants' and sex workers' lack of agency and to consequently project a victim identity onto them. By the same token, it is also common—though rarely commented upon—to elevate traffickers to a perfected omnipresent and powerful entity resembling a shady Nietzschean Übermensch. The assumptions are that traffickers are well organized, they are calculating, they adapt to situations, they are global, they run highly professional cartels, and their profit exceeds those of most other economic enterprises (Phongpaichit 1999; Salt and Stein 1997). In short, whereas the victim is portrayed as unaware, innocent, and weak, traffickers are imagined as evil, dominant, cunning, and all-knowing.

Where do such imageries of traffickers and victims come from? One would perhaps think that such information would be found in court cases. Although the number of prosecutions of traffickers has increased worldwide over the last few years (UNODC 2009), case studies—pre-

sented in trafficking workshops, training manuals, or media stories—
constitute the main source of descriptions of traffickers and victims.[1]
The following case study is typical:

> Sonia began working as a prostitute in a Latin American country
> when she was evicted from home at the age of 14. She tried to get
> other jobs as well, but always returned to prostitution. When she was
> 17, a taxi driver invited her to go to Europe. The taxi driver said she
> was very pretty and would make a fortune if she moved to Europe
> and worked there. With her looks, he said, she could probably work
> as a model, and he would take care of all the arrangements. Sonia
> was very tempted but still afraid. After a while she accepted his offer.
> It took him a month to arrange everything for her. Three other girls
> went with her. When they got to Europe, another taxi driver took
> their passports and said they needed to trust him since the city was
> very dangerous. They had to work everyday from 6 p.m. to 6 a.m.
> as prostitutes and were told that they would not get their passports
> back before the house manager was paid back for the travel arrange-
> ments. Sonia says she expected prostitution but had never imagined
> she would be a prisoner, threatened day and night. (UNODC 2006b,
> xvi)

Some credit should be given to the publisher of this case study for not
using the stereotypical image of a young girl being kidnapped. The reason I draw attention to this case study is to illuminate how documents
that are intended to support anti-traffickers in their work[2] construct
a particular narrative. The document in which this study appears, for
example, contains several short case studies presented in ruled boxes,
which leave limited room for complexity in narrative structure. As a
result, the representation of human trafficking is reduced to a small
number of characters. It takes on a theatrical quality. In the case study
above, we are introduced to the main actor, "Sonia," who is the trafficked victim. In addition to Sonia, there are four other actors: two
traffickers, a house manager, and a group of anonymous co-victims.
Sonia is merely given a short introduction, and the other characters
are only mentioned in passing. The chief villains (the traffickers)
appear on the stage from nowhere, exploit, and then disappear from

the story line. When one reads newspaper stories about trafficking, watches trafficking movies, and examines trafficking reports, one finds that the narrative structure is surprisingly similar to that of the story about Sonia (Hughes 2000; McLachlan 2007). Traffickers and victims are depicted as a dyadic asymmetry without any sociality. This formulaic construction of trafficking cases is partly due to the discursive necessity to create a separation between the victim and the perpetrator, a point to which I will return. The narrative is melodramatic, and individuals appear decontextualized and desocialized. We learn nothing of the social context in which trafficking supposedly takes place. Other than implicit relations between traffickers and other shady villains, all actors are presented as atomized individuals bereft of any sociality.

Traffickers are not simply depicted as amoral criminals. Assumptions are also made about their attributes and skills. Portrayals of traffickers' supreme adaptabilities commonly take on a mechanical reading. A report from Laos, for example, attempts to account for the lack of progress in combating trafficking:

> Another explanation [for the limited reduction of trafficking] has been the comparison of trafficking to a squishy balloon, where pressure applied in one place simultaneously leads to a local reduction in the problem and its "ballooning up" in another place, with traffickers dynamically adjusting to changing environments. Thus, through displacement of the problem, every actor or organisation working on trafficking will have genuine "success stories" to tell, yet the problem's overall magnitude will remain intact. Displacement can be geographical (with traffickers targeting other villages, provinces or countries), social (with traffickers targeting different social groups), or a displacement in time (for example[,] with traffickers waiting until an intervention is over). (UNIAP et al. 2004, 6)

We see here an image of highly adaptable traffickers who preemptively and systematically address potentially disruptive actions of trafficking projects. Trafficking is presumed to operate as a zero-sum game, with clear cause-and-effect relationships. Indeed, the metaphor used here is derived from the laws of physics. In this way, the imagery of traffickers takes on a superhuman and prescient character: they are mystical creatures who operate in global dark corners, they are ghosts we never see, they stand behind us and breathe over our shoulders—yet when we quickly turn our heads, they have disappeared. Still, they are able in a most frightening way to exploit the innocent through their invisible threads. They are undetectable yet omnipresent.

Organized Crime

Trafficking has often been portrayed in terms of poor, corrupted, and heartless parents selling their daughter to a brothel owner. This stereotype is well depicted by anthropologist and filmmaker David Feingold, who in an interview stated:

> Too often—in film or print—you have little Apsu, naïve little Aka girl who has been sold by dad, who is a heroin user. She is sold to a trafficker, who sells her into a brothel whereupon she is rescued by a dynamic NGO. Then, there is the compulsory interview that says Asians don't care about their daughters. . . . This sort of myth that everyone is sitting around waiting to sell their children is not characteristic of most cases. (Quoted in Silverman 2003)

It is certainly correct that such narratives have been fashionable in media. Other forms of narration also dominate, such as the notion of organized crime within a global marketplace. The cliché of morally deficient parents selling their daughters and the notion of organized crime are not necessarily mutually exclusive, however, and at times appear within the same trafficking narrative. As I suggested earlier, the ascendance of the term "trafficking in persons" stems from concerns about national security. Such anxieties have also penetrated the perception of traffickers. A trafficking training manual by the United Nations Office on Drugs and Crime (UNODC 2006a, 36), for example, asserts that human trafficking poses multiple strategic risks for a nation-state:

> Organized trafficking crime does not occur in isolation. Once established, the trafficking networks quickly diversify and develop mutually

beneficial affiliations with existing organized criminal organizations that operate in other spheres, such as terrorism, drugs and weapons trafficking as well as smuggling of migrants. . . . Trafficking of human beings on a significant scale can destabilize populations at the micro and macro level.

UNODC is not reticent in pointing out how human trafficking may affect world order. Yet UNODC is far from alone making such claims. The battle against trafficking is often depicted by anti-trafficking organizations as just that—a battle with traffickers whose powers are not to be trifled with. One representative from an NGO working in the Mekong region writes:

> Many of us are honest in admitting that trafficking is on the rise in our region and in the world: in the battle between traffickers and anti-traffickers it may be said that "we" are losing and "they" are winning. . . . While traffickers have agents in every village and networks that reach all the way to policymakers and law enforcers, we struggle to form networks of community partners committed to combating trafficking. (Aye 2002, 3)

Similarly, Kevin Bales, a well-known anti-trafficker in the United States, has warned that "many a good researcher has been wounded on that battleground and has retired to pursue other, less dangerous subjects" (2005, 89). The "battle" between traffickers and anti-traffickers has even led to the claim that traffickers are infiltrating anti-trafficking programs (Hughes 2002). Although such seemingly incendiary accusations may not be daily fare for most anti-traffickers, it is after all not too far removed from a common perception that I described earlier: the notion that trafficking is a smoke screen that benefits governments' anti-immigration and capitalist hegemony.

The lack of careful empirical attention to the organization of mobility appears not to have dawned on a number of academics who have taken great interest in the "transnational" and "organized" element of human trafficking. Although empirically based studies on trafficking networks are rather limited, this has not prevented several academics from attempting to understand its operations. A quick search through the literature on trafficking reveals a perpetual use of business-cum-mafia jargon and market metaphors (Ruggiero 1997; Schloenhardt 1999). John Salt and Jeremy Stein (1997) are among the more ambitious authors who have attempted to develop a model of trafficking networks. However, they admit to a thin empirical foundation for their own research even before commencing their analysis:

> Our hypothetical model of trafficking as a business . . . presents trafficking as an intermediary system in the global migration business facilitating movement between origin and destination countries. It is not a description of actual trafficking organizations, nor does it assume any particular size of operation, but it is an attempt to understand how such organizations operate. (Ibid., 476)

"Our hypothetical model," we are told, "is not a description of actual trafficking organizations." Yet Salt and Stein's self-admitted paucity of primary sources did not deter them from asserting:

> Trafficking system involves planning of smuggling operations, information gathering, finance and a set of specific technical and operational tasks. There are clear inputs and outputs to the system. (Ibid., 477)

We are left with an image of an international form of enterprise that is calculating, professional, transnational, hierarchical, and, most of all, profitable (see Wheaton et al. 2010). Yet at the same time the empirical basis for such claims is often flimsy.

Among UN agencies, UNODC has a primary mandate to address transnational organized crime. Over the last several years it has taken on a larger role in combating trafficking along with the United Nations Children's Fund (UNICEF), the United Nations Development Programme (UNDP), and the International Labour Organization (ILO), to mention a few. This has resulted in a proliferation of trafficking training manuals for police officers, prosecutors, and the courts. As trafficking is framed within a law enforcement perspective, due attention is given to the organizational structure of trafficking. Profiling of traffickers is highlighted, though it rarely goes beyond mentioning nationality, gender, and other generic characteristics. In some cases, attempts are made to develop typologies of different forms of organizational structures. Yet many of these reports are methodologically weak and conjectural.[3]

I am not alone in highlighting contentious claims regarding organized crime (van Schendel and Abraham 2005). Other researchers who have focused on the closely related topic of people smuggling and Chinese migration to Europe (Pieke et al. 2004) and the United States (Zhang and Chin 2002) point to a similar trend. One would have thought that wide spatial movements between these three continents would be a strong precursor for necessitating mafia-style operations, yet academics who have studied such operations in detail, such as Sheldon Zhang and Ko-Lin Chin (ibid., 737), report:

> Contrary to widely held conceptions about Chinese organized crime, most alien smugglers are otherwise ordinary citizens whose familial networks and fortuitous social contacts have enabled them to pool resources to transport human cargoes around the world. They come from diverse backgrounds and form temporary alliances to carry out smuggling operations. With the exception of a shared commitment to making money, little holds them together.

That being said, I emphasize that I am aware that both mobility and sex commerce can be facilitated by official complicity. In Thailand, for instance, it is well known that some police officers take an active role in allowing entertainment venues to operate (Wilson 2004). In addition, some Thai military personnel have been known to take part in facilitating cross-border movements. For example, in the early 1990s a senior Thai general infamously explained the presence of Burmese sex workers in Ranong Province by proclaiming: "In my opinion it is disgraceful to let Burmese men frequent Thai prostitutes. Therefore, I have been flexible in allowing Burmese prostitutes to work here" (*Nation* 1993). Yet one must avoid jumping to conclusions regarding such incidents. Human trafficking presumes a particular form of recruitment trajectory that suggests that the facilitation of sex commerce and migration is intimately connected with coercive or deceitful recruitment practices. Although it is not difficult to point to complicity of officials in the operation of prostitution and cross-border movements, this is not nec-essarily the same as organized crime syndicates being engaged in the trafficking of persons. Nor is it entirely accurate to portray commercial sex as organized. As Mark Askew (2002, 259–261) has pointed out in his critique of Thai prostitution analyses that have a political economic orientation:

> The persistent use of the term sex industry and sex tourism by research-ers implies a monolithic system: in reality it is multilayered and dis-articulated. It is united (but not coordinated) only through the con-centration of complementary venues—coffee shops, bars, hotels, night clubs in several locations, the component venues of which gain from the agglomeration economies of proximity, but whose ownership pat-terns and workers are diverse.

Although claims alluding to the involvement of organized crime must be treated with caution, one cannot categorically rule out its occurrence in Thailand, Laos, and elsewhere. The primary concern in this book is how such images compare with Thai-Lao practices of migration and sex commerce in the specific locales where this research was carried out, as well as how they shape action within the Lao anti-trafficking sector. Furthermore, not everyone who is working to combat trafficking (or commenting on the phenomenon) adheres to the view that trafficking is necessarily well organized. There is a growing con-sensus that although trafficking may at times be systemic (Caldwell et al. 1999), its organization is often small-scale and involves a highly fluid form of networks (see Feingold 1997; and Marshall 2001). Even the UNODC training manual (2006a) quoted above mentions cases of "informal recruitment." In fact, the trafficking literature contains a fair amount of ambivalence regarding organized crime. For example, Thai academic Pasuk Phongpaichit (1999, 76), writes:

> Agents include organized gangs controlled by the underworld, aided by corrupt police and other government officials in the immigration office, the airport authority, and other offices.

Yet, a few pages later (ibid., 95), a different picture emerges:

Young women who go to work as prostitutes learn the skill of luring others to follow them. Migration to work in sex services in Bangkok shows a similar pattern. An elder sister goes first. Once she is too old to continue working in the trade, she entices her younger relatives or neighbours to follow suit in order to sustain the earnings. Similarly those who make money overseas often return to lure other young women to follow in their footsteps.

The suggestion now is that trafficking is not an organized crime but more of a localized affair governed by informal family ties and networks. However, later on (ibid., 97), we are again told that trafficking is an organized professional enterprise:

In the mid-1990s traffickers began to diversify their supply source by recruiting immigrant women from Burma, Laos, China, and other neighbouring countries.

At the end of the essay, we are offered four "case studies" on trafficking, which do not substantiate any clear evidence of organized crime or professional business enterprise. They all include vague references to "agents" whom we learn little about. One of these case studies tells the story of a Thai woman and her Japanese husband who collaborate in facilitating migration of Thai women to Japan, but no clear indication is given that deception or coercion is applied in the recruitment process.[4] Such double narratives of organized crime and informal recruitment are commonplace in the trafficking literature, and as we will see in later chapters of this book, this is also a trend within the Lao anti-trafficking community.

Despite such lack of coherence, the notion of the involvement of calculating and organized crime remains conjectural and tenacious in the anti-trafficking sector. Indeed, the UN trafficking protocol itself is placed within a legal framework that criminalizes what is deemed transnational and organized in character. The way that trafficking in persons is defined in the protocol presumes the existence of an organized modus operandi, and it makes criminalization contingent on traffickers' awareness of the labor conditions they move migrants into, hence implying collusion between employer(s) and recruiter(s) (Anderson and David-son 2004; Davidson 2006).

Regardless of what the real connection between trafficking and organized crime is, many reports and trafficking programs have a ten-dency—despite lack of empirical research—to interpret trafficking into formulaic models of organized crime. In fact, it is the very lack of, or the shaky state of, data that becomes the "evidence" for organized crime. An important reason for this is that, as with any topic relating to security, claims by governments and international organizations are much less likely to be questioned, for it is assumed that their sources cannot be revealed. So when information is provided that points out the less structured, ad hoc, and fluid character of "organized crime," then the "fluid structure explain(s) why . . . organized crime groups are quick at adapting to, and diversifying into, new criminal markets" (UNODC 2002, 8). Or if a trafficker is identified and has no appar-ent connection to an organization, then this is taken as evidence of a cellular structure of operation. In other words, information that might make cracks in the organized crime paradigm is turned into cement to support it.

Finally, it is important to note that when trafficking is placed within the framework of organized crime, there is a silent assumption of agglomeration and scale. If trafficking is an organized and transnational crime that generates enormous profits, then it is a short step to imagin-ing trafficking in terms of trends, patterns, and hot spots. We will now turn to how the logic of agglomeration is reinforced when trafficking is imagined as a marketplace.

Market and Spatiality

It is common for development organizations to focus on "risk groups" and "vulnerability factors" in their anti-trafficking programming (IOM 2004b). Both governments and aid programs manage scarce resources and—at least in theory—seek to put their efforts into areas of most need. Therefore efforts are made to identify individuals or groups who are considered to be at particular risk of trafficking. Risks, or vulner-ability factors, can be aspects such as poverty, lack of education, and ethnic background. Vulnerability is not necessarily conceived in the social body (i.e., who is vulnerable?). Spatial notions of vulnerability (i.e., where does trafficking take place?) are also commonplace. In this context, it becomes possible to talk about hot spots, and here international borders become ample vessels for the logic of agglomeration. Underpinning this is a strong assumption that trafficking in persons operates first and foremost according to a unified market logic.

The most common spatial imagery depicting trafficking in persons is arguably that of traffickers preying on poverty-stricken migrants who move from a poor country—usually across an international border—to a place of opportunity. For example, Jyoti Shangera (2005, 7) asserts:

> The sites of work that draw this supply of migrant livelihood-seekers are contingent upon demand from particular sectors of the economy for certain types of labor that would enable maximization of profit. . . . The drive for maximizing profit under a competitive economic regime fields a demand for workers who are the most vulnerable and therefore the most exploitable and controllable.

An image of a marketplace composed of atomized economic actors engaging in frictionless transactions across international borders is evoked (Caldwell et al. 1999). Economic terms, such as "demand" and "supply," are used frequently, and borders are seen as demarcations of migration flows from areas of poverty to places of opportunity. This conception is often taken at face value and rarely problematized among anti-traffickers. On the contrary, this unacknowledged economism can be considered as part of anti-trafficking sector's habitus that straddles debates regarding migration and prostitution. For example, the Global Alliance against Traffic in Women (n.d.) and the Coalition against Trafficking in Women (Leidholdt, 2004) take opposite positions regarding prostitution (legalization versus criminalization), yet they both frequently frame their discussions in terms of supply and demand. As Bridget Anderson (2008a, 4–5) has pointed out, anti-traffickers, despite stark differences in their take on the subject matter, have a tendency to be "concerned with rescuing the market."

Classical economic theory perceives migration as a response to market disequilibrium (Callon 1998; Massey 1998), and it is not difficult to miss how this somewhat outmoded proposition speaks through anti-traffickers, as it were, in their reports, media statements, and pro-gramming. Indeed, it is ironic that many anti-traffickers' critiques of trafficking argue that it is caused by freewheeling global capitalism, yet they have seamlessly adopted a language of neoliberal economics to articulate this very same point.[5] The tacit and habitual evocation of market metaphors is of course not confined to the anti-trafficking sec-tor. Neoliberal assumptions about individualistic entrepreneurialism have hazily influenced development programming for years (Olivier de Sardan 2005). More broadly, as Ben Fine (2002) has observed, the market has itself become a metaphor for globalization. And have not anthropologists themselves perhaps been hasty in depicting migrants as flows (Appadurai 1996), as if human beings had weightless properties similar to those of a bank transfer?

Human trafficking, the market metaphor, and its spatial dimension raise questions about where trafficking takes place. The most common conceptualization of trafficking is as an enterprise occurring within larger patterns of cross-border labor migration that flow from poorer to richer areas, where cross-border migrants' vulnerability (e.g., socio-cultural alienation, illegal status) is commonly taken as a weak spot that traffickers methodically target in their operations. It is in this con-text that it becomes possible to talk about "migrant flows," depicted on trafficking projects' websites with red arrows, usually across borders, to indicate trafficking "trends." Indeed, trafficking and migration are com-monly articulated in aquatic terms (Beare 1999), such as "flow," "tide," "swell," "surge," and "wave." At times, such liquid properties are tied into how traffickers are assumed to operate:

> There is a growing acknowledgement of the displacement, or push-down pop-up (PDPU) effect surrounding trafficking. This name is used to describe a phenomenon whereby the problem is reduced or pushed down in one place, only to emerge somewhere else. Trafficking is a dynamic phenomenon and traffickers can quickly adjust to changing environments, in particular, but not only, by shifting geographic focus of their activities. Evidence of PDPU raises questions about the effi-cacy of a range of current programs and its acknowledgement is fun-damental to developing more effective interventions. (Marshall and Thatun 2005, 44)

In this conceptualization, traffickers are all-knowing and are capable of adapting to changes in the market. This conforms neatly with the tendency of classical economic theory to depict human subjects as atomized, desocialized, and frictionless (see Callon 1998; Fine 2002; and Massey 1998). This approach is problematic for two reasons. First, conceptualizing traffickers in this way obfuscates how agency ought to be articulated. As Pierre Bourdieu (1998, 24–25) has remarked with reference to rational choice models:

> For, granted perfect knowledge of all the ins and outs of the question, all its causes and effects, and granted a completely logical choice, one is at a loss to know wherein such a 'choice' would differ from pure and simple submission to outside forces or where, consequently, there would be any 'choice' in the matter at all.

Second, the market metaphor appears to work differently for traffickers and victims. Classical liberal economic theory presumes agency in order for an economic actor to maximize utility, and agency is something trafficked victims are unable to exercise, as they are by definition in an exploitative situation controlled by traffickers. Indeed, trafficked victims are often depicted, not as subjects, but as commodities (Molland 2010a). However, in much of the trafficking literature in the Mekong region (Feingold 1997) and elsewhere (Anderson and Davidson 2003), it is widely acknowledged that trafficking commonly begins as voluntary migration, where migrants seek better opportunities but somehow along the way end up in trafficking situations.[6] As will become evident, the emphasis on the ability of risk groups to make rational choices is also implicit in anti-trafficking programs in which removing incentives (thereby implying the ability to make rational choices) to migrate through the provision of rural development is a key strategy. In these instances, the assumption that migrants act according to the logic of a marketplace also adheres to them. Hence, although the rational choice model at first glance appears to apply only to traffickers who prey on a market disequilibrium that straddles borders, human trafficking discourse implies a much broader notion of a marketplace. As several of the aforementioned quotations suggest, although traffickers play the role of bringing supply to demand, the common picture is that they do so in the context of preexisting flows that are underpinned by discrepancy within the marketplace. In other words, traffickers prey on migration flows but do not create them. The consequence of applying such market metaphors to an understanding of trafficking is that it furnishes cause-and-effect notions of agglomeration and hot spots. And this conceptualization has not only a spatial dimension but also a bodily one that emerges most clearly in presumptions about profitability and the demand side of trafficking.

Demand: Correlations of Bodies, Profit, and Value

The trafficking literature makes two intertwining assumptions about profit in relation to production and exchange value. The reason for the enormous profitability of trafficking is often deductively presumed by juxtaposing it with drugs: "An ounce of cocaine wholesale is $1200 but you can only sell it once, a woman or child [is] $50–$1000 but you can sell them each day over and over and over again (30 to 40 customers a day), and the markup is unbelievable" (Keefer 2006, 2). To canvass profitability in this way is nothing short of a tautology. The first of the two assumptions at play here is the notion of trafficked victims being resold "over and over," either by being sold to a customer (such as a client in a brothel) or being transferred from one trafficker and resold to another. However, the purchase and subsequent sale of any commodity do not in themselves explain its profitability, (which depends on purchase price relative to sale price). It is here that the second assumption is smuggled in—that is, the possibility (and often fact) that traffickers and exploiters repeatedly deprive the victim of earnings (often in the form of debt bondage). Again, this is nothing other than stipulating a Marxian conception of surplus value. Indeed, within a capitalist logic, surplus value is the definition of profit. The repeat income extracted from surplus value does not denote a qualitative difference between trafficked and other forms of labor. Just as a trafficker extracts surplus value from his or her victim "each day over and over and over again," so is the case for bank managers and their employees, university chancellors and their lecturers, and UN agencies and their technocratic officials. Profitability, or surplus value, is a relative property and needs to be considered in light of a range of factors (surplus value relative to exchange value; total trade volume; price relative to production cost, etc.). Trafficking may well be profitable, but the exact reason for that profitability becomes an empirical question and cannot be determined from axiomatic comparisons with the drug trade.

The notion of profitability also refers to how the body is valued as a function of exchange. From the point of view of a law enforcement agency or a trafficking project, an obvious question is, who is likely to be trafficked? It is common in the development sector to try to understand who may be "at risk" in village communities by profiling villagers according to age, gender, ethnicity, education levels, poverty, and "lack of awareness." This constitutes a strange teleological projection, in which anti-trafficking programs attempt to formulate outcomes of complicated migration patterns retrospectively using generic village-based socioeconomic data. It is therefore no surprise that over the last few years it has become fashionable to shift focus toward the demand side of trafficking.

Concentrating on demand directs attention away from risk factors in migrants' source communities and toward questions about production and consumption, which take place at migrants' destination points. In other words, the demand side attempts to understand the roles employers and consumers play in engendering deceptive or coercive recruitment that leads to exploitative labor situations. The challenge of demand-side reduction for a trafficking project is well depicted by Bridget Anderson and Julia O'Connell Davidson (2004, 26) in one of the best-known studies on the demand side of trafficking:

There is no reason to assume that individuals who wish to exploit others are only or specifically interested in trafficked persons. It is hard to imagine an abusive plantation manager or sweatshop owner turning down the opportunity to subject a worker to forced labour or slavery-like practices because s/he is a "smuggled person" rather than a "victim of trafficking," and harder still to imagine a client refusing to buy the sexual services of a prostitute on the same grounds. It makes more sense to assume that the niceties of international and national law on trafficking, and the details of a person's journey into vulnerability and unfreedom, are irrelevant to those who exploit or consume their labour/services.

Neither migration nor labor exploitation in itself accounts for the demand side of trafficking. From a trafficking project's point of view, the question then becomes, why does a factory owner employ trafficked labor as opposed to voluntary labor? Or, why does a brothel owner employ trafficked women as opposed to voluntary sex workers? In other words, reasons for trafficking are being directly associated with and linked to the modus operandi of business enterprise.

When it comes to the commercial sex industry, how one understands the demand for trafficked labor depends on what view one takes on prostitution. Those who take an abolitionist stance on prostitution see all sex work as constituting trafficking, thereby equating the demand side with client demand (Davidson 2006; Hughes 2004). In legal terms, several governments are considering criminalizing customers who seek commercial sexual services. The first country to do so was Sweden. The criminalization of customers also informs many discussions around trafficking, including influential reports such as the US State Department's annual trafficking report (Weitzer 2005).

There is already considerable controversy in regard to the "Swedish model," mainly around the question of the practicality of criminalizing clients. One may want to ask, why not just simply target third parties, such as pimps and traffickers? One reason this approach is not taken has to do with an implicit abolitionist stand on prostitution. Focusing only on third parties would imply that sex commerce without third-party involvement is benign, and by extension prostitution itself becomes neutralized and removed from any moral-political gaze. However, another, more fundamental issue at play is the relationship between criminalization and state intervention on the one hand and the implicit understanding of a marketplace on the other. By criminalizing clients, one assumes that law enforcement has the ability to have an impact on or even undermine a market, as reflected in the following statement by Thomas Eckman, a prominent Swedish police officer involved in investigating trafficking cases:

> It will be more difficult to earn money. I believe there must be more focus on those who purchase sex. It is them who create the demand and consequently the problem . . . Trafficking is a business like any other business. There are some who want to earn as much money on

their investment in shortest time possible. If it is difficult for buyers to find their way, then this is clearly disruptive for the procurers. (Quoted in Storvik 2006; my translation)

Supporters of targeting demand do not constitute a homogenous group, however. Organizations and individuals who believe there is a distinction between voluntary and nonvoluntary sex workers have also shown an interest in "demand." Just as with the frequent recycling of the word "market," the "demand side" of trafficking is eagerly written and talked about in several quarters. The Palermo Protocol recommends that state parties "discourage the demand that fosters all forms of exploitation of persons, especially women and children, that leads to trafficking" (UN 2000, 6), and the United Nations' *Recommended Principles and Guidelines on Human Rights and Human Trafficking* sees demand as a "root cause" of trafficking and encourages governments to "[analyze] the factors that generate demand for exploitative commercial sexual services and exploitative labour and [take] strong legislative, policy and other measures to address these issues" (ECOSOC 2002, 12). Again we see how individuals and organizations that may have different views when it comes to legalization of prostitution write about trafficking in conceptually similar ways.[7] In part, the ubiquity of an emphasis on demand can be explained by the previously mentioned shift in focus to the migrant's destination point. Many organizations emphasize the demand side to draw attention away from migration and toward what many believe is the main problem: labor exploitation at the destination point of migration. Targeting demand can also be framed within an explicit law enforcement objective based on the argument that increased prosecution of traffickers will act as a deterrent and consequently reduce demand (ECOSOC 2002; US State Department 2007).

From an analytical perspective, it is clear that an abolitionist stand on prostitution makes any analysis of demand tautological—that is, because all sex commerce equals trafficking, all consumption of commercial sex equals demand for trafficking. In contrast, when one makes a distinction between voluntary and trafficked sex workers, the question of demand becomes far more intriguing: that there is a demand for sex commerce does not in itself explain why there is a demand for trafficking. Hence, a missing link must be identified to account for the presence of trafficking.

To date, most research on the demand side of trafficking has emerged from development organizations and UN agencies. These reports tend to vary in quality and style and do not constitute anything approaching a coherent body of theorized scholarship.[8] This is perhaps not surprising. As Arjun Appadurai notes: "Part of the reason why demand remains by and large a mystery is that we assume it has something to do with desire on the one hand (by its nature assumed to be infinite and transcultural) and need on the other (by its nature assumed to be fixed)" (1986, 29). Nonetheless, trafficking literature does provide some clues to what demand may entail. First of all, when one asks for the reasons for employment of voluntary and nonvoluntary sex workers, one is interested in, not only the consumption of sexual services (i.e., clients), but also the role of employers and recruiters in facilitating the availability of sex workers and sexual services. It is common to suggest that traffickers and exploitative employers are likely to hire workers who are docile and easy to control. Migrants, women, children, and ethnic minorities are the usual suspects. Along these lines, sex industries have focused on diversification. It has been noted that some customers desire women who are socially or culturally different them or are imagined to be socially subordinate (Anderson and Davidson 2003). Hence, some commentators have suggested that trafficking is found at the low end of the sex industry: "A rationale indeed for many bar owners to provide trafficked women is that they cost less and therefore, they can correspondingly charge their clients less" (Long 2004, 19). According to this view, the demand for trafficking is explained by low profit margins. In a Marxian sense, the employers and third parties are in a particularly good position to reap the most surplus value. This suggests that trafficking should be more frequent in certain segments of a commercial sex market because of profit maximization and cost-cutting strategies. This is one of the most common assumptions being made about trafficking demand, and the contradiction between the assumption of low profit margins and the assumption that trafficking is one of the most profitable illegal enterprises in the world appears to go unnoticed.

In relation to this view, some anti-traffickers have focused on particular preferences among clients in the commercial sex industry. Under conditions of capitalist logic, the value of sexual practices becomes contingent on scarcity, which is to say that there is a generative disparity between demand and supply (Singer 1993). Value, in turn, must be constructed with reference to needs and desires, which within the commercial sex industry are fashioned by the double enticement of erotic desire and commodity fetish. The connections between desire, value, and availability become reinforced through diversification and proliferation of commercial sex. Linda Singer writes: "The economic advantage of specialized sexuality is not only proliferation (more kinds of sex, more kinds of supportive instrumentation), but the creation of differential economy of access and availability, a kind of erotics of supply and demand, which allows certain sexual practices to be proffered at premium prices, given their presumed relatively limited availability" (1993, 48).

It is here that other assumptions about both vulnerability and profitability sneak into the equation of trafficking and demand. Physical attributes (skin color, bodily appearance) and personality (demeanor), as opposed to factors such as poverty and lack of awareness, are features that are deemed relevant in explaining a person's vulnerability to trafficking. In this context, it becomes common for anti-traffickers to associate direct correlations between profit, value, and essentialist notions of female bodies. As Sigma Huda, a former UN special rapporteur on trafficking herself, has stated: "The fairer, taller, and prettier they are, the more desirable they are, the higher the price" (1999). The claim of congruence between beauty, market value, and trafficking vulnerability is also commonplace in trafficking reports (Berman 2003; Hughes 2000) and somewhat contradicts the aforementioned proposition of low profit margins. In this view, it is the large profit potential, and not low profit margins, that entices recruiters to apply nonconsensual recruitment methods. If the demand for a particular type of woman is strong and the number of such women who work voluntarily in the sex industry is limited, then this situation could lead third parties to use deception and coercion in order to meet market demand. A similar proposition is made with reference to particular sexual services. There may be a demand for particular transgressive sexual services for which it is difficult to solicit enough sex workers to perform voluntarily. Consequently, the client demand for transgressive sexual services may engender coercive or deceptive recruitment practices.

In some cases, there can be a convergence between particular types of women and types of sexual services, as exemplified by the sale of virginity and pedophilia. Pedophilia and the sale of virginity may overlap, and they are similar in that they irreversibly change—in an intensely embodied way—the status of the person who provides, or is made to provide, the sexual service. In the case of the selling of virginity, the female body is categorized according to binaries (one either is or is not a female virgin; see Molland 2011). Consequently, one would expect direct correlations of demand, profit, and female bodies to be particularly intelligible. Although in theory the sale of virginity does not necessarily need to involve minors, it is heavily associated with underage prostitution. And it is with regard to this type of trafficking that most abolitionists and advocates of sex worker rights often hold a similar view of the demand side. I pointed out in chapter 1 that the UN trafficking protocol makes a distinction between adults and children. In legal terms, underage girls by definition cannot consent. Consequently, any recruitment, whether deceptive or not, into prostitution is deemed to be trafficking. Here we see a discursive shift from a dyadic to a universal conception of agency. This suggests that congruence between profitability, the value of female bodies, and trafficking should be particularly lucid for anti-trafficking programs. However, for reasons that are explored in later chapters, projecting such models onto the social reality of cross-border sex commerce along the Thai-Lao border entails its own difficulties. But first we need to consider how the market metaphor of trafficking resonates with the everyday life practice of sex commerce and mobility along the Thai-Lao border. That is the subject of part II.

PART II

LOCAL IMPERFECTIONS

On-the-Ground Realities and Ambiguities

4 Teens Trading Teens

Entry to Thailand by being fraud, Treat [*sic*] or force, kidnap
Did you come with agent?
The work that you do is not the same one that the agent told
    You [*sic*]
You did not get any payment or get less than you were premised
    [*sic*]?
Did you get the Physical violence? [*sic*]
Have you been impeded by your employer or not?
Have you expereinced [*sic*] Sexual violence?
Do you get sick or have any accident from your work
Did you work more than 8 hours/day?
Did you work more than 12 hours/day?
Can you go back home by yourself after being sent to the
    Border?
    —Guidelines for the first stage in identifying trafficked persons,
        by a Thai NGO working with Lao migrants

LEGAL DEFINITIONS of trafficking presuppose a dyadic conception of agency. Determining whether trafficking has occurred is primarily a question of whether a third party has applied deception or force in an active way with the intent to exploit a migrant. Whereas trafficking literature commonly implies that recruitment is inherently nonconsensual, academic literature on prostitution has tended not to address this question directly. Academics who research trafficking by and large ground their critiques of trafficking discourse in analytical and conceptual arguments, without reference to detailed empirical studies of how recruitment is carried out (Doezema 2000; Sullivan 2003). In contrast, scholars who focus on commercial sex in Thailand and Laos have tended to draw attention to circumstantial reasons for women entering the sex industry, consequently giving less prominence to the logistics of how women become sex workers. Some authors have commented on "informal" recruitment (Muecke 1992; Phongpaichit 1982), often referring to involvement of community members (relatives). Others have highlighted regional differences in Thailand, where the presence of "agents" has been more prominent in the north and informal kinship-based recruitment more common in the northeast (Lyttleton 2000). Attention has also been given to recruitment of Thai men and women abroad (Sobieszczyk 2000). Yet few have problematized recruitment itself with regard to the particular question of coercion and deception involving third parties. This constitutes a general gap of knowledge in research. In this chapter I discuss some of the different ways recruitment is carried out, as well as implications for interpreting them in the context of trafficking definitions.

This chapter describes the significant divergences that exist between how human trafficking is articulated through legal regimes, such as the Palermo Protocol, and the way recruitment is carried out in the sex industry along the Thai-Lao border. These divergences are important backdrops for later chapters that examine both spatial and embodied images of trafficking, as well as the ways anti-traffickers attempt to reconcile these divergences.

Sociocultural Aspects of Prostitution

Nort and Da

The following incident occurred after I had made numerous visits to the Friendship Bar in Vientiane, Laos.

Phut [my research assistant] and I arrive at the Friendship Bar around eight o'clock in the evening. We enter the main room. Two men are sitting together with two *sao borigan* [female sex workers], drinking beer in a corner. Loei, a new recruit, greets us. Another sex worker recognizes us from earlier visits. She reassuringly proclaims, "Nort will come soon. Do you want to wait for her?" We usually sit and drink with Nort when visiting the Friendship Bar. Here women are careful not to step on each other's toes by "stealing" regular customers from each other. We say it is OK and we just want to sit down and have a few beers.

We go out on a small veranda that is elevated over the rice fields. Rice paddies stretch out into the dark horizon that is occasionally lit up by distant lightning. There is a slight cool breeze as a thunderstorm is approaching. Outside the bar, there are a few cows. One of them gave birth the day before, Loei tells us.

Loei gets a few bottles of beer and joins us while we wait for Nort. Loei has worked in the bar for only two months. She was introduced to the bar by another young woman whom she knew from her hometown in Udomxay Province in northern Laos. Loei is wearing a traditional *sin* [sarong] and a faded old shirt. She is not wearing any makeup; her hair is in a ponytail. She looks like *phu ban nork* (a country person) who has come straight from her village. Loei's appearance contrasts with that of the other women who have worked in the bar for a while. They wear makeup, fashionable clothes (knee-length skirt or mini-skirts; fitted or tight tops or blouses), modern hairstyles, and neatly decorated fingernails.

While we sit drinking, family and friends of the *mamasan* and *papasan*,[1] a couple who own and manage the Friendship Bar, arrive and congregate outside between the bar and the adjacent family house. The *papasan* is in full swing barbecuing. The air is filled with the smell of burning charcoal, Laotian dance music, and humming voices. Suddenly a boy about eight years old comes running into the bar, then vanishes. A group of kids are playing hide-and-seek. Children's giggles and quick footsteps add an audible, buzzing backdrop to our conversations.

Nort arrives. She is wearing a knee-length skirt, a white blouse, and a modern hairstyle. She looks like she has come straight from the hairdresser. In contrast to her usual attire, she is wearing a gold bracelet and necklace. It turns out that it is the *mamasan*'s birthday, which explains Nort's ostentatious attire as well as the small party that is evolving outside the bar.

Nort is in a good mood. She is chatty and constantly smiles. She tells us that she just returned from her village in Ban Kheun. Her family is doing well. The reason she went back home this time was to leave prostitution, she proclaims. She wanted to open a shop in her village. But then the *mamasan* called her and asked if she could work a bit longer, suggesting that Nort postpone quitting until after the rain season. Nort agreed and returned to the bar.

While we sit talking, one of the other sex workers leaves with a customer who is a *tuk tuk* driver.[2] He has paid *ka ok han*—a fee for taking a sex worker outside the venue—to the *mamasan*, and he and the sex worker are on their way to a guesthouse. Nort and another woman shout jubilantly, "Het peua koy, deh! Het peua koy, deh!"[3] The woman and the *tuk tuk* driver giggle; then they drive away.

Nort talks about a regular customer she has been seeing. They get along well. He has given her gifts, and recently he gave her a refrigerator, she tells us. But she is angry with him because he visited another bar last week.

A bit later Nort's regular customer, by chance, turns up. Nort runs up to the car. They talk, but we cannot hear what they say. Nort returns and looks upset. He walks toward the neighboring bar, which is located about hundred meters away. Nort is emotional. I can see tears running down her cheek. While he walks toward the other bar, Nort shouts after him, "Ma lin, ma lin!" [Come and "play" here, come and "play" here!]. The *papasan* comes out on the veranda. "Nort, don't shout at customers like that. It is his choice. If he does not want to come here this time, then you have to accept that." Nort is quiet. She turns her back halfway from us. She cries. Loei tries to comfort her. Nort stands up abruptly and storms off to the toilet, slamming the door behind her.

Loei and another woman stand outside the toilet door, trying to calm Nort down. "Forget him," they say. "He's an idiot! Don't worry, Nort." Eventually Nort comes out again and joins our table. She does not want any more drinks. Phut and I look at each other. We don't know what to say. We quietly finish our drinks, pay our bill, and leave a tip. Nort thanks us. We agree it will be better if we come back another time.

At the time of this incident, Nort was eighteen years old and had worked at the Friendship Bar for about a year. She came from a village that is approximately seventy kilometers from Vientiane. She was adopted at a young age after her parents died. Her stepfamily are rice farmers. Several times Nort complained about her stepmother. She does not treat her well, Nort alleges. The stepmother blames her for everything that goes wrong. "I started to work [in this bar] to get away. I wanted to show them [her stepparents] that I can earn money," she proclaims. Nort started working in the Friendship Bar when she was seventeen. She was introduced by "a friend," she says. She did not sell sex the first four months but debuted as a sex worker by selling her virginity for 10,000 baht (US$315) to a Thai businessman. She has worked in the Friendship Bar ever since. Nort once told me, "My stepmother wants to buy a piece of land. I will save my money and buy the land for them." A few months earlier . . .

Phut and I arrive at the Friendship Bar in the early evening. Nort sees us and comes running toward us. She is merry and flirty, which is a common identity posturing in such venues, perhaps in the hopes of whatever material benefit might trickle from visitors. We sit down inside the bar. A new recruit joins our table. Her name is Da, and she comes from the same village as Nort. She does not conform to Lao conceptions of feminine beauty (light complexion, skinny, and young). She is in her early twenties, dark skinned after considerable time spent farming, and of a rather generous proportion. After a while, Da says, "This is the first day at work for me." Then she says, "My stepmother sold me to the bar." Her family, who live close to a river, had bought a boat and had a debt of 600,000 kip [US$60] to pay off.

Da is not forced by the bar owner to be in the Friendship Bar. In contrast to the other young women there, Da does not get a commission on beer sales, and she feels guilty eating the food in the bar, as she is not officially "employed." It seems to be the case that the owners hesitantly allow her to hang around without controlling her in any way or supporting her. Da tells us that she does not want to work as a prostitute. Her stepmother had complained that she had taken care of Da all these years of bringing her up, and now it was time that Da made herself useful to the family. Da tried to refuse, but the stepmother beat her and brought her to the bar.

These stories about Nort and Da pose two sets of questions. First, they call attention to analytical and methodological challenges as to what constitutes trafficking in persons. Second, the coexistence of family parties, playing children, the social status of customers, and mothers who force their daughters into prostitution raise questions about morality and norms of work, sex, and reciprocity. Before discussing the specificity of recruitment, we will first examine some of the social and cultural aspects of both prostitution and labor migration in the Thai and Lao context.

Modernity and Tradition: The Interplay of Kinship, Reciprocity, and Morality

The literature concerning both labor migration and commercial sex is far larger for Thailand than for Laos.[4] Despite obvious differences in politics and socioeconomic development, the two countries share linguistic, cultural, and social similarities. This is particularly so for the lowland Lao in Laos (the dominant ethnic group) and the predominantly ethnic Lao of northeastern Thailand. Hence much of the literature that analyses Thailand, particularly the northeast, can—with some caution—be projected onto Laos as well. Much has been written about why women enter prostitution in Thailand. In what follows I will recapitulate some of the main arguments pursued in the literature, in order to assess its relevance for the social context of Lao women who work in the sex industry along the Thai-Lao border.

SEX: FROM PATRONAGE TO CASH

A lot of writings on commercial sex have tended to focus on tourist-orientated prostitution. However, prostitution in Thailand is also very much a local affair and dates at least back to the Ayudhaya period (1350–1767), when it was legalized and taxed by the government (Montgomery 2001b, 41; Van Esterik 2000). Meanings of prostitution at this point were different. Mia klang todd (slave wives) were common—a wealthy man would pay a poor woman in return for his sexual monopoly over her (Montgomery 2001b; see also Turton 1980). In 1805, prostitution was introduced as a legal category in Thailand, and the term ying nakorn sopheni (prostitute) came into use, which both formalized the position of women who sold their bodies, and was a factor in the intensification of their stigmatization (Montgomery 2001b). These changes need to be seen in the context of expanding Chinese labor migration to Bangkok and other Thai ports, as well as the importation of Chinese female prostitutes (Askew 2002; Kirsch 1996). Sukanya Hantrakul (1988) argues that prostitution increased in Thailand after the abolition of slavery in 1905 (see also Feeny 1989; and Van Esterik 2000). Hence women who had earlier been under the patronage of men now entered a more explicit commercial sphere, and the outlawing of polygamy in 1935 reinforced this process. Hantrakul (1988) argues further that prostitution has always been embedded in Thai nobility and trickled down to the lower classes. Although the outlawing of polygamy did not diminish prostitution, its criminalization, along with the abolition of slavery, contributed to an increasing supply of women entering prostitution as well as a larger pool of men who could afford commercial sex. This shift of availability of female bodies from patronage toward a more explicit commercial sphere needs to be understood in a context of patron-client relationships.

FREEDOM AND POWER: PATRON-CLIENT RELATIONSHIPS

Historically, slavery was commonplace in Southeast Asia. Historians and anthropologists point to the combination of a scarcity of people and an abundance of land to account for this phenomenon. Anthony Reid (1983, 8) explains:

The key to Southeast Asian social systems was the control of men. Land was assumed to be abundant, and not therefore an index to power (with the partial exceptions of Java and Central Thailand in relatively modern times). It is this that distinguishes traditional Southeast Asian states from feudal ones. Society was held together by the vertical bonds of obligation between men.

This type of social system is commonly referred to as a galactic polity, where state power was spatially configured from a royal center and radiated outward toward its peripheries (Tambiah 1976). Although this sociospatial conception of traditional power has been criticized (Day and Reynolds 2000; Walker 1999), there is broad consensus in the literature that one important source of power was the control of people, in contrast to the appropriation of land. Captured enemies, whose numbers could be considerable, were often turned into slaves (Stuart-Fox 1997; Terwiel 1983). For instance, when the Kingdom of Siam invaded Vientiane in 1826, no fewer than six thousand families were taken captive as slaves (Turton 1980). Indeed, slavery was often an interethnic affair, placing minorities in particular on an unequal footing with more powerful lowland polities. This observation led James Scott to suggest that "the historical basis of freedom in precolonial, and much of colonial, Southeast Asia was physical mobility—the capacity to flee the reach of the state" (1998a, 50). Defining freedom in this way has some relevance to this book. As will become evident, one of the main minority groups in Laos, the Khmu, is overrepresented among Lao sex workers, and I will return to reasons why this is the case. The historical unequal relationship between minorities and majorities in both Thailand and Laos has its contemporary manifestations in the form of exploitative wage labor in the mountains of Laos, the lack of citizenship among many Thai minorities, and the use of the word *kha* (slaves) by many Thai and Lao even today to refer to several minorities derogatorily.

To say that slavery is a reflection of unequal relationships between lowland and highland ethnic groups is, as Stanley Tambiah (1976, 121) has pointed out, to tell only half the story. Commenting on the relationship between freedom and slavery, Igor Kopytoff notes that "ethnographically, the opposite of slavery in most societies (and with the striking exception of the modern West) is some notion not of autonomy but of citizenship, of civic belongingness, of attachment to structure rather than detachment from it (so the 'freeman' of colonial New England was the locally anchored property holder—the very opposite of the autonomous wanderer)" (1982, 220–221; see also Patterson 1982). Indeed, freedom in Thailand and Laos has historically not necessarily meant fleeing but rather seeking a patron. Whereas the power of a patron (*nai*) was dependent on mustering a following of clients—whether they were commoners (*phrai*), bonded persons, or slaves (*that; kha*)—the poor and the weak could find both opportunity and security in being aligned with a powerful patron (Reid 1983; Terwiel 1983). In large parts of Southeast Asia, including what is today Thailand and Laos, the majority of the population fell under such hierarchical relationships (Carné 2000; Feeny 1989). A numerical hierarchical system called Sakdina indicated the social rank of entire populations and articulated rights and obligations all the way from the king down to commoners and slaves.

Translating "slavery" in the classical liberal sense, in which it is opposed to individual civic freedom, is hence problematic: "In general, life in Old Siam was insecure and harsh. Little legal and financial security was available from the state to commoners or even nobles. Freedom from other people, especially potential supporters and patrons, was not desirable or even imaginable" (Aphornsuvan 1998, 170). As human beings are the index of power, collateral took the form of people, not property (Turton 1980). This applied not only to patrons but also to clients: "Pawning one's dependants or oneself (and in modern times one's property), or else entering a very unequal partnership with the creditor who became the patron if not the master, were the common Southeast Asian means of obtaining capital" (Reid 1983, 11). David Feeny notes the same trend: "One popular avenue to debt slavery was gambling. The Thai government extracted considerable revenue from fees for licensing alcohol, opium, and gambling establishments, especially in urban areas. Gamblers pledged their wives, children, and themselves as collateral" (1989, 294). Pointing to subtle regional and historical differences, Andrew Turton (1980) has critiqued this tendency to portray old Siam as a place where people happily bonded themselves to patrons. That being said, reciprocating labor for debt was often seen as an accepted obligation embedded in patron-client relationships (Reid 1983). Hence bondage was—and still is in many cases—not seen as a moral problem. Indeed, as Akin Rabibhadana has observed: "Thai words for buying slaves are interesting. It was not *su that* (buy a slave) but *chuai thai* (help to redeem). The reason for using the term 'help' was that one helped the poor by lending money to him" (1969, 110).

As we will see throughout the remainder of this book, there is indeed a fine line between bonding (i.e., trafficking) and helping someone. The types of slavery discussed here, such as the Sakdina system, are of course long gone in both Thailand and Laos. However, it is important to recognize their legacy in shaping social relations in modern times and encouraging "the growth of structural and normative patterns useful for the maintenance of control of people" (Lande 1977, 82). Several scholars (e.g., Girling 1981; and Scott and Kerkvliet 1977) have described such patterns in terms of patron-client relationships. Carl Lande (1977, 77) writes:

The distinguishing feature of archetypical patron-client relationships is a broad but imprecise spectrum of mutual obligations consistent with the belief that the patron should display an almost parental concern for and responsiveness to the needs of his client, and that the latter should display almost filial loyalty to his patron—beliefs reflected by the tendency for familial appellations to be employed in the relationship.

Patron-client relationships are characterized by face-to-face interaction but also inequality. However, this inequity of power has a limit:

While a client is hardly on an equal footing with his patron, neither is he entirely a pawn in a one-way relationship. If the patron could simply issue commands, he would have no reason to cultivate a clientele in the first place. His need for a personal following which can be mobilized on his behalf requires some level of reciprocity. Thus, patron-client exchange falls somewhere on the continuum between personal bonds joining equals and purely coercive bonds. (Scott and Kerkvliet 1977, 442)

Hence neither the patron nor the client necessarily sees such a relationship as exploitative. As will become evident, in the context of migration and sex commerce along the Thai-Lao border, a penetrating market economy and modern aspirations have an important bearing on how interpersonal relationships take shape and are understood by the social actors themselves. But such relationships are unstable and can quickly alter or break down if one or both parties perceive that the reciprocal flow has turned in their disfavor. Indeed, the unpredictable nature of such relationships has been one of the main conundrums within Thai studies.[5]

Although the significance of patron-client relationships has been modified by a range of processes, such as population growth, colonialism, and increasing state and market penetration (Scott and Kerkvliet 1977), its endurance must be acknowledged. Several scholars have commented on the importance of hierarchical personal alliances in rural contexts (Phillips 1974; Paul Cohen and Wijeyewardene 1984). Although traditional sources of patronage such as landownership may have withered (Lande 1977), patrimonial relationships have made inroads into a range of modern institutions, whether it is political parties, bureaucracies, military institutions, or development aid programs (L. M. Hanks 1977; Lande 1977). In contemporary Laos, patron-client relationships have been noted to be influential in politics (Evans 1998) as well as in rural, suburban, and urban contexts (Rehbein 2007).

Such patron-client relationships remain central to both Thai and Lao sociality, for they structure interpersonal behavior and the ways in which emotional and sexual aspects of social relationships are understood and experienced. Emphasizing patron-client relationships is not intended to suggest that they are all there is to Thai and Lao sociality. It is precisely how patronage meshes with other social parameters that is analytically significant, and academic literature points to how these shape both out-migration from villages and sex commerce.

CONTEMPORARY NORMS: BUNKHUN, THAN SAMAY, AND THE MONETIZATION OF MORALITY

Contemporary writings on Thailand (Keyes 1984; Mills 1999), and to a lesser extent Laos (Ngaosyvathn 1993; Rigg 2005), have drawn attention to reciprocal relationships between parents and their sons and daughters to account for both female labor migration and women entering prostitution. The Buddhist term "Bunkhun" (debt of merit) is central. Parents give life to their children, who reciprocate through respect and material support throughout their life (Mills 1999; Montgomery 2001b; Muecke 1992). In this sense, in the Thai and Lao countryside children are seen as an investment in both religious terms (strengthening of karma through enactment of Bunkhun) and material terms (through children's contributions on the farm) (Montgomery 2001b). Daughters and sons reciprocate differently, as is succinctly recapitulated by Penny Van Esterik: "In rural contexts, women express the idea that one raises a child in expectation of explicit returns. A daughter repays the debt to her mother by remaining in the parental household to care for her parents in old age, while a son ordains as a Buddhist monk to pay his mother back for her breast milk" (1996, 27).

Traditionally, Lao and Thai ethnic groups are characterized by uxorilocal matrilineal kinship systems (Ireson-Doolittle and Moreno-Black 2004; Van Esterik 2000; Whittaker 1999). Matrilocality has been common, with usually the youngest daughter staying on the parents' land and looking after them when they get older. Although this residence pattern is lessening, it still informs reciprocal norms among family members. Therefore a stronger pressure is exerted on daughters to provide material support and care for their family than on sons (Keyes 1984; Kirsch 1996). Additionally, although inheritance is commonly split between sons and daughters, it is usually the latter—particularly the youngest daughter—who inherit land. Hence women have had a relatively strong material and economic position in Lao and Thai societies. However, within increasing marketization of the countryside (introduction of wage labor, monetary consumption), both the power and the traditional means of fulfilling reciprocal obligations through the principle of gratitude (Bunkhun) have diminished (Whittaker 1999). Labor migration and sex work have thus become new ways of fulfilling traditional obligations through the sending of remittances (Muecke 1992).[6] One of the first studies to draw attention to this is one on Thai sex workers, conducted by Pasuk Phongpaichit (1982). Based on her findings, Phongpaichit argues that women entering the sex industry do not depart from traditional norms but, on the contrary, fulfill daughters' cultural normative obligation to provide material support for their families. This is why the prostitution stigma can be mitigated through remittances and merit making. Chris Lyttleton writes: "Widespread acceptance of this practice [prostitution] is couched in the village rationale that the woman's ostensible deviance is mitigated by the merit she accrues for supporting her family" (1994, 259). Or as Wilson has so aptly put it: "It is the desire to be appropriate daughters that makes them inappropriate women" (2004, 93). Simultaneously, Bunkhun has been used as an explanation for why families allegedly pressure, or outright sell, their daughters into prostitution (Muecke 1992). Indeed, the aforementioned commonality of using persons as collateral in older times, as well as the account of Da's being forced by her stepmother to work in a Lao beer shop, resonates with this point. Scholars disagree as to what extent Buddhism engenders the debut of young women into prostitution. Although most would agree that Buddhist teachings do not contain explicit prohibitive commandments against remunerated exogamous sexual liaisons, it remains a point of controversy as to whether Buddhism legitimizes gender hierarchies that facilitate prostitution (Muecke 1992) or whether Buddhism plays more

of a complementary gender role that has less of a bearing on prostitution than does capitalist consumerism (Keyes 1984).

This debate is perhaps more than anything a question of emphasis. Although it is true that Buddhism places moral obligations on
young women to provide for their families, it gives little purchase to
account for prostitution using singular parameters (Lyttleton 1994).
Bunkhun does not alone account for prostitution (and more generally,
labor migration) in Laos and Thailand. As is so abundantly evident in
many parts of the world, modernization allows for new identity positions (Derks 2008). The desire for modern and fashionable status symbols, as well as modern life experiences (*chiwit thansamay*), also shapes
women's decision to leave their villages (Mills 1999). Mary Beth Mills
(ibid.) has drawn attention to how the increasing female labor migration from rural northeastern Thailand to Bangkok challenges traditional notions of gendered space. Whereas male mobility is accepted
and an important source for masculine identity markers, female mobility challenges norms regarding women's and girls' morality and com-
munal obligations. This tension is accentuated by how modernity and
the female body are portrayed in mainstream Thai culture: "Women or
women's bodies represent powerful images of modernity and progress.
The active, mobile, beautiful 'modern Thai woman' is celebrated and
promoted in the entertainment media, beauty contests, shopping malls,
beauty salons and a wide range of advertisements, all of which tend to
link feminine beauty and sexual attractiveness to the acquisition and
display of the latest market commodities" (Mills 1995, 259). Consequently, according to Mills (1999), there are two contesting selves for
young rural Thai women: "good daughter" (enacted through Bunkhun)
and "modern woman" (enacted through *chiwit thansamay*). And it is
precisely during visits to their home communities that these two selves
can be reconciled through gift giving, provision of money, and ostentatious display of modern status symbols. However, although there are
intimate associations between modernity, beauty, and the young female
body, "only a fine line separates it from the stigma and moral degrada-
tion of the prostitute" (Mills 1995, 259). We will later see that Lao
female migration and sex work also exhibit this dichotomy.

Accounting for prostitution through the nexus of modernity and
tradition has also been analyzed from a different angle: how sexual

transgression (premarital sex, adultery) is mediated in village settings in northeastern Thailand (Lyttleton 2000) and in Laos (Lyttleton 1999a; Ngaosyvathn 1993). When sexual transgression comes to the attention of the village community, the man's (or boy's) family has to compensate the woman's (or girl's) family. Such compensation takes place irrespective of consent between the couple. Lyttleton writes: "Fines in reference to sexual transgression on the village level appear to stem from traditional beliefs in village spirits which required ritual placation in such cases. However, now this has more and more taken on a form of money exchange. The result is that the commodification of the female body becomes internalized by villagers (both men, women, boys and girls)" (2000, 166–167). In some cases such fines can be considerable, even as much as bride-wealth, which also entails the compensatory logic of Bunkhun. Instead of perceiving bride-wealth as a contribution to raising the groom and bride's children in her home, in Thailand (and Laos) it is widely perceived—by both academics and village people—as the obligation of the groom's family to repay in-laws' efforts in raising the bride (ibid., 113). Indeed, bride-wealth is sometimes referred to as "the price of the mother's milk" (*kha nam nom*). It must be emphasized that the payment of fines for sexual transgression is not practiced everywhere and predominantly occurs among ethnic Lao in northeastern Thailand, as well as Lao and Khmu in Laos (Lyttleton 2000, 2008). Nor is the payment of fines as common as before. Nonetheless it still occurs and informs normative understandings of gender relations in rural areas of northeastern Thailand as well as Laos.

That there is a monetary value on both bride-wealth and fines for sexual transgression creates an association between marriage and the commoditization of female bodies (Lyttleton 1999b). This association is reinforced by the observation that bride-wealth can be reduced if there is suspicion about the bride's premarital sexual experience (Mills 1999). Van Esterik explains: "Marriage and prostitution articulate different but complementary spheres of existence for Thai men. Both are commodified, and reflect the expectation that a man should pay to have access to a woman's body. Daughters repay debts to their parents by marrying wealthy men who can supply bridewealth, or by becoming a prostitute and sending remittances home" (2000, 190). The material association between village fines and bride-wealth also accounts in part for why a woman's status in sexual relationships can assume several forms, including wife, mistress (*mia noi*), "rented wife" (*mia chao*), and prostitute. Prostitution must therefore be understood in light of sexual relationships that are inherently hierarchical and reciprocal in character. As Lyttleton puts it: "The point is that aspects of material exchange associated with a patron-client framework are frequently entwined with notions of love and sex. This is so much the case, that, in the context of the everyday concerns that people bring to relationships, the combination of intimacy and gender inequality inherent in heterosexual relationships means patronage can seldom be usefully disentangled from emotional and physical exchange" (1999b, 37). In other words, social stratification is intimately linked with emotional and sexual relations. Patron-client relationships and the broader social order become embodied in how intimacy is understood and experienced (Lyttleton 2000).

This also has consequences for adolescents and sexual experimentation prior to marriage. There is no doubt that premarital sex is now more common in Laos (Lyttleton 1999a) and far more so in Thailand (Allen et al. 2003; Fordham 2004). However, boyfriends are unstable currency (they might not commit to marriage), which means that prostitution is sometimes considered as a possible alternative to nonremunerated intimacy with boyfriends. As one female Vientiane resident told me, "Premarital sex is very bad [*baw di*]. It is a shame for the family. Prostitution is equally bad, but at least a *sao borigan* can send money to her family." Many Lao sex workers consider prostitution to be "better" than "wasting time" with untrustworthy boyfriends, and we will later see that such views further an increase in the commoditization of virginity. The sale of virginity, no doubt, can involve deception and "sweet talk" by third parties, but it can simultaneously be perceived as a maximization strategy among young Lao women (and girls). Saying this does not equate with applauding entrepreneurial agency among young Lao women. On the contrary, this is an expression of the highly marginalized position in which many young Lao women find themselves, where they have to make very difficult choices within a society that provides few opportunities for young rural women.

Nor is there a lack of moral sanctioning of prostitution. Sex work is far from celebrated among Thai and Lao culture and is in many respects considered a threat to public order (Jeffrey 2002). Stigmatization in the

form of gossip, social exclusion, and the jeopardizing of marriage credentials among women who have worked in, or are suspected of working
in, the sex industry are common concerns (Mills 1999). Premarital sex
also carries a strong moral sanctioning. We have seen this already in the
historical example of fines that apply irrespective of consent (Lyttleton 2000). Although it is the man's (or boy's) family that must provide compensation, "a crucial task of feminine restraint is to guard the
body's virginity and sexual purity (*khwaam borisut*)" (Mills 1999, 98).
Hence sexual transgression carries a far heavier moral weight for women
than for men. While marriage—at least in theory—provides a woman
with a respectable status and material support, being a prostitute secures
the latter (which in turn partly mediates the former), whereas having
a boyfriend might secure neither (unless it results in marriage, that is).
It is therefore no surprise that scholars point to the commonality of
women from the northeastern parts of Thailand entering prostitution
after breaking up with a partner (Askew 1999, 2002; Lyttleton 2000).[7]

Finally, we must keep in mind that in Thailand and Laos the social
body is contextual and fluid, with an emphasis on, in Goffman's words
(1981 [1959]), the stage of a social actor. Van Esterik writes: "In brief,
surfaces are transformable, temporary and aesthetically pleasing, while
the self—who he/she really is—remains hidden and ultimately unknow-
able, a worldly accommodation to the Buddhist concepts of *anatta* (non-
self) and *anicca* (impermanence)" (2000, 203). Thus, along with gossip
regarding what a given family's daughter is *really* up to while working
in a faraway city, Lao—and even more so Khmu—villagers also learn
to ignore such questions in a public sphere (Lyttleton 2008). I earlier
mentioned the disproportional number of Khmu women in the Lao sex
industry, and the distinction between public appearance and conduct on
the one hand and actual practice on the other might be even more relevant in Khmu communities. Literature on norms around sexual transgression among the Khmu is limited indeed. However, one recent study
(Lyttleton 2008) suggests that although the imposition of fines for certain forms of sexual transgression is practiced, just as among the ethnic
Lao, moral sanctioning is more closely linked with its spatial anchoring.
Extramarital sexual practice away from the village household carries far
fewer normative consequences in Khmu villages than among the Lao,
because it does not evoke spiritual sanctions of village spirits.

The Changing Faces of Prostitution: Thailand and Laos

Commercial sex takes multiple forms in both Thailand and Laos, and there are important differences and similarities between them. In some respects the two countries are moving in opposite directions with regard to commercial sex. The Thai sex industry has for a long time operated in a far more liberal sociopolitical context. In big cities, commercial sex venues are often explicit and ostentatious in their marketing. However, the anxiety surrounding the HIV/AIDS epidemic since the late 1980s has led to increasing regulation of the sex industry, commonly operationalized through the medical apparatus (Fordham 1998). This development has had a direct effect on the types of venues that cater to sex commerce, as well as the forms of social interactions and identities that such regulation enables. Whereas sex commerce prior to awareness of the HIV/AIDS epidemic tended to take place in classic brothel settings with a unitary script for both sex workers and clients, these days sex commerce has moved toward a more indirect sphere (restaurants, entertainment clubs, etc.), where more open-ended forms of social interactions take place between sex workers (insofar as they identify as such) and their customers (Lyttleton and Amarapibal 2002). Furthermore, although Thai sex workers are subject to far less punitive actions from state authorities than those administered in Laos, this is not the case when it comes to the influx of migrant sex workers from neighboring countries. Over the last few years there have been several reports on migrants, including sex workers, who are deported and at times allegedly abused by Thai police (Amnesty International 2005; *Bangkok Post* 2007; *Nation* 2004).

During the heyday of the Vietnam War, Vientiane had a sex industry resembling that of contemporary Bangkok, albeit on a small scale. A report on prostitution in Vientiane from the late 1960s portrays a varied sex industry with brothels catering to the lower classes and specialized venues offering fellatio and more acrobatic forms of sexual entertainment:

The most famous of Vientiane's whorehouses is the "White Rose." A long-standing bar-brothel of dubious repute. International word-of-mouth fame has made it an instant Mecca for visiting potentates such as American congressmen presumably on "fact finding" missions on the U.S. involvement in Laos. The "White Rose" has the usual rooms upstairs for assignations but it thrives, not so much on this service, as on the activities which go on in the dimly-lit bar. Fondling, groping, undressing are common. For 500 kip, a prostitute will strip and dance nude. Instances of customers performing cunnilingus on a woman atop a table have been reported. The special house show, however, is a nude dance. For the price of several drinks, the dancer will light several cigarettes, insert them in an inappropriate female receptacle, and contract the muscles of her stomach to "puff" them. (Jackson M. Wolff and Donnan 1970, 182)

Such practices came to an abrupt halt when the communist Pathet Lao came to power in 1975. In addition to individuals who were on the wrong side of the political divide, those who were deemed deviants, such as prostitutes and hippies, were sent off for reeducation (Askew et al. 2007; Stuart-Fox 1997). Since then commercial sex has been subject to severe scrutiny. However, in the context of a political program of economic and social liberalization since the late 1980s, the Lao sex industry is today slowly moving from state regulation and surveillance toward a more liberal and deregulated atmosphere. This is not to say that sex commerce has reached explicit styles comparable with those of contemporary Thailand or of Vientiane's former decadent self. Indeed, the Lao government prides itself on its "purer" moral credentials relative to those of its neighbor, as reflected in a tourist brochure published by the Lao National Tourism Administration (2006, 21):

Gallantry: Gentlemanly behaviour at all times!
  Those seeking romance with Lao people in mind may be disappointed. Laos, unlike many of its neighbouring countries, forbids the liason [sic] between foreign gentlemen and local persone [sic] consequently the HIV virus is not the only risk involved. Police inspections of hotels sometimes occur and one may be subjected to a hefty fine and expulsion while the locaux [sic] participant faces a far harsher penalty. So be careful.

Hence it is not only sex commerce but even extramarital liaisons between Lao citizens and foreigners that are subject to policing.[8]

However, although sex commerce was—and still is—discreet and indirect, it is simultaneously proliferating in both scale and variety. A decade or two ago, men could not assume sexual availability among women in entertainment clubs. One way of assessing a woman's willingness for more intimacy was to take note of how close she would allow her body to be to the customer during dances (see Lyttleton 1999a). In contrast, during my fieldwork it was commonplace that venue managers, or sex workers themselves, explicitly flagged monetized sexual availability. Additionally, there are now other ways of obtaining commercial sex that were not readily available a few years ago. During the few years I lived in Laos (2002–2006, mostly in Vientiane), three main changes occurred. First, female and transvestite (khatoey) streetwalkers along main roads in Vientiane emerged, many of whom were explicitly promiscuous in terms of their dress (gaudy makeup, miniskirts, high heels) and their body language (posturing; eye contact with men walking by; audible marketing).[9] Second, facilitated by the ubiquity of mobile phones, many hotels and guesthouses can—and do—provide guests with phone numbers of escort services. At the same time, in response to general societal liberalization, there are now far fewer restrictions on bringing outside companions to guests' bedrooms. Third, along some of Vientiane's main roads tuk tuk drivers eagerly—yet discreetly—make no secret to (male) passersby of their ability to provide both drugs and women.[10] At the same time, there are clear limitations to overt commodified sexual hedonism in Laos. At times, Lao government officials state in international and regional forums that "there are no brothels in Laos." This might come across as an expected conservative defense mechanism that is difficult to take seriously. However, such statements contain a grain of truth. The overwhelming majority of venues that facilitate prostitution in Laos do just that: facilitate. Entertainment clubs and beer shops in Laos rarely provide opportunities for on-site sex, although this is also gradually changing, particularly in the north (Lyttleton 2008). Thus the classic brothel is still a rare sight in Laos.

Although commercial sex, like Lao society more generally, is going through a process of liberalization, it nonetheless remains a site of unpredictable state surveillance and social control. The development aid community in Laos is aware that at times sex workers are subject to harassment, fines, and arrest by authorities. And entertainment clubs would most likely find it very difficult to survive unless they paid informal "taxes" to local authorities in addition to formal taxes.[11] It is therefore not a surprise that venues are sporadically shut down only to reopen sometime later.

Although Vientiane (or anywhere else in Laos for that matter) does not yet have anything comparable to the overt red-light districts found in Bangkok, I must point out that when I make comparisons of towns and cities in a border context, such as Vientiane and Nong Kai, the sex industries are similar in terms of their styles and forms, although major differences still remain. I will return to comparisons of types of venues, as well as differences and similarities between Nong Kai and Vientiane, in the next two chapters. Here, however, I limit the discussion to an exploration of the specificity of recruitment into Lao beer shops.

LAO BEER SHOPS

A beer shop (*han bia*) is usually owned and managed by Mae ("Mother," or a *mamasan*) or Pho ("Father," or a *papasan*). And in some cases—as with the Friendship Bar, where Nort works—a family runs the beer shop. Conversely, it is common for owners and managers of such venues to refer to their staff as *luk* (children). In both Lao and Thai culture, real and fictive kinship terms are frequently used in many social settings. However, the use of fictive kinship terms reflects a social reproduction of a family ethic (Lyttleton 2008) that has clear euphemizing effects on power relationships within these venues. Beer shops can vary in size but typically consist of a wooden or brick shack, with a few tables and chairs and perhaps a couch. They are usually equipped with a stereo karaoke system and a refrigerator (full of Beer Lao), and sometimes strings of lights and Beer Lao flags decorate the walls. The *mamasan* or *papasan* employs from three to ten young Lao women.[12] Predominantly Lao men of different ages and socioeconomic backgrounds frequent beer shops. They come either in groups or alone.[13] When they enter a beer shop, they sit down, and a *sao borigan* will bring drinks and join their company. Hence the initial role of a sex worker is similar to a hostess service—a feminine companion to both pamper the customers and take part in their drinking sessions. Beer Lao is by far the most common drink consumed, sometimes accompanied by snacks (*khap kaem*) such as dried meat (*sin haeng*) or fried insects (*maengmai jun*). As the drinking session proceeds, the customer might become more insistent. The *sao borigan* gets a commission from the beers consumed, so the increase in beer consumption entitles the customer to an increase in physical intimacy with the *sao borigan*. Eventually the drinking session might lead to the couple negotiating the terms for sexual services to take place elsewhere, commonly in a nearby guesthouse. Lyttleton (1999a) describes a very similar pattern, which suggests that the venue settings, as well as the style of social interaction, have not changed much over the last decade or more.

I will describe economic aspects and reciprocity within these dealings later on, but here I want to point out that the relationship between the *sao borigan* and the customer can take different forms. The *mamasan* and *papasan* rarely take on an active role in the negotiations between sex workers and customers (Askew 1999; Lyttleton 1999b). Rather, the terms negotiated between the two parties depend to a large degree on the relationship they build during joint drinking sessions in the beer shop. Repeat customers can establish status as a *kaek prajam* (regular) or even a *faen* (boyfriend), with both monetary and emotional transactions between the two becoming far more open-ended.

Just as the interactions between customers and sex workers take on a fluid and unpredictable character, the recruitment of sex workers does not adhere to a straightforward pecuniary logic. Because the Palermo Protocol's definition of trafficking in persons places great emphasis on the nature of how a person is recruited into an alleged exploitative situation, we will now explore recruitment within Lao beer shops in more detail.

Recruitment

Rather than exploring moral-philosophical arguments concerning agency, I seek to illuminate the process of recruitment in the context of definitions of trafficking. Doing so does not discount that a wide range of reasons for entering prostitution exists. Indeed, many informants both explained and rationalized their reasons for working in prostitution in numerous ways: poverty, debt, abusive stepparents, family conflict, boredom in the village, desire to become rich and possess nice clothes, aspirations to travel and see the world, following friends, death of a family member (and consequent need to earn extra income), support of siblings' education fees, breakup with a boyfriend or husband, loss of virginity to a boyfriend who does not want to marry, unwanted pregnancy, and so on. The point is that because trafficking definitions privilege a dyadic conception of agency, it becomes necessary to pursue the specific question of the role of who is involved in recruitment and how such a person goes about recruiting others.

Thia, Daeng, and Sei are three young women in their late teens who all come from the same village in Vientiane Province. They all work in the Factory—a small beer shop in one of Vientiane's suburbs. A middle-aged couple runs this shop, and sometimes their teenage son helps out with various errands (such as buying more beer). In addition to Thia, Daeng, and Sei, approximately five other women work here. The *mamasan* rarely goes out to recruit women to work in the shop. Nor does she use professional agents. Instead, staffing of the venue relies entirely on the ability of currently employed sex workers to recruit friends and acquaintances in their home communities, during their oscillations between the bar (for work) and their home village (for recreation, remittances, and gift giving). Thia was introduced to the bar through a friend. After working for a little while, she took part in introducing Daeng to the bar, and Daeng in turn later introduced Sei. Thia told Daeng about the real work she was supposed to perform when she was recruited, and Daeng in turn told Sei the same. All of them explain their debut into sex work as due to "poverty" and difficult family situations, and not in terms of force or deceit by a third party.

The way Thia, Daeng, and Sei were initiated into becoming sex workers conforms with what has been observed by others (Askew 2002; Lyttleton 1999a, 2000; Montgomery 2001a), and in my research this form of debut in the sex industry appeared to be common. Other sex workers at the Factory provided a different picture.

Gop comes from the same district as Thia, Daeng, and Sei, albeit a different village. Before becoming a sex worker, Gop had a sexual relationship with her boyfriend. Later on, a friend said she knew of a good job for her. "She told me that I was going to work in a noodle shop and that I would get good pay," Gop recalled. "I was very surprised when I realized that it was a beer shop. I did not want to sell sex." Responding to Gop's despondency, the *mamasan* suggested to her that she did not have to sell sex or go out with customers. Instead she could do chores around the bar and only sit and drink with customers. In explaining how she ended up selling sex after all, Gop said, "I saw how much more money the other women earned. And some customers are not that bad; some of them are handsome[*laughs*]." It took about one month from the moment Gop arrived in the bar until she went out with her first customer.

The way Thia, Daeng, and Sei recruited each other contrasts sharply with commonplace imageries of trafficking that emphasize the coercive and desocialized nature of recruitment into the sex industry. Yet although Gop's story far from depicts consensual, innocent, and cozy recruitment among friends, neither does she exemplify a prototypical trafficking case. Early on in my research, I encountered similar gray-area cases in a small beer shop in Houaxay (northern Laos).

> Nut is an eighteen-year-old woman from Xaygnabouly Province, and she has worked in a beer shop for only a few weeks. A friend who returned to her village told Nut she could arrange a good job in Houaxay. Nut was eager to earn money and came along. She was very surprised when she arrived in Houaxay and realized it was a beer shop where there was an expectation to sit and drink with men and to provide physical intimacy and sex.

Although Nut was deceived, there appeared to be no physical restraint that stopped her from leaving the beer shop. However, there are clear constraints for some new recruits once they are in a bar environment, as exemplified by Nok, who works in the same beer shop as Nut.

> Nok is twenty years old and comes from a Phou Noi [ethnic minority] village in Udomxay Province. "I do not go out with clients," Nok alleges, limiting herself to accompanying customers in drinking sessions. A friend from her neighboring village recruited Nok to the beer shop. "I was tricked," Nok says. Her friend told her that she was going to work in a shop in Houaxay, but instead she was taken to this bar. Nok stayed in the bar for two days but did not like it at all. She left the bar and moved to a guesthouse but could afford to stay only three nights. She did not know what to do. She wanted to go home. The

third day, she went to the market. By chance, the bar owner was there and persuaded Nok to come back to the bar. The owner said that Nok did not have to sell sex and could instead only entertain customers. Nok agreed, as she felt she didn't have any other choice.

Khao, another sex worker in Houaxay who had previously worked as a peer educator for an HIV project, was one of the first persons to explain deceptive recruitment among peers to me. Khao confirmed that sometimes recruitment occurs among the women themselves. Often they know each other, sometimes lying about the real form of employment. The recruiter gets a commission, and the amount depends in part on the income and price levels for sexual services in the beer shop, Khao said. For example, if a woman gets 3,000 baht per month from the bar, the commission might be as high as 10,000 baht. Then the recruit has to pay this amount back to the owner over a three- to four-month period, Khao alleged. Another sex worker in Vientiane also confirmed this practice and simply said, "Sometimes women recruit other women, and they do it for money. They can get up to 10,000, even 20,000 baht for it."

I will later return to price and income stratification within different venues. The different amounts referred to here, however, most probably reflect variety in how sex workers are remunerated within different venues, as well as the fragmented and situational nature of how recruitment occurs. Furthermore it is not uncommon for sex workers to bring in friends without receiving any commission. In some cases the venue owner might sponsor a trip home for some of the workers, with the implied reciprocal obligation of bringing friends back with them when they returned (see Lyttleton 2008).

Women who are recruited sometimes need to start working right away, including selling sex. In such instances the type of venue setting appears to be a contributing factor. As Gop's case illustrates, women who have been newly recruited to a beer shop by deceit are not immediately required to sell sex. Leu, who works in a small beer shop in Vientiane, tells a similar story: "When I started working in a *han bia*, I did not really know what the job was about. The *mamasan* is good at keeping the women here. In the beginning I did not sell sex. I helped with washing clothes, doing the dishes, and so on. After a while I saw how much the other women could earn by going out with customers, so I thought, 'Why not?'" In other cases an additional transaction is introduced that makes the *mamasan* more directly involved in inducing the woman to enter sex labor: the *mamasan* provides a bonus to the woman if she starts going out with customers and selling sex. Here the recruiter is herself a sex worker, and commonly such a recruiter is an acquaintance of the woman she recruits. I will now consider how the stories of Nut and Gop may be read in light of the trafficking definition as articulated in the Palermo Protocol.

DEFINING TRAFFICKING, VICTIMS, AND NONVICTIMS

Article 4 of the Palermo Protocol states:

> This Protocol shall apply, except as otherwise stated herein, to the prevention, investigation and prosecution of the offences established in accordance with article 5 of this Protocol, where those offences are transnational in nature and involve an organized criminal group, as well as to the protection of victims of such offences. (UN 2000, 3)

The Convention against Transnational Organized Crime defines an "organized criminal group" as

> a structured group of three or more persons, existing for a period of time and acting in concert with the aim of committing one or more serious crimes or offences established in accordance with this Convention, in order to obtain, directly or indirectly, a financial or other material benefit. (UN 2001, 4)

A "structured group" is to be understood as

> a group that is not randomly formed for the immediate commission of an offence and that does not need to have formally defined roles for its members, continuity of its membership or a developed structure. (Ibid.)

These definitions do not necessarily mean that state parties will consider cases only when at least three persons are involved in the crime,[14] yet such stipulations undoubtedly place emphasis on crimes that involve some level of professionalism and scale.

The recruitment I described earlier contrasts with these definitions, as only one person recruits in collaboration with the venue owner. But even though the recruiter may be a friend, the recruitment is not necessarily consensual. Nut and Nok, for example, were not physically restricted, yet they appeared to have limited ability to leave the job. They found themselves in a town they had never been to before and where they knew nobody. With no money, they both said they did not know what else to do other than to stay on working.

The three cardinal principles of trafficking—movement, deception/coercion, and exploitation—appear to be present in the cases outlined earlier. Gop, Nok, and Nut were all moved from their village to a different town, and one of the means for enabling this movement was deceit (they were lied to). And finally, the purpose of these actions appeared to be to place them in a labor situation that involved selling sex, something they did not expect or consent to when they left the village. However, with a more careful reading, things are not that straightforward.

With regard to the recruiter's intent, it is difficult to imagine that it was anything but a conscious deception. Furthermore, "giving or receiving of payments or benefits to achieve the consent of a person" (UN 2000, 2) also occurred, for the mamasan paid an existing sex worker to recruit Nut and Nok. Hence, it can be argued that one of the means applied here was deception and that the purpose was to place the person in a nonconsensual labor situation. However, the actual process from leaving the community to entering the exploitative situation was not sequential fashion but occurred over a period of time and involved a socialization process within the venue. This has implications for our understanding of agency and consent in relation to temporality.

Considering the intent of the recruiter, it appears that the women who recruited Gop, Nok, and Nut were well aware that they had brought the newcomers into a labor situation without informing them about the intended work. But exactly what situation were they deceived into? After all, they were deceived in real time, not into selling sex, but merely into doing chores, selling beer, and entertaining customers in drinking shops. As some of the cases above show, it was only later, after a few weeks or months of socialization into a bar environment, that the women themselves—at least in a procedural sense—took the step to selling sex.

To Choose to Be Exploited

Deceit in cases like those of Gop, Nok, and Nut involves two steps. Women are arguably deceived into working in a bar only to serve drinks, but within this scenario is the presumption that once the woman is in the bar, the likelihood that she will decide to sell sex is high. The recruiter's intent includes the outcome of selling sex, but only after presuming that the women have "consented" to do so (i.e., have been socialized into accepting their situation). In this way, "consent" reenters—through the back door, so to speak—and becomes part of the equation before the exploitative situation takes place. In short, a socialization process within the bar forms a bridge between a dubious recruitment practice that, technically speaking, is free of deception with the intent to sell sex, and an outcome that the migrants would consider exploitative prior to recruitment but not after socialization within the bar. We will later see that this has important consequences for how recruiters, recruits, and anti-traffickers perceive employment trajectories and agency.

With regard to women taking the step to sell sex, it is important to acknowledge the range of parameters at play. Most migrants initially leave their villages voluntarily for a range of reasons, as is true for the examples I have provided and is also acknowledged in both academic and development literature (IOM 2004a; Rigg et al. 2004). As we have seen, although sex work might result in stigmatization, this can in part be mediated through material support for the women's families, as sex work provides relatively good opportunities for income. Furthermore, going home empty-handed can also carry a stigma, for it is commonly perceived as unsuccessful migration.[15] In this sense, as Linda Singer has pointed out, "The regulatory force is represented and enacted through a currency not of coercion but of desire" (1993, 59).

It is these types of social obligations and aspirations that bar owners and recruiters—more or less knowingly—take advantage of. A bar owner, or a young woman who has just recruited her friend, knows that the recruit desires to "see the world" and to earn money and will find it very difficult to return empty-handed to her village. The recruiter also knows that most new recruits have limited means of redress and no one to turn to once they are in a bar environment, especially given that they often have not previously been outside their village. In other words, *mamasans* and women who recruit take advantage of what they know marginalizes newcomers once they are in a bar. This marginality means that the bar owner does not necessarily need to take many active steps to ensure that the women working there sell sex. In other words, coercion is not applied through active conduct but is imposed by the very situation in which the newly recruited woman is placed. We can assume, however, that threats and perhaps even physical coercion might occur, although no informants admitted this to me. Indeed, I will subsequently draw attention to the use of physical confinement in some venues. However, overt coercion is not the main method employed to achieve the consent of women to sell sex.

This raises an important question regarding how the various means (deception, coercion, etc.) listed in the UN trafficking protocol ought to be understood with reference to its purpose (i.e., exploitation): At what point in time is the determination of a situation as being exploitative contingent on deception or coercion in order for it to be considered trafficking? The UN protocol does state that "the abuse of power or of a position of vulnerability" (UN 2000, 2) shall be considered one of the means that nullifies consent. Yet what constitutes "the abuse of power or of a position of vulnerability" is not defined and is open to speculation and selective interpretation by governments and anti-trafficking organizations. Furthermore, many trafficking programs emphasize that trafficked victims can be subject to a process of "normalization" (IOM 2004b), whereby they come to accept their working situation. We see a very fine line emerging here between deception, socialization, and normalization. The result is that the protocol's definition of trafficking allows for the possibility that migrants *can consent to be exploited.* Hence, in the cases of Gop, Nut, and Nok, where there was a time lag between the deception and the exploitation, it becomes possible to interpret their stories along these lines. The effect is that agency can be read either way.

In order to understand recruitment trajectories, we must grasp not only the complexity of how "consent" can be understood in the cases outlined above, but also the nature of the social relationships within recruitment and commercial sex venues. In contrast to the neat categories of victims and voluntary workers that are stipulated in trafficking literature, in the bar environment these categories overlap and social statuses are fluid and porous. Further complicating this murkiness is that the "traffickers"—if we see these cases as trafficking—are themselves sex workers and are subject to the same labor situation as the "victims." Indeed, in light of trafficking definitions, the type of recruitment outlined in this chapter is paradoxical, because the recruiter is usually also a sex worker. She embodies what trafficking definitions deem "exploitative"; she is both exploiter and exploitee.

Later chapters will explore how trafficking programs interpret the stories of Nort, Da, Nut, Nok, and Sei and will assess how venue owners, recruiters, and recruits perceive such recruitment practices. However, interpretation of such stories is not only an analytical endeavor but also a methodological one, raising questions about how the truths of such stories are established (through interviews, outreach services, and so on). We now turn our attention to these questions.

Identifying the Victim

The way identity posturing takes place within the Lao sex industry is difficult to grasp in only a few short visits to a site. Repeated visitation allows for a better comprehension of the context in which informants act. Hence Phut and I returned to the Friendship Bar.

There are now seven women working in the Friendship Bar and notably more customers than before. Phut and I are sitting with Nort and another sex worker. They are used to us hanging around the bar, and our identity as "customers" has been toned down. We talk about all sorts of things, such as festivals that are coming up and a recent hailstorm. The other woman is quiet at first but soon starts talking. Her name is Jai, and—just like Da—she looks like a *sao bannok* (countrywoman) who has come straight from the countryside. She is dark skinned and is wearing a traditional Lao sarong (*sin*). She tells us that she is from Luang Prabang and that this is her first day at work.

Nort mentions that she has heard rumors that Da has been back to her village, but Nort is not sure about the circumstances. Da's mother has called the bar several times.

Jai tells us that she used to sell vegetables at a market in Luang Prabang. She says it was hard work and usually lasted eight hours a day. Some of her friends brought her to the bar, she alleges. She has never been in Vientiane before. "My friends work in a factory in Vientiane," she says. "I thought I was going to work in a factory too." We ask, "What do you mean?" Jai responds, "I thought my friends were going to introduce me to work in a garment factory, but they left me here. I don't know where the factory is." Later on, Jai excuses herself and goes to the toilet. This gives us an opportunity to ask Nort what is going on. Nort confirms to us that what Jai is saying is correct. Yet Nort seems indifferent.

Like Da, Jai does not fit common notions of beauty in Laos. She is dark and older. I thought her story had many similarities to Da's. Jai returns to our table. She seems calm. We ask her why she went with her friends. She says that her friends came back to the village with nice clothes. She wanted to earn money like them, so she came along. Then she says, "My friend will come and get me tomorrow. I do not want to be here."

After Phut and I left the bar, we discussed what was happening. I said I thought it was strange that Jai's friends would bring her to the bar and leave her like that. As with Da, I could not see the rationale for the *mamasan* having her in the bar. Phut also thought this was strange. He gave one possible explanation that I thought was plausible. Phut's theory is as follows: There is no doubt that women who go back to their village inspire others to migrate because the others can see that the migrants earn money and have nice clothes. At the same time, sex workers who have not told their families about what work they do are afraid that anyone in the village will find out. They will therefore be quiet about the real work they are doing and probably say they work in a garment factory or a restaurant. On the one hand, they will go to great lengths to prevent any suspicion that they are sex workers. Yet they face considerable admiration and amusement among young people in their village. When their village friends want to come along to Vientiane, they find themselves in a dilemma. They can tell the truth to their friend, but then the whole village will know they are prostitutes. The other alternative is to not say anything and to let the friend come along and somehow get rid of her along the way to maintain the secret about their actual work. And by dumping their friend in the bar, the friend will be subject to the same potential stigma and will therefore be silent about her real work too. In other words, this form of trafficking arises due to sex workers' dilemma of lying about their work in order to avoid stigma and simultaneously being admired by their fellow villagers. The implica-tion of Phut's theory is that perhaps the other women work in another bar. When they came to Vientiane, they dumped Jai in the Friendship bar and moved on to the venue where they were working. That way they could still conceal the real work they were doing in Vientiane.

As noted earlier in this chapter, although extramarital affairs and prostitution are not as strongly sanctioned in Laos as in many parts of the world, a stigma regarding them certainly exists and can in many instances (but not all) make sex workers hide the nature of their employment. What is fascinating about Phut's explanation is that it can be seen as trafficking in the sense that a woman is being deceived into working in a bar, and many anti-traffickers would probably argue that this is indeed a trafficking case. However, the reason it happens has nothing to do with profit or organized crime.

A few days later, Phut and I visited Nort's bar again.

Today Nort is not here (she is out with a customer), but Vong joins us. Vong is Nort's friend, and we have met her several times before. Vong is cheerful and a bit tipsy. It is difficult to keep up a conversation with her. She is joking a lot and more interested in talking to some of the other women in the bar than to us.

We notice that Jai is not in the bar anymore. We ask Vong what happened. Vong says, "Oh, that lady, she is full of problems. She brings bad spirits to the bar. She is a liar [khi tua]!" Vong tells us that Jai has worked as a prostitute for several years. She used to work in Vong and Nort's bar a few years ago. "Now she left for Xiengkhuang," Vong says.

It was very difficult to know what the truth was about Jai. I did not feel that Vong's story made sense, for she did not explain—nor could I see—the rationale behind a sex worker's lying to customers by telling them that she did not want to be there. Of course, I have seen many sex workers play on pity, but this was quite different—a woman saying she did not want to be there, without any other attempt to sensualize, eroticize, or market such subjectivity to a customer. And she had made no attempt to ask us to take her out or give her money. And who knows? Perhaps Vong is lying to us. After all, she knows that we do not buy sex in the bar and that we sit, talk, and are interested in bar work. Perhaps she senses danger in giving us information about trafficking in the bar and is trying to tone this down by lying about its occurrence. To cross-check this information, I needed to ask Nort and possibly others in the bar about it. The opportunity to do so arose on a later visit. . . .

We are again back in Nort's bar. It has been a little while since we met up with Nort. We sit down. Nort brings a few beers to our table. She tells us that she has some news about Da. Nort heard that Da is apparently living somewhere in Vientiane and that she had been back to visit her home village. The village chief is upset because Da allegedly stole a mobile phone. "Was it true what Da told us when she was here?" I ask, wondering if Da's stepmother really had sold Da to the bar. Nort confirms that this was the case.

Then we ask about Jai. Vong is not in the bar, so it's a good opportunity to cross-check her assertion that Jai lied to us. Nort tells us: "Oh, Jai. She is dishonest. She must have lied to you. She used to work here, but she was kicked out of the bar. She stole 500,000 kip from me once." "But why would she lie to us?" I ask. "She wants customers to feel sorry for her," Nort says. "Does she get any customers then?" "Yes, some customers feel sorry for her, and they take her out." "Have you heard of other women doing this?" I ask. Nort responds, "No, never, but Jai is a bit of a nut!"

Later Phut and I went back to the Friendship Bar. I thought it was still unclear whether Jai actually went out with customers for sex or whether she merely got tips by playing on sympathy. The following field notes describe our next encounter with Nort:

"Do you remember the woman from Luang Prabang who did not want to work here, but lied? Did she actually go out with customers?" I ask.

Nort responds, "No, but she did not lie. She did not want to be here." Now Phut and I are very confused. "But you told us earlier that she lied to us!" Then Nort says, "Well, my sister said she told her what the work was about." Now we are even more confused.

We soon realize that we are talking at cross-purposes. Nort is talking about Da and not Jai. And now Nort had revealed to us that her sister—and most probably Nort herself—took part in getting Da to the bar. It does not mean that they deliberately lied to Da, but they must have been the link. I ask, "Was it your sister who took Da to the bar, then?" Nort replies, "No, the [step]mother took her, and it is true that Da refused but couldn't do anything."

I was never able to confirm Da's story with another woman in the Friendship Bar. It relies solely on Nort's information. There is a possibility that Nort is not being entirely truthful, but I see this as unlikely, because through the course of my research she kept her story straight four times. It is reasonable to assume that Da was indeed forced against her will by her stepmother to work in the bar and that Jai lied and pretended she did not want to be there possibly as a marketing strategy or simply to seek emotional support. I continued to receive information about these stories through numerous bar visits over seven months. It is interesting to speculate as to how anti-traffickers would approach this. Would anti-trafficking projects that provide support for victims have a bias toward such stories, depending on how the stories fit within their objectives? Do not Da's and Jai's stories legitimize the very existence of a trafficking project? Is it plausible that both would be identified as victims of trafficking? And with an acceleration of trafficking projects on the ground, how would sex workers interact with such institutions?

The stories of Nort, Da, Jai, and the other sex workers discussed in this chapter pose serious challenges both analytically and methodologically as to how one reads a bipolar model of agency. It may be useful to reflect on the types of recruitment discussed here, in light of a recent research method for trafficking that has been developed by a group of academics and anti-trafficking practitioners. This model has received an award from a regional UN program operating in the Mekong region (UNIAP 2008b) and thus is of interest, for anti-traffickers might in the future apply it in the same venue settings discussed here.

Measuring Trafficking?

I have pointed out the commonplace tendency of many anti-traffickers to make unsubstantiated claims with regard to both the scale and the nature of trafficking in persons. In response to this unfortunate tendency, Thomas Steinfatt et al. (2002) have developed a methodology to measure numbers of trafficked victims. The method involves the use of taxi drivers to identify venues catering to commercial sex, the numbers of sex workers within those venues, and the numbers of indentured (i.e., trafficked) workers.

Steinfatt et al.'s positivistic method (ibid.), which is based on statistical geographic mapping of the Cambodian sex industry, argues for a model that is transcultural and can be tested and replicated elsewhere. The authors' urge to communicate the validity of their method is such that they find it necessary to point out that their method is "scientific" more than a dozen times throughout the report. Although their rhetoric can be read as a critique of organizations and individuals who use hyperbole and unsubstantiated claims regarding trafficking, this methodology nonetheless has two serious shortcomings. First, one of its main ways of identifying venues that cater to commercial sex involves the use of taxi drivers, and the authors rationalize this approach as follows: "Taxi drivers in any urban area of the world are generally quite familiar with locations of sex areas in their territory, since they make money from both passengers who want to go there and from the business, which may give them a kickback from the customer's payout" (ibid., 4). As will become clear in the next chapter in light of how venues operate in Nong Kai, this assumption is a rather crude inductive projection that is ethnocentric in regard to how information spreads within sex industries.

The second shortcoming has to do with the way trafficking figures are derived. After a geographical enumeration is conducted to identify venues catering to commercial sex, taxi drivers are used to visit these venues. The taxi driver does so under the pretext of scouting the venue, which presumably allows him to avoid unwarranted suspicion. The taxi driver asks the venue manager about the number of sex workers that are available, price differentiation, and the ethnicity of the sex workers. The main method of establishing numbers of trafficked victims is achieved by "the driver . . . [asking] how many of the workers were or had at one time been working off a debt or were otherwise not free to leave . . . as some customers were particularly interested in being with such workers" (ibid., 5). Here Steinfatt et al.'s method is revealed as unconvincing. Although it is true that clients sometimes have specific preferences and that eroticism can be associated with the level of sex workers' docility, one cannot help but suspect that such a query would come across as both highly peculiar and outright suspicious. Furthermore, in their efforts to develop a quantifiable method to estimate trafficking, Steinfatt et al. force themselves to work with a shallow and one-dimensional conception of agency. Translating a complex legal definition of trafficking into a method that requires only a few simple verbal exchanges in a brothel is clearly problematic. Although the authors promise to provide a "scientific" method to estimate trafficking numbers, they introduce a subtle slippage by gradually equating "debt," "contract," and "bondage" with trafficking. That debt has both historically and in contemporary times been a means of maximizing one's lot seems to go unnoticed by the authors. The fallacy of conflating debt with trafficking is fairly well known among several anti-trafficking programs and is brilliantly critiqued by Teresa Sobieszczyk (2000), who demonstrates that debt bondage can just as often be a maximization strategy and that in some cases migrants prefer such arrangements to other recruitment channels (including legal ones).[16] Ironically, Sobieszczyk's research has been praised by the former program manager of the very same organization that gave the award to Steinfatt's model: "Raising awareness of the dangers will not suffice—as Teresa Sobieszczyk's research demonstrated, people often know more than we realise and debt bondage can actually be a conscious choice to reduce the risks of migration" (Marshall 2003, 5). Steinfatt et al. even admit the problem of unconditionally conflating contract, debt bondage, and trafficking midway through their report, stating: "Not all indentured workers are trafficked. Some workers are well aware of the implications of signing an indentured contract and do so willingly. For purposes of this study so as not to miss any possibly trafficked persons, all persons ever trafficked, those with indentured contracts past or present, are counted . . . as currently trafficked" (2002, 9).

To be fair, the method developed by Steinfatt and his colleagues has merit in the sense that it goes a long way to demonstrate that commonly quoted numbers of trafficking in Cambodia are most probably exaggerated, since the authors' own numbers—which conflate debt and trafficking—still produce lower estimates. Yet these estimates are also unsatisfactory, as they fail to consider that debt bondage is just one of many means by which a person may be placed in an exploitative (i.e., trafficked) situation. Nor is it clear how Steinfatt et al.'s model addresses the question of legal age. Hence the authors' claim of offering a reliable method to measure trafficking falls far short, and one is left wondering what explanatory power is left in this form of crude reductionism.

How would Steinfatt et al.'s methodology play out in the Friendship Bar? Nort debuted by selling her virginity when she was below the legal age, but she has no debt to the venue. Would this then be considered trafficking? And Da was in debt, but to her own stepmother, not to the bar owner; would this then qualify as trafficking? And what about Jai? She claimed to have been deceived in order to be brought to the bar, but she had no debt and her claims appear to have been a bogus form of identity posturing to get sympathy (and money) from customers. What information would Steinfatt et al.'s taxi drivers obtain from someone like Jai?

The real problem with Steinfatt et al.'s model is that it attempts to measure something that does not lend itself easily to measurement. The way human trafficking is discursively articulated necessitates a multidimensional reading of agency; one simply cannot determine trafficking measurements according to a bipolar logic. Reinforcing this limitation is that recruitment within the sex industry itself can be immensely multifaceted.

Steinfatt and his colleagues attempt to project a simplistic transcultural methodology that is somewhat antitechnical. According to them, no local knowledge of culture or the society in question is necessary, nor do those collecting the data require much training in the social sciences—taxi drivers will suffice. Consequently, the method can be applied and replicated everywhere. It is difficult not to miss that this method appears to be better suited to the needs of anti-trafficking programs than to the actual social reality they are attempting to address. It is a simple recipe that any organization can implement, and as it promises to be both scientific and replicable, it makes itself particularly fitting for donor funding.

When one has read through Steinfatt et al.'s research on trafficking in the Cambodian sex industry, one is left with an epistemology similar to that of the individuals and organizations he seeks to criticize. The assumption is that there is an ontological truth, whereby trafficking is perceived as something with a real and independent existence "out there," and it is just a matter of getting our tools right to detect it. Steinfatt et al.'s model appears not to provide more-objective descriptions of trafficking but rather affirms a discursive field that legitimizes the continuing combat against trafficking.

And here we see contours of a particular logic: anti-trafficking programming has a tendency to move toward ideal types. As will become evident in the next chapter, this is pertinent where anomalous recruitment trajectories tend to regress into economic models and to be rationalized with reference to those models.

5 Hot Spots and Flows

An analysis that begins . . . with the givens of the peasant
household budget, and deduces peasant needs and interests from
them . . . risks treating the peasant purely as a kind of marketplace individualist who amorally ransacks his environment so
as to reach his personal goal—that is, the stabilization of his
subsistence arrangements. The individual and society are set
apart from this perspective and society is simply the milieu in
which he must act.
  —James Scott, *The Moral Economy of the Peasant*
  (1976, 165–166)

DURING THE COURSE of my research, Phut and I revisited the Papaya
Bar, which is located not far from the Factory, where Thia, Daeng, Sei,
and Gop work. The following account is from one of those visits:

Gin, one of the sex workers at the Papaya Bar, joins Phut and me
at our table. We have met numerous times before, and our drinking
companionship is now routine. Gin is of Khmu ethnicity and comes
from Luang Prabang Province. Her journey into sex work exemplifies
that of many Lao sex workers: an informed decision based on a mix
of circumstance and informal friendships and connections. When she
initially came to Vientiane, she began working in noodle shops (*han
foe*). The pay was poor. She heard about bar work through a friend,
and one day she decided to try this type of work. She is now making
far more money than she did when was working in the noodle shops.

There are notably fewer sex workers in the Papaya Bar since I
last visited. Gin tells me that since I have been away, the owner had
to reduce the number of workers because the local authorities had

clamped down on the numbers of *sao borigan* working in the district. Some of the women had to leave, so Gin temporarily moved on to another bar in Vientiane before returning again to the Papaya Bar. Gin describes the location of the bar she moved to, and it turns out that it is the Friendship Bar, where Nort works. What a coincidence! Phut and I tell Gin that we are well acquainted with Nort. Gin laughs at this happenstance, as she opens a new bottle of beer Lao with her teeth.

Gin tells us that while she worked in the Friendship Bar, Nort moved on to Nong Kai. The *mamasan* at the Friendship Bar has a cousin who runs a similar establishment in Nong Kai and arranged a job for Nort there. Gin suspected that the *mamasan* must have received some money for this—why else recruit away one of your own employees? Or perhaps she was reciprocating favors with her relative. Nort did not work long in Nong Kai and returned to Laos later. Gin tells us that Nort had saved up 40,000 baht by working in Nong Kai but was paid only 30,000 baht by the owner. The prices were also lower. Despite this, Nort still went back to work there sometimes, moving between Laos and Thailand and hoping to get her money back. Gin laughingly adds, "Nort has had her heart broken many times by Thai men who she thinks will marry her."

Borders, Flows, Money, Women

Nort is the only one of my informants who I know, with some certainty, worked in both Vientiane and Nong Kai. Nort is therefore far from typical, yet her story does touch on several conundrums in regard to how a cross-border sex market supposedly operates: Why does Nort choose to cross the border to Thailand to sell sex for allegedly lower prices than those in Laos? Or is such a move an indication of nonconsensual movement constituting trafficking? What do such cross-border movements indicate in terms of risk and marginality produced by border zones? More generally, how can cross-border migration and recruitment within the Lao and Thai sex industries be grasped in light of the economic models that trafficking organizations often imply in their reports?

This chapter explores cross-border oscillations of Lao sex workers and some of the conundrums these oscillations raise for how anti-trafficking programs envisage trafficking and mobility to take place. I have earlier highlighted that human trafficking reports commonly portray an image of a market that has both a bodily dimension (who gets trafficked?) and a spatial dimension (where does trafficking take place?). It is the latter notion we will explore here. The depiction of migration flows as a response to market disequilibrium is also evident in the local anti-trafficking sector. Besides the use of economic jargon in reports, a strategy common to several trafficking projects in Laos is to provide vocational training and microcredit schemes in villages with out-migration. Not only do such projects, perhaps naively, assume that a "trafficking situation" is "prevented" by removing incentives for leaving the village, but such project activities also reflect a profound internalization of classical market theory. By providing opportunities "at home," these projects tacitly reason, one is contributing to a labor market equilibrium. That is, if equal opportunity exists at home, then why leave?

Furthermore, the Lao anti-trafficking sector views such a marketplace as being intertwined with spatial notions of vulnerability, produced by international borders. Most Lao anti-trafficking projects are located in border areas. Five are part of regional anti-trafficking programs (hence implying the importance of borders), and many have "cross-border" in the name of their project.[1] The border also contributes to the way migration is imagined among trafficking programs. In the previous chapter we learned of informal yet deceitful recruitment among sex workers within the borders of Laos, a practice that contrasts with the common perception that trafficking is first and foremost a problem of transnational organized crime. The local anti-trafficking community in Laos has in many respects a nuanced understanding of cross-border mobility, acknowledging that Lao trafficking occurs within the context of a larger labor migration to Thailand. Several trafficking reports from Laos point to how migration is often initially voluntary but might later lead into an exploitative (i.e., trafficked) labor situation (IOM 2004a; UNIAP and Ministry of Labour and Social Welfare 2001). Nonetheless, the imagery of socioeconomic differentiations across borders is so dominant that—for reasons we shall discover—it has distorted understandings of actual migration practices within the arena of sexual commerce. In order to explore all of these assumptions, this chapter widens its focus to compare the sex industries of Nong Kai and Vientiane.

Mobility: Thailand and Laos

National borders maintain important political functions as both gateways and protective shields within the realpolitik of nation-states. However, national borders also have important symbolic aspects. Borders transcend nation-states and "are also meaning-making and meaning-carrying entities" (Donnan and Wilson 1999, 4). Borders fashion certain forms of engagement. In this sense borders are productive in character (Rosaldo 1989), and much literature perceives borders as particularly illuminating sites for grasping social, political, and economic processes of late modernity (Chapin 2003; Rosaldo 1989; Vila 2003). It has become commonplace to assign frictionless and disembedded properties to borderlands, and it is therefore no coincidence that words such as "flows" have been in vogue within the academic literature (see Hannerz 1997; and Tsing 2000). Simultaneously, borders are productive by their very disjunctive character (Donnan and Wilson 1999). National borders divide and control. Yet the very demarcating logic of borders has its allure: "Borders are made to draw attention, they constitute a cultural signal system. The line drawn in the sand, the pause in the conversation, the door that must be opened, the ritual that has to be carried out—they all signal 'Look out! Something is happening here,' something starts, ends, or is radically transformed" (Löfgren 2002, 254). The simultaneous articulation of borders as sites of both flow and disjuncture is apt in the case of Laos and Thailand (Lyttleton and Amarapibal 2002). Vientiane, being the capital of Laos and situated along the Mekong River, is a point of gravity within Laos itself in terms of business, governance, tourism, and travel. By regional standards, however, Vientiane is remarkably small to be a capital, and in several respects it is comparable to many rural town settings in other parts of Asia. One of the most obvious comparisons would be with Thailand's Nong Kai, which is located across the Mekong River only forty kilometers or so downstream from Vientiane.

Nong Kai and Vientiane are connected not only by proximity but also by the fact that the main legal crossing point by land between Laos and Thailand is in Nong Kai, via the Friendship Bridge.[2] There is thus considerable movement of tourists and visitors, including Thai and Lao migrants, between the two cities. Over the last few years there has been a considerable increase in Thai visitors to Vientiane, some for business but even more for short holidays (Askew et al. 2007). Lao cross at the Friendship Bridge into Nong Kai for a number of purposes, including shopping in Nong Kai and beyond,[3] visiting relatives, or finding work in Nong Kai or farther afield. Although Nong Kai is smaller than Vientiane and a small town by Thai standards, the Friendship Bridge's location at the edge of Nong Kai gives the town a symbolic significance as an entry point to Thai modernity.[4]

Similarly to the way the anti-trafficking sector produces an image of migratory flows between poor and rich countries, the physical infrastructure surrounding the Friendship Bridge reflects Thai and Lao hierarchies of "poor" and "advanced" nations. When entering Laos from Nong Kai, visitors are met with a checkpoint in the form of a large building with a tilted roof imitating the roof of a Buddhist temple (*wat*). Surrounding this building are smaller shops, a few small eateries, a travel agency with information about package tours, a car insurance office, and a sizeable duty-free shop well stocked with French wine. The checkpoint itself is overstaffed with luggage handlers. Besides the migrants present at the Friendship Bridge, family members also greet or bid farewell to traveling relatives and friends there, which reinforces a bustling atmosphere. *Tuk tuk* drivers and a growing number of taxi and limousine drivers offer rides into Vientiane. Surrounding the checkpoint are large billboards advertising hotels and mobile phone companies. The infrastructure surrounding the bridge says to those arriving, "Welcome to Laos. You have come to a place of significance." In other words, visitors are reminded that they are arriving in Laos through the front door—that is, the capital city.

The welcoming infrastructure is not reciprocated, however, for those traveling from the Lao side to Nong Kai. Although the border checkpoint is similar to that of Lao, there is a dearth of other buildings and bustling activities. The architectural style of the checkpoint building is modernist, with no attempt to imitate Thai culture. There is no duty-free shop, no luggage handlers, no billboards. Besides the checkpoint, there is only one small kiosk selling drinks, cigarettes, and candy. A few *tuk tuk* drivers are hanging around. The bus station is not even adjacent to the immigration checkpoint; for some obscure reason, it is located some five hundred meters away. To the Thai, Nong Kai is a back door at the nation's periphery. And by extension, back doors lead only to places of insignificance and underdevelopment, places that at the same time offer more private and unadvertised zones for undisclosed activities.

Hence Vientiane and Nong Kai reflect—through the public infra-structure and border movements via the Friendship Bridge—the very asymmetry between Laos and Thailand: Laos as the impoverished, yet-to-grow-up little brother of the sophisticated developed and prosperous big brother, Thailand. Crossing to Nong Kai is for the Lao a gateway to modernity, whereas crossing to Vientiane is for the Thai a back door to an impoverished yet nostalgic past.

Nevertheless, the Thai-Lao border is not a stereotypical border that features sharp disruptions between the two sides. Due to strong cultural, linguistic, and kinship ties that straddle the Mekong River, the border constitutes both otherness and a shared social community (Lyttleton and Amarapibal 2002). As Vatthana Pholsena suggests: "In spite of their cultural, linguistic and geographical proximity, the two peoples on the opposite banks of the Mekong River retain this peculiar combination of closeness and strangeness for one another" (2006, 54). Border crossings do not necessarily take place at checkpoints, however. Unlawful crossings are commonplace and occur without much fanfare. In the Lao imagination, unlawful crossings connote risk and danger but, simultaneously, access to a modern, enriching, and even liberating world that is out of reach at home (ibid.).

It is worth noting that here we are talking about a migration pat-tern that has changed several times historically (Askew et al. 2007). The river has always been more of a highway than a border, and the flow of migrants from Laos to Thailand went in the reverse direction only a few decades ago. The Vientiane plains, with their low popula-tion density, attracted many ethnically Lao farmers from what is today northeastern Thailand, as settlers, wage laborers, and religious pilgrims (Evans 2007). The Vietnam War and the subsequent takeover of Laos by the communist Pathet Lao regime resulted in an exodus of Laotians, as well as estranged relations with Thailand and the closure of their shared border. More than four decades has now passed, and Thailand has become the biggest economic force in mainland Southeast Asia. At the same time, Laos has opened its borders in the context of general economic, social, and (to a lesser degree) political liberalization. These changes have not only brought peoples on both sides of the Mekong River closer together but also accentuated the socioeconomic differences between the two countries.

Although thorough data are limited, it appears that cross-border movements from Laos to Thailand have increased dramatically in tandem with the gradual liberalization of Lao society since the early 1990s (Rigg 2005). An ILO report from 2003 on labor migration from three southern Lao provinces found that 6.9 percent of the total population migrated, of whom 80.5 percent migrated to Thailand. Another report, by UNIAP and Ministry of Labour and Social Welfare (2001), documented villages where as much as 20 percent of the village population migrate on a seasonal basis to Thailand. These reports are vague in defining migration,[5] but they do indicate that a common reason for both cross-border and internal migration is for labor purposes. The ILO report notes that approximately half of the migrants who go to Thailand send remittances back to their families.

Thailand not only is a point of gravity in economic terms but also informs much of Laos' cultural orientation. That many Laotians watch Thai television is well known. Among Lao teenagers, Thai television celebrities and pop artist function as role models, and Thai TV commercials reinforce enthralling models of modernity through plush lifestyles, ideals of beauty, and leisure experiences. The role of Thailand as a gateway to modern experiences for young Laotians has been commented upon in several trafficking reports (O'Connor 2006; Phetsiriseng 2001), as well as in the media (*Vientiane Times* 2007c) and academic literature (Pholsena 2006; Rigg and Jerndal 1999). At the same time, "going to Thailand" is still very much seen as both a risky and unpatriotic endeavor that is officially condemned in political practice (UNIAP et al. 2004). Before 2007, Lao citizens who wanted to leave the country, whether for a holiday, official business, or labor migration, were required to obtain an exit visa, and a failure to do so could result in fines and even reeducation for returning migrants (see Ginzburg 2002a). Since 2007, Lao citizens who possess a passport have been allowed to travel freely to Thailand and other ASEAN countries, a policy shift that constitutes a considerable liberalization in Lao migration regimes. Nonetheless, crossing the border is still politically precarious. As late as June 2007, *Vientiane Times* reported cases where Lao migrants with valid passports were being fined by local Lao authorities upon their return home (see Phouthonesy 2007c). Considering that most Lao people cannot afford a passport and cross either with border passes or without any documents, punitive measures still strongly inform public norms around migration.

The anti-trafficking sector too has participated in articulating meanings of cross-border migration, as reflected by the erection of a UNICEF-sponsored anti-trafficking billboard at the Friendship Bridge in 2005 and a subsequent Thai government billboard on the Thai side of the border. These billboards hence symbolically mark the Friendship Bridge as a "hot spot" for trafficking.

It is in this context that migration trajectories within both the Nong Kai and Vientiane sex industries must be considered. Although Nong Kai is merely a small country town within Thailand, it constitutes a risky yet exciting doorway to modern life experiences. Vientiane has over the last few years gone through a process of considerable economic, political, and social transformation, drawing rural migrants from various areas of Laos (Askew et al. 2007). Hence Vientiane and Nong Kai are analytically significant, for they both constitute "pull" areas for migration and contain notable commercial sex industries, yet at the same time they are metaphorically a link—physically articulated by the Friendship Bridge—between poverty and modernity.

Given that human trafficking is supposedly parasitic on migration flows from poorer areas to destination points with better economic opportunities, we need to explore more carefully the price and income hierarchies within the Vientiane and Nong Kai sex industries, as well as the styles of recruitment and migration that they entail.

Income and Price Stratification in Laos

As has been discussed, social interactions in a beer shop (*han bia*) allow multiple and open-ended styles of relationships to form, establishing a framework for monetary flows and reciprocal relationships between *sao borigan* and customers. Let us now consider the income sources of a *sao borigan* in a beer shop.

A *sao borigan* can obtain her income from two main sources. First,

she receives a commission from the amount of beer she sells. This commission is typically 1,000 to 2,000 kip per bottle.[6] This in part explains
why a *sao borigan* participates in drinking sessions with customers. By
serving beer and taking part in its consumption, the *sao borigan* maxi-
mizes the amount of commission she earns, based on the quantity of
beer bottles both she and the customer consume. That the customer
indirectly pays for the *sao borigan*'s time through the commission on
beer sales is reciprocated by the customer's increasing entitlement to
intimacy (flirting, touching, kissing, etc.) throughout the drinking session (see Lyttleton 1999a). As a result, it is not uncommon for both the
customer and the *sao borigan* to become rather drunk.

The amount of beer the sex workers can sell varies significantly. For
example, in the Papaya Bar, where Gin works, the *mamasan* pays the *sao
borigan* a salary every fortnight that constitutes their accumulated commission from sales of Beer Lao. Sometimes this is as little as 10,000 kip,
or it can be as much as 100,000 kip, depending on how many customers
have visited the bar.

The second potential income for *sao borigan* derives from selling
sex. In the majority of cases, the price for sex is negotiated between
the sex worker and the customer. There is some standardization in the
prices sex workers will initially quote, but the actual price a *sao borigan*
and a customer agree on depends on the type of relationship the sex
worker and the customer have. In addition, sex workers often receive
tips.

For example, in the bars where Gin and Nort work, the price for
"short term" (going to a guesthouse for two hours or so) is 500 baht.
Prices are also quoted as "long term," which implies that the customer
and the *sao borigan* will spend the whole night together. Long-term
prices tend to be more open-ended, and sex workers commonly charge
1,000 to 1,500 baht. It is important to note that quoted prices do not
equate with what customers actually pay. In these venues sex is negotiated, which renders sex workers' income subject to considerable fluc-
tuation. Younger customers in particular can be notorious for haggling
over prices. One customer told me that he sometimes gets the price for
short term down as low as 250 to 350 baht. Some sex workers admit
that if they happen to like the customer, they might be less insistent
on receiving a particular price. Conversely, sums can exceed quoted

prices. Daeng exemplifies this. In the shop where she works, 500 baht is the standard price for short term, but sometimes long-term prices can be considerable. "*Farangs* [Westerners] have sometimes given me 4,000 baht," Daeng says. Although most of the customers are Lao, she can earn large amounts of money. "Sometimes I receive 3,000, and it is not uncommon that I get 2,000 baht," she says. Although both prices and customer frequency vary, Daeng is usually able to earn around 2 million kip per month (approximately 8,000 baht). In cases where the customer has the status of *kaek prajam* (regular customer) or *faen* (boyfriend), reciprocity takes on a far more open-ended and generalized form of gift economy, and it becomes increasingly difficult for the *sao borigan* to extrapolate income.

The main way a bar owner earns money from the commoditization of sex—as opposed to sales of drinks and food—comes through *ka ok han* (literally, "leave-shop price"). This is better known in tourist-oriented parts of the Thai sex industry as a "bar fine" and is discussed in the literature on the tourist-oriented sex industry in Thailand (see Askew 2002; Bishop and Robinson 1998; and Wilson 2004). A *ka ok han* is a fee the customer has to pay to the venue owner to take a sex worker outside the venue for a period of time. Besides being an indirect charge for sexual access to a *sao borigan* in a beer shop, it can also be seen as a compensation for the lower marketability of the venue due to the resulting decrease of sex workers in the bar. In both of the bars discussed above, *ka ok han* amounts to 40,000 kip. I will return to *ka ok han* and how managers generate profit later on, but for now I will merely note that it adds a small amount to the total cost for a customer to purchase sex.

The beer shop is only one of many venues and social contexts where commercial sex is negotiated in Vientiane. Elaborating the diversity of the Vientiane sex industry is beyond the scope of this book. However, to give an idea of its complexity and its variety in terms of price and income stratification, I will make a few observations from some of the high-end entertainment venues.

High-end venues differ from beer shops in that they are considerably bigger and the sex workers are more elegantly dressed and make a more consistent effort with makeup and hairstyles. Also, the furnishing ("classy" fake leather lounges), the decor (blinking disco lights, plastic flower decorations), and the general feel of these venues (e.g., size of the karaoke machine) are more extravagant. These venues cater to older men who can afford to spend considerable sums, and the targeting of this market is reinforced by the tendency to overstaff these clubs with male (and sometimes female) waiters, a live band, and in some cases even valet parking. These plush venues also provide an aura of value-added pampering, exemplified by the renowned shoulder massage provided by a male masseur in the restroom so that guests can wind down while using the urinal or washing their hands. The way sex workers treat the customers in these venues can at times verge on the baroque; not only is due care taken to provide snacks and whiskey, but even spoon-feeding of customers can at times be observed.

The Naga Club is a large entertainment venue that offers a spacious lounge room as well as private karaoke rooms where customers—not unlike in a beer shop—can sit and enjoy drinks and female company. Around fifty women work here. The Naga Club has on-site bedrooms (it is formally a hotel) where customers can take sex workers for an extra charge of US$4 for short term or US$6 if they need the room for the night. Sources of income for sex workers are similar to those of a beer shop. The workers sell sex for prices ranging from 1,000 baht for short term to 2,000 baht for long term. Nhut is the *mamasan* in this venue. She used to be a sex worker herself, debuting by selling her virginity for 45,000 baht, and has several years of experience in the sex industry under her belt. With regard to sex workers' income, Nhut said, "The sex workers here earn very well. None of the sex workers working here get less than 20,000 baht per month. Some ladies have as many as four to five customers a day.[7] Sex workers who are disciplined can earn enough money after one year to buy a house." A similar situation is found in another larger entertainment venue in Vientiane called the Mekong Lounge. More than sixty women work in this venue, and prices for sex range from 1,000 to 2,000 baht. An additional element in this venue is a *kha nang*, or sitting fee, of 18,000 kip. This is a fee the customer must pay for sitting with a sex worker. Women here also receive tips and commissions from drinks.

Souksavan is the *mamasan* at the Mekong Lounge, and she has a similar employment trajectory to Nhut's. Souksavan started working as a *sao borigan* ten years earlier and gradually worked her way up to become a *mamasan*. She has been a *mamasan* for six years and has considerable experience. Income came up several times in our conversations. "Do women in the Mekong Lounge earn more than in *han bia*?" I asked. "Oh, yes," said Souksavan. Then I asked her, "What is the highest income sex workers can make here in a month?" Souksavan replied, "Once we had a Lao-American who paid 100,000 baht for a lady [*phusaw*] for a whole week. He was very kind. After he returned to America, he sent gifts to the sex worker. I think they still keep in touch." Such high incomes are not representative, but earnings are similar to those at the Naga Club. As well as opportunities for greater income, high-end venues give sex workers the opportunity to socialize with older men who are often wealthy and of high social standing. It is not uncommon for sex workers to become mistresses (*mia noi*) of wealthier men, and this is undoubtedly another motivating factor for seeking work in such venues. Both Nhut and Souksavan have no difficulties recruiting workers and are in a position where they have to turn down applicants. Considering that an average teacher's salary is approximately 1,000 to 2,000 baht and that working in a garment factory provides a monthly salary of 250,000 to 500,000 kip ($US25–50) (Sene-Asa 2007), sex workers in Vientiane can earn quite a high income. Given the large numbers of Laotians who migrate to Thailand for work, one might expect that income opportunities for Lao women in the Thai sex industry might be even better than those for Thai women.

Income and Price Stratification in Nong Kai

As Nong Kai is slightly smaller than Vientiane, it should be no surprise that the sex industry in Nong Kai is comparably smaller. One NGO official in Nong Kai told me that about 90 percent of sex workers there came from Laos. Although I am not in a position to validate this claim with thorough statistical data, I would say that this might be an exaggeration. I would not hesitate to accept, however, that young Lao women dominate the Nong Kai sex industry. It is significant that one night when I was walking along one of the main streets of Nong Kai, a *tuk tuk* driver came up to me and asked, "Au phusaw Lao baw?" (Do you want a Lao lady?) The prominence of Lao sex workers in Nong Kai appears not to be well known—let alone recognized—either among government officials on a national level in Bangkok or among aid agencies who work with human trafficking in Laos and Thailand. As I pointed out earlier, despite two reports referring to Nong Kai as a trafficking destination (UNICEF and Ministry of Labour and Social Welfare 2004; Wille 2001), no trafficking projects in Laos and Thailand that I consulted about potential research sites could identify specific locations where Lao women were trafficked, let alone worked in prostitution voluntarily. Early on in my research, I corresponded by e-mail with the Thai Department of Social Development and Welfare and received the following response to my question regarding the presence of trafficking and prostitution in Nong Kai: "Women and children who are victims of human trafficking were convinced or brought to work there by agents or networks of human trafficking. They were brought into Thailand through borders in Nong Khai Province to work in Bangkok. Most of the victims do not work in nearby provinces or along the area bordering Lao PDR." It was further claimed that Lao sex workers in Nong Kai were older and had come to Thailand voluntarily by themselves. However, among local health workers in Nong Kai, it is known that there are considerable numbers of Lao sex workers there, including some cases of trafficking and deceptive recruitment. This split in knowledge probably has to do with variation in the mandates of different ministries and aid programs. Public health programs that focus on HIV/AIDS prevention tend to work far more closely with the entertainment industry than do agencies whose mission is to combat trafficking. This difference arises partly because anti-trafficking work allows governments and others to emphasize prevention in source communities, which indeed remains one of the most common anti-trafficking activities in Laos. Although there are many trafficking programs in Thailand, the focus on Lao victims is still limited[8] (the main focus being on the Burmese), and targeting commercial sex venues directly was still a novelty within the anti-trafficking sector in the Mekong region at the time I carried out my research ("Community Action" 2002).

Nothing in Nong Kai mirrors the Lao beer shops, but some restaurants and karaoke clubs are very similar to the ones in Laos. The social script of drinking, socialization, and flirting with female staff is common and is often followed by negotiated sex elsewhere. In these venues, both a sitting fee (particularly in karaoke clubs) and commissions from drinks are common. In some places sex workers also receive a set salary (*ngern duan*) ranging from 1,000 to 3,000 baht. Prices too are comparable to those in Vientiane, where short term can be around 1,000 to 1,500 baht and long term as much as 4,000 baht.

Just as recruitment into the Lao sex industry involves a co-presence of deceptive and nondeceptive practices by recruiters, so it is in Nong Kai. Moreover, as in Vientiane, such different recruitment trajectories can be found within the same venues. Lae from Laos started working in a Nong Kai restaurant after she met an old school friend on a shopping trip to Nong Kai. Her friend already worked in Nong Kai as a waitress, and her job also involved sex work. Considering the supposedly higher income potential as well as the excitement of working across the border, Lae decided to try this too. Another Lao woman, Amporn, also obtained work in the same venue through informal acquaintances. However, in contrast to Lae, Amporn was not aware that she was expected to go out with customers, which in some cases meant providing sexual services. Two weeks later she left the venue after she was pressured by the owner to go out with a customer.

Alongside these similarities between Nong Kai and Vientiane's sex industries, there are also clear differences. For example, Nong Kai has what I call "off-site brothels," which are similar to what Marc Askew (2006) has documented along the southern border of Thailand. Off-site brothels are similar to other brothels in the sense that sexual services are detached from any other form of social script. In contrast to entertainment clubs, these venues have no prelude of flirting or other forms of interaction between the sex worker and the customer besides the sexual encounter itself. Moreover, sex workers reside on the premises, in some cases with considerable restriction on their movements. At the same time, these networks are similar to hostess services, in the sense that the availability of women is arranged through mobile phones, and sexual services are offered off-site, usually at the customer's choice. Since customers do not enter these venues as in a classic brothel, the venue manager relies instead on agents to solicit customers. These agents build up a customer base using a mobile phone. Customers call an agent when they want to purchase sex, and the agent brings a sex worker to the customer's location (guesthouse, hotel, or private house).[9] Lao women dominate these off-site brothels. "Thai students" are also available through these networks, though they work part-time. In contrast to the Lao sex workers, they reside independently and are far more expensive.

Kham is one such agent, and he collaborates with five off-site brothels, as well as some ordinary brothels on occasion. His main role is to develop a customer base, but he also from time to time takes part in recruiting Lao sex workers into this network. Kham was initially a customer. Sometimes friends and acquaintances asked him for advice when they wanted to obtain paid sex, and he directed them to these off-site brothels, which he himself frequented. Gradually he realized that he could make money by charging the customer a fee. He has now collaborated with these off-site brothels for a few years and makes a good income. Kham's client base consists of approximately one hundred regular male customers, with considerable spin-off from one-time customers who hear about the network by word of mouth. This type of operation poses methodological problems for the model Steinfatt et al. (2002) developed for measuring trafficking (discussed in chapter 4). Kham's network solicits customers through the use of mobile phones and word of mouth, not through a network of *tuk tuk* drivers. More broadly, on both sides of the border, I recall only a few incidences of seeing Thai or Lao men arriving at a venue using a taxi or a *tuk tuk.*

The five off-site brothels have a similar pricing structure. When Kham arranges a customer for a sex worker, the customer pays 700 baht for short time. Kham keeps 200 baht in commission, 250 goes to the *mamasan/papasan,* and the sex worker keeps the remaining 250 baht. Thai students have a higher social status within the Nong Kai sex industry's pricing hierarchy. Short time with a Thai student can cost up to 2,000 baht. Customer frequency is relatively high. Rattana, a *mamasan* in one of the off-site brothels that collaborate with Kham, explained, "The sex workers here usually have two to three customers per day, most of them being short term customers." When I asked her about the cost of long term, she replied, "If it is after midnight, then they can be with the sex worker until the morning." Kham confirmed this, stating that sex workers typically have about two customers a day, but popular women can have as many as five. According to Kham, some of them "have to take medication; otherwise their vagina becomes swollen." It is common for the women to work about twenty-five days per month, taking a few days' break during menstruation as well as for a return trip across the bridge to renew border passes. The total income is often around 10,000 baht per month, but for popular sex workers it can be as high as 50,000 baht.

The off-site brothel network does not offer the cheapest available sex in Nong Kai. There are also other venues that conform more to the stereotypical image of a brothel. The Boutique is a small venue located in a dark alleyway out of sight from the general public. The Boutique comes alive at night. A group of young Lao women stand outside attempting to attract customers passing by. The *papasan* usually sits right outside the entrance, watching television along with some of the workers. Inside is a small dirty room with four tables and a karaoke machine in the corner. There are a few Western soft-porn posters on the wall. The bar has bedrooms upstairs, and the women's lodgings are in adjacent houses. As with the off-site brothels, Lao sex workers dominate the Boutique.

Beer is sold at the Boutique, and it is possible to sit down and drink, but it is not encouraged. The sex workers do not receive any commission from selling drinks, and the establishment is geared toward selling sex, quick and ready. Customers come and usually only spend a few minutes to decide which woman they want to bring to the bedroom. When men decide to sit down and have a drink, it is usually because most of the women are busy, so the men must wait until one is available. Thus the bar is essentially a waiting room. The bar on occasion assumes an additional social function similar to that of a *han bia* in Laos: a social space for negotiating commercial sex. A visit by my research assistant and I exemplifies this:

> While we sit and drink our beer, I recognize two Lao women we previously met in Si Chiangmai.[10] They are sitting with Thai men who look like manual laborers. We can hear them talking: "199 baht. Take it or leave it." One of the women recognizes us and comes over to our table. She was very surprised to see us here. Both women join our table. They tell us that they lost their jobs in the bar in Si Chiangmai and have just moved to Nong Kai. After a while, they go back to the other men's table, but they return to our table later on. This oscillation between the two tables continues a few times. Later on, one of the men comes over to one of the women, and we can see him putting 200 baht notes

in her hand. "Take it or leave it. I'll wait outside," he says. She looks embarrassed but eventually walks outside to the customer.

Although negotiation of prices sometimes takes place, they are fairly standardized at the Boutique. In contrast to both karaoke venues in Nong Kai as well as entertainment venues in Laos, *ka ok han* is rarely applied here, as many sex workers are not allowed to leave the premises. Instead, it primarily offers on-site sex. The venue owners, an old couple in their sixties, make a profit similar to that produced by Kham's brothel network—they simply take 50 percent commission from the sex workers' earnings. In other words, the women who work in this venue receive only 100 baht per customer.

We see here contours of two radically different types of sites specializing in sex commerce. On the one hand, there are entertainment clubs—such as restaurants, karaoke clubs, and beer shops—on both sides of the Mekong River (with the exception of beer shops that are found only in Laos). These venues allow for open-ended forms of interaction where remunerated sex follows a prelude of socialization (see Lyttleton and Amarapibal 2002). In contrast, the off-site and on-site brothels in Nong Kai do not allow for such encounters prior to the provision of remunerated sex. Although some of the managers in these venues claim that women are free to choose customers, the level of choice is limited in comparison with that in beer shops and karaoke clubs. Although I have not been able to personally observe any direct negotiations between sex workers and clients in the off-site brothels, I have witnessed customers choosing sex workers in classic brothel settings.[11] When a customer enters, all sex workers have to line up to allow the customer to indicate his choice by pointing to her. Although venue owners might intervene on behalf of sex workers if a customer is particularly unruly or violent, beyond this, room for negotiation hardly exists. In contrast, other types of venues, such as beer shops and karaoke clubs, allow for a more negotiated space, not only when it comes to prices but also regarding rejection of customers. In these venues I have seen sex workers apply a range of strategies to avoid going out with customers: pretending to be sick or menstruating, pretending to go to the toilet (and not returning to the same table), pretending to talk to someone on her mobile phone, tricking another coworker into joining the table (so that the first worker can subsequently leave the table), or simply disappearing out of sight. There is a clear difference in the way sex workers can apply various strategies in the two types of venue settings, and it is reflected in the large cut that venue managers take in off-site and on-site brothels (50 percent), whereas sex workers in beer shops and karaoke venues keep the whole amount.[12] With this in mind, what concerns us here are the differences in price hierarchies.

Contrary to what one might expect, prices for commercial sex are similar on both sides of the border, and in many cases they are even more expensive in Laos than in Nong Kai. Short time costs around 620 baht (including *ka ok han*) in a beer shop in Vientiane and 700 baht in off-site brothel networks in Nong Kai. However, sex workers in Vientiane can often negotiate higher prices than that. In glaring contrast, Nong Kai has low-end brothels where sex costs as little as 200 baht. Despite active inquiry, I have not heard of comparable cheap sex in Vientiane.[13] Furthermore, women who work in establishments in Nong Kai keep far less of the revenue from selling sex than do sex workers in Vientiane. The women in the off-site brothels keep only 250 baht per customer, and those in the low-end brothels earn as little as 100 baht per customer, whereas women in Vientiane *han bia* make 500 baht per customer. At the same time, there are venues in Nong Kai where sex workers also receive higher income, often comparable to that earned in high-end venues in Laos.

We see here that price levels within the sex industry in Vientiane and Nong Kai appear to be the reverse of what would be expected according to the commonly understood image of migration, which informs much of the anti-trafficking sector. One would assume that Thailand, being the advanced, developing "big brother" of Laos, would on the whole have higher prices for commercial sex than Laos.

That high prices for commercial sex are found in a poor developing country like Laos is in itself not surprising, given that it is a land-locked country where many goods are imported. Hence it is not only commercial sex that is pricier than in Thailand. Air tickets, a bowl of noodles, and taxis—to mention a few random goods and services—are more expensive in Vientiane than they are across the border. It is precisely for this reason that each weekend a considerable outflow of Laotians (and expatriates) crosses the Friendship Bridge to the Tesco Lotus store in Nong Kai (or beyond in Udon Thani, Bangkok) to do their weekly shopping. The presence of cheaper sex in Nong Kai most likely reflects a more diverse sex market in Thailand (with cheap, moderate, and expensive sex) than that in Laos. Furthermore, it can be argued that the comparatively pricier sex in Laos functions as a monetary compensation for devaluing the worth of female bodies. Such compensation resonates with the practice of assessing fines in response to sexual transgression in both Thai (Isaan) and Lao villages (Lyttleton 1999a), as discussed in the previous chapter. Despite all this, the notion that Laos is poor, and by extension cheaper than Thailand, remains strong. During and after my research I repeatedly encountered Lao, Thai, and expatriates who expressed great surprise upon learning that prices for commercial sex were at times cheaper in Nong Kai than in Vientiane.

However, this disparity of prices raises another conundrum. Although prices appear to be the same or even lower in Nong Kai than in Laos, Lao women nonetheless still migrate to Nong Kai. In other words, Lao sex workers who cross the border to work in Nong Kai seem to go against the current of classical market logic (i.e., maximization of utility), for they appear to seek places where prices are lower. I was able to discuss this puzzle with several colleagues working with anti-trafficking and HIV/AIDS prevention. As will become evident, most explanations are expressions of a functionalist classical economic view of cross-border migration.

Explaining Migratory Trajectories: Customer Frequency

Officials working with either anti-trafficking or HIV/AIDS programs commonly point to customer frequency when explaining Lao sex workers' pursuit of work for lower prices in Nong Kai. Although prices for commercial sex in Nong Kai can be lower, some suggested to me that the number of customers might be higher. Hence sex workers' total earnings might after all be superior in Nong Kai. In order to examine this claim, we will need to extrapolate income levels in the different venue settings of Vientiane and Nong Kai with reference to prices and volumes of customers.

From the ethnographic descriptions above, it certainly appears that sex workers in Nong Kai have more customers than do workers in Laos. According to the off-site brothel agent Kham, the number of customers—usually between two and five a day—varies according to how popular the women are. Let us now consider the lower income bracket within this brothel network. If a sex worker has on average two customers per day for twenty-five days a month[14] and earns 250 baht per customer, then her monthly income totals 12,500 baht. As we see from the discussion above, this is a bit higher than what many sex workers earn in a *han bia* in Vientiane, which is around 8,000 baht monthly. A downside for sex workers in Nong Kai, however, is that they have many more customers—fifty a month in the calculation above—whereas in Laos a *sao borigan* in a Vientiane beer shop will typically have fewer than ten, according to my informants. Furthermore, women in a *han bia* have far more negotiating power in choosing and rejecting customers than do workers in on-site and off-site brothels in Nong Kai.

If it is correct that the more popular women in Nong Kai off-site brothels have five customers a day for twenty-five days a month, earning 250 baht per customer, then their total income would be 31,250 baht. But to earn that income, a woman would have to have 125 customers per month. Although 30,000 baht is a considerable sum, there are only a few women who would be able to get that many customers. By contrast, in a *han bia*, sex workers can be found who are able to earn an income above 20,000 baht but with far fewer customers.

When considering the low-end venues, the picture is clearer. In places such as the Boutique, sex workers earn 100 baht per customer. For a sex worker to earn 8,000 baht per month, which is comparable to the income in Vientiane beer shops, she must have eighty customers per month. To earn this income, a sex worker needs an average of 3.2 customers per day for twenty-five days per month. Some sex workers will have this level of frequency of customers, and some even more, but for most the average number of customers will be fewer. Hence, economically it is clearly a far worse deal to work in a brothel in Nong Kai—even with high customer volumes—than in a beer shop in Vientiane. Added to this are the physical and emotional implications of having far more customers and less ability to negotiate and reject such interactions.

Thus it appears that in terms of income, parts of the Nong Kai commercial sex industry are comparable to that in Vientiane, albeit with more labor-intensive work, but when considering other parts of the Nong Kai industry, the picture points toward a more favorable income working "back home" in Laos. In short, as with price levels, the actual income generated by sex workers along the Thai-Lao border is to some extent the reverse of what the trafficking sector implies. Can the explanation for this contradiction then be found in the notions of risk and vulnerability—which trafficking programs also perceive to be significant for border crossings?

Risk and Illegality

Earlier I pointed out that exploring cross-border trafficking with reference to income maximization strategies can appear incorrect, as migrants who are considered trafficked would, in contrast to other migrants, be deprived of agency to function as "rational economic actors." I have drawn attention to how this objection is somewhat misplaced, as it is largely recognized in the Lao trafficking literature that trafficking is usually an outcome of migration that is initially voluntary. A statement by the manager of one of the regional projects in the Mekong is exemplary of this view: "As many people migrate first and are trafficked later, there is a need to look at what went into the decisions around leaving villages—such decisions are often rational given the range of choices and information" (Berger 2001, 5). This distinction reappears in conversations with anti-traffickers, but from an opposite entry point—that is, that deprivation of agency becomes the explanation for maintaining a rational-choice model of cross-border migration. When I point out the apparently contradictory movement of Lao women to Nong Kai, some simply see this as evidence of trafficking: the women work for lower pay because they have been forced into such working conditions. This proposition is intriguing because it would both account for the existence of trafficking and preserve the notion of a classical market logic as promulgated by the trafficking literature. Consequently, the presence of Lao sex workers in Nong Kai is not due to rational maximization strategies, simply because these migrants are deprived of exercising such choices.

In the late 1990s a social survey was carried out on Lao attitudes toward Thailand. Although positive views are commonplace, Laotians, particularly adolescent females, who have never been to Thailand simultaneously perceive it with suspicion. The following responses are telling:

We're not going with them [those who go and find work in Thailand]. We're scared that they would take our eyes.

They have a bad society, with no laws, and people do whatever they want.

They will sell us as prostitutes, and then the police will catch us and we'll go to prison, and we're scared that someone may rape us. (Cited in Pholsena 2006, 53)

The depiction of Thailand as risky is also commonplace among sex workers, and I repeatedly heard the claim that "Thailand is scary [yarn]." No doubt, anti-trafficking programming has given such anxieties an arena in which to be articulated politically. However, it would be a mistake to suggest that such views are a direct result of a governmental process enacted by anti-trafficking programming. Historically, Thailand and Laos have had a difficult relationship, and such attitudes predate contemporary concerns regarding trafficking. For example, the survey quoted above was conducted before trafficking programs existed in Laos.

I have earlier pointed to deceptive recruitment in Laos as well as entertainment clubs in Nong Kai. The same style of recruitment operation is also present in both escort- and brothel-style venues, as is evident in the following conversation with Kham:

SVERRE: You mentioned earlier that most sex workers get a job by knowing another friend who already works in your network. Are there other people involved in this recruitment process?

KHAM: Sometimes the owner [of a venue] crosses to Laos to recruit, but this is rare. Other times mothers bring their daughter to a brothel. They do this because they are poor. Mothers of sex workers who already work as prostitutes in Nong Kai recruit other sex workers sometimes.

SVERRE: How are the sex workers introduced to the work they are going to do? What are they actually told?

KHAM: In most cases they are told they have to work as prostitutes, and they tell them how much money they will earn.

SVERRE: So in most cases they are told this. But what about other cases?

KHAM: They tell them that they will perhaps work in a restaurant.

SVERRE: So what happens when the sex workers arrive and they realize what they are supposed to do?

KHAM: They have to work. Sometimes the recruiter has paid 4,000 baht in advance to the parents, and the sex worker has to pay it back. The sex worker has to find the money somehow.

SVERRE: But what if the sex workers do not want to sell sex? Have you heard of sex workers who have earned 4,000 baht in an alternative job that does not involve selling sex?

KHAM: Hmmm. No. Sometimes sex workers escape from the venue.

Rattana, one of the *mamasans* in Kham's network, also admitted that sometimes new recruits are "surprised" to learn what the work is about upon their arrival in Nong Kai. As in Laos, current sex workers often recruit acquaintances back home for a commission. In Rattana's place, sex workers usually receive 1,000 baht in commission for recruitment, but the amount can vary, depending on the "beauty" of the sex worker. In some of these cases the recruiters use deception when they recruit acquaintances back in Laos. Family members, particularly mothers of sex workers, are also involved. Kham told me on another occasion that although some mothers deliberately deceive young women and girls in their home communities to work in Nong Kai, other mothers actively recruit back home in Laos but believe their daughters are working in normal restaurants. Hence they are instrumental in luring Lao women into sex work in Nong Kai without themselves knowing it.

Thus, just as in the Vientiane sex industry, there is evidence that deceptive recruitment is taking place. Before considering this as an explanation for cross-border oscillation of Lao women between Laos and Nong Kai, it is worthwhile taking note of the implication of illegality when recruits cross the border for sex work. After all, trafficking is intimately related to the notion of risk and vulnerability, which border crossings presumably produce.

Most Lao informants I encountered cross the Friendship Bridge by using a border pass, which is valid for three days. Kham, Rattana, and NGO officials working in Nong Kai confirmed this practice. Lao sex workers travel between their workplace and the bridge every three days, many of them simply to renew their border pass and immediately return to Nong Kai. It is not uncommon that a relative waits at the Lao border checkpoint to collect a sex worker's earnings.

Many sex workers also possess a valid Lao passport, which permits them to stay and work in Thailand for longer periods of time. In contrast to a border pass, which allows legal mobility only within provinces close to the Lao border, a passport enables free movement throughout Thailand. In most cases sex workers obtain a passport in Laos, where the cost is approximately 3,000 baht.

In addition to acquiring the necessary travel documents, there is an issue of legal status of employment. In the last few years, cooperation between the Thai and Lao governments has been increasing. In 2002 they signed a bilateral memorandum of understanding (MOU), which seeks to register Lao migrants in order to legalize and regulate their labor status in Thailand (Government of Lao PDR and Government of the Kingdom of Thailand 2002). Officially, this MOU does not apply to commercial sex workers, but that has not stopped local venue owners in Nong Kai—nor the government authority that approves the registrations—from registering Lao sex workers under this program. In one karaoke venue I visited several times in Nong Kai, the Lao sex workers even carried official worker identity cards. Several informants told me that that the labor registration cost 4,000 baht for a year and that in some venues the cost is passed on to the migrant whereas in others the employer covers this cost.

Not all Lao sex workers in entertainment venues in Nong Kai possess a passport, border pass, or work permit. This lack of documentation appears to have limited impact on how recruitment and migration operate, with the obvious caveat that sex workers who cross illegally do not cross the river at official border crossings. Regardless of the migrants' legal status, recruitment is predominantly carried out among individuals who know each other and who are in some cases connected through kin networks. However, the legal status of Lao sex workers does seem to have an impact on the nature of their working conditions.

The different venues Kham collaborates with vary considerably in how they restrict the Lao women's freedom of movement. Some require the women to be present only during work hours and they are otherwise free to come and go as they please. Rattana's venue exemplifies this policy. All of her Lao sex workers have passports and work permits. Otherwise there would be "a lot of difficulties with the police," she admits. However, other places are more restrictive, and the workers are not allowed to leave the premises, because—in Rattana's own words— "they do not have their papers in order."

I once visited one of these more restrictive venues with Kham. Before we entered, Kham told me that we could only go in and "have a look" and not do any interviews with the owner, for he was "very strict." Later on Kham told me that the sex workers there are not allowed outside the venue during the day. The owner locks up the place. The reason, according to Kham, is that the owner is afraid of the police, but he also wants to prevent the sex workers from developing relationships with customers and negotiating prices directly. One method of achieving this is to prohibit the women from leaving the premises outside working hours. The same restrictive policy is also evident during the women's working hours. Another person always accompanies the sex worker when she meets a customer. This person will wait while the sex worker is serving the customers and then will accompany her back to the off-site brothel. Kham told me that if a sex worker is caught engaging in selling sex on the side, she would have to pay a fine of 500 baht, or she may even be fired. Such restrictive styles of operation can in part be seen as a contest between sex workers and venue owners in controlling the market product. Another obvious possibility—which was never suggested by either Kham or Rattana—is of course that sex workers' movements are restricted because the owner wants to prevent them from leaving the premises altogether. Indeed, both Kham and Rattana admitted that sometimes women escape. Kham also alleged that the sex workers who "struggled the most" in venues with restrictions on movements were not sex workers who were new to the industry but those who had first worked in establishments with a more open and relaxed policy and were far less willing to adapt to a more restrictive working regime.

At first glance, the suggestion that Lao sex workers work for less in Nong Kai due to trafficking seems plausible. Deceptive recruitment and restrictions of movement are carried out in some venues. However, just as in Vientiane, women who were deceived into sex work and others who entered prostitution voluntarily are found in the same venue settings. Furthermore, sex workers who have been deceived are subject to the same price and income hierarchies as their fellow workers, many of whom entered the venues knowing the work conditions. In other words, although in theory the fact that those Lao sex workers were deceived into working in the sex industry in Nong Kai would account for why they are working for lower prices, this does not account for the presence of other Lao sex workers who entered these venues voluntarily. Also, we must remember that most sex workers oscillate frequently across the border. This is particularly the case with sex workers who have border passes. That many return to their workplace every third day suggests that they work in these places voluntarily or have accepted their work situation. Moreover, the nature of their recruitment appears not to be very different from how recruitment is carried out on the Lao side—where current sex workers receive a commission for recruiting acquaintances in their home communities, sometimes using deception. Nothing suggests that a qualitative difference in recruitment exists on either side of the border or that trafficking is more frequent on either side.

Hence the migration of Lao women to the Nong Kai sex industry does not seem to fit well with explanations based on a market logic geared to distinct forms of profit making or with those based on notions of deceptive recruitment or the nature of migrants' legal status. How can we then explain such migration trajectories? To answer this question, it is helpful to consider how some informants themselves understand the reasons for crossing the border to work in Nong Kai.

Border and Attraction

Mary Beth Mills (1997, 1999) has written extensively on labor migration from northeastern Thailand into Bangkok, and she argues that an important motivating factor for migrants is *chiwit thansamay*—that is, a taste for the modern life. There is no doubt that this motivation also extends across the border into Laos. The anti-trafficking sector in

Laos is keenly aware of this dynamic (UNIAP et al. 2004; UNICEF and Ministry of Labour and Social Welfare 2004), and in conversations with anti-traffickers this suggestion often comes up to explain Lao women's continuing migration to Nong Kai, in spite of its less favorable income prospects. There is nothing surprising about this. Indeed, borders are symbolic markers that take on a particular meaning when transgressed. At the same time, borders function as "free zones" (Donnan and Wilson 1999) and facilitate forms of escapism. Several Lao sex workers who work in Nong Kai accordingly see their reason for working in Thailand as such. Crossing the border not only provides a taste of life in Thailand but also allows them to escape social policing and surveillance by community members at home. Several informants said that if they worked in Laos, they would be concerned that relatives and friends would find out what type of job they were doing. Hence, working in Nong Kai can be seen as a strategy to control information. There is no denying that the twin processes of *chiwit thansamay* and this getaway effect contribute to cross-border migration to Thailand. However, some caution needs to be taken with regard to this idea. I earlier highlighted that Nong Kai is by Thai standards a backwater, and at the same time Vientiane is both larger and more rapidly modernizing, making it in many respects comparable to Nong Kai. Indeed, in certain respects Vientiane is far more cosmopolitan and urban than Nong Kai, due in part to a large aid presence and a booming tourism, and it is currently experiencing an increase in wage labor migration from rural areas (see Askew et al. 2007).

Although the two cities are demarcated by an international border and have key differences, they also constitute a shared social space, similar to the relationship of the southern border towns of Mukdahan and Savannakhet (Lyttleton and Amarapibal 2002). Whereas Nong Kai offers a symbolic destination for those desiring *chiwit thansamay*, Vientiane increasingly has the same appeal for rural women. Gin, who was introduced at the beginning of this chapter, exemplifies this. Coming from a poor Khmu village in Luang Prabang Province, she often points out the contrasts between her village and the modern and busy life in Vientiane. And just as working in Nong Kai allows sex workers to do their job away from the scrutiny of relatives and friends, so does working in Vientiane for many Lao sex workers. It is widely known that

Lao sex workers move on to different provinces within Laos' borders precisely for this reason (PSI 2005; UNICEF and Ministry of Labour and Social Welfare 2001), and Gin also rationalizes her work in this way. Vientiane is far away from her parents, who think she is working in a noodle shop (*han foe*) and are unlikely to ever find out what type of work she really does. Hence the sociospatial configuration of Vientiane and Nong Kai as sites for both escapism and modern experiences blurs to some extent the emphasis on the significance of borders in shaping migration flows. This does not refute the general claim that a large motivating factor in Laotians' migration to Thailand is the thrill of experiencing a form of modernity. However, subtle nuances that disturb the explanatory models commonly applied to Lao cross-border mobility must be taken into account.

There are two points I wish to make here. First, in a border zone such as that of Vientiane and Nong Kai, where both cities constitute points of gravity, sex workers can draw on a wide register of pros and cons—or in Pierre Bourdieu's (1977 [1972]) terms, different sources of capital—in rationalizing their migration and employment decisions. Therefore the migration rationale can tip either way. Second, the mechanical models implied by anti-traffickers do not offer convincing explanations for the apparent contradictory movement of Lao sex workers to Nong Kai. One aspect that is peculiarly absent from such models is social relationships and how information is shared in the recruitment process of Lao sex workers. We will now consider this aspect.

Information and Social Relationships

During my research I tried to engage informants in discussions about migration by asking, "What do you think it is like over there?" Surprisingly, not a single informant admitted to having work experience on both sides of the border. Opinions and beliefs about what it is like "over there" exist, however.

Like anti-traffickers, many Lao women in the Vientiane sex industry assume there is much more money to be earned in Thailand. Sei, a sex worker in a beer shop in Laos who earns around 10,000 baht per month, was convinced that Lao sex workers in Nong Kai would earn much more than in Laos. And just as anti-trafficking programs focus on the risk of crossing borders, Sei too reasoned that migrating to Thailand was too risky and dangerous to make it worthwhile. She was surprised when I told her that I knew of places in Thailand where sex workers received only 100 baht per customer. Similarly, many Lao sex workers in Nong Kai believed that they were earning more money in Nong Kai than what was possible to earn in Laos. Lae, who was introduced earlier in this chapter, asserted, "In Laos, there are big differences between rich and poor. There is no opportunity there. For example, if you work as a teacher, you get only 1,500 baht per month. There is a lot of corruption, and you need connections in the government to get anywhere. That's why I am working here." I later asked Lae if she knew of income opportunities in the Lao sex industry, but she was not sure. That she made comparisons of income with public sector jobs, not income potential within the Lao sex industry, is noteworthy. Some informants, however, gave different responses. They told stories of how they either knew of other Lao women working in Nong Kai or other places in Thailand or had themselves been approached by agents with job offers but turned them down due to perceived low prospects of income. Daeng was a case in point. Commenting on whether Lao women earned more across the border, she simply stated, "Some earn more, some earn less." Daeng knows four other women who work across the border, but she alleges that none of them appear to earn more than she herself does. Hence information about prices and income is spread unevenly among sex workers.

Anthropology has for several decades focused on the social embeddedness of markets, where conventional economic theory has come under attack for projecting empirically misleading depictions of social reality (Appadurai 1986; Carrier 1997). Commenting on the limitations of the classical market theory model, James Carrier (1997, 18) writes:

> One of the reasons the model has the force and appeal that it does is that it roots the Market in what is construed as fundamental human nature. The Market is presented as embodying essential humanity and the ethics that spring from it. It is, in effect, what people would do spontaneously among themselves if left alone, if their propensity to truck, barter and exchange were not constrained. Consequently, any

arrangements and practices that depart from the Market model require the expenditure of energy and resources, which those who adhere to the model are prone to attack as wasteful and inefficient.

In response, several authors within both anthropology and migration studies have shifted attention toward social networks (Brettell and Hollifield 2000; Massey 1998). This shift of focus is well-taken, but with modifications. Goss and Lindquist are quite right when they point out the pitfalls of some of the presumptions about social networks: "Social networks are conceived of as 'the result of universal human bonds' . . . or locally-circumscribed affective ties, governed by informal norms of reciprocity and sustained by personal interaction. Second, migrant networks are presumed to expand opportunities for migration throughout the community as they evolve, ultimately providing near universal access to the members" (1995, 330). In other words, the assumption that information somehow spreads automatically among migrant populations must be treated with caution. This ties in with Foucault's (1980) attention to the confessional nature of Western models of truth, which is sometimes implicitly—and perhaps unintentionally—projected onto understandings of how information is shared within sex commerce in Thailand and Laos. Several health programs use peer education strategies in their outreach work, thereby presuming harmony, camaraderie, and support within a social space that is inherently hierarchical in character. Without denying that genuine social support and trust exist within many entertainment venues (Askew 1999), it is also clear that backstabbing, lying, and distrust are common. This should come as no surprise, as, after all, sex workers are in a competitive relationship with each other. Within the Vientiane and Nong Kai sex industries, infighting with coworkers is a common reason sex workers leave a venue to work elsewhere (Askew 2002). More broadly, deeply personal issues are often not subject to social sharing, a tendency that has been commented on with direct reference to commercial sex in the context of the HIV/AIDS epidemic (Lyttleton 2000), as well as in both older (Phillips 1974) and more recent (Van Esterik 2000) ethnographic studies on Thailand.

The spurious nature of the relationships among sex workers affects how work opportunities and information sharing materialize within the sex market. Although in some cases sex workers might move on to another venue for a short period to check its earning potential, it is far more common that employment in a given venue is triggered by being introduced by "a friend" (see Sobieszczyk 2000). Ironically, several trafficking reports mention, but do not reflect upon, the importance of friends and relatives in the migration process, as well as the notable lack of confirming employment information before migrating (IOM 2004a). Yet the anti-trafficking community projects a tenacious ignorance of social relations, viewing the intentional subject (i.e., the rational agent) as being external and prior to social interaction. The way recruitment is carried out in the Vientiane and Nong Kai sex industries is modeled, not on a system based on the free flow of information, but through informal networks of patronage.

I have pointed out the importance of current Lao sex workers in Nong Kai to both voluntary and nonconsensual recruitment back home. And in previous chapters we have seen a similar pattern in Laos as well. Hence, decision making about migration is triggered by informal social networks, not by a coherent understanding of a market. This is not to say, however, that no market information is available. As we have seen, at times informants have knowledge of the "other side," and over time sex workers undoubtedly develop numerous connections and networks. But this is exactly the point: information is produced through informal networks and not in a preexisting transparent marketplace with atomized economic actors. And recruitment operates through intimate and associated networks of exchange, not through externalized instruments of market assessment. As Sanford Grossman and Joseph Stiglitz (1980) have pointed out about markets generally, there is a conflict between how markets spread information and incentives for acquiring information. Mitchel Abolafia observes: "The transaction is not a simple dyadic exchange. Its outcome is a reflection of the social and cultural, as well as the economic, forces shaping it. These forces determine who may transact, how the commodity is defined and a variety of other conditions of transaction that affect buyers and sellers" (1998, 69). The limited knowledge that sex workers have about prices and income was neatly summed up by Kham when I asked why Lao women worked for such low pay in some of the venues in Nong Kai. "The reason," he said, "is that the women do not know that you can earn much better elsewhere. Most of the women are introduced by other friends, and they simply don't know much about other places or prices." As Kham illustrates here, market information is limited in the venues he collaborates with, and what triggers a change in employment (or a debut into sex commerce for that matter) depends on social connections. In contrast, the anti-trafficking sector seeks explanations that reference a register of individual rational choices and maximization, where a focus on the actual migration process itself is peculiarly absent. Thus we have canvassed a pattern that will become clearer when I later discuss anti-trafficking activities in more detail—that is, when confronted with anomalies, anti-traffickers have a tendency to ricochet back to ideal type models of knowledge. It has now been noted several times that we are studying a commercial sex industry that employs both deceptive and nondeceptive recruitment practices. Human trafficking literature commonly reads such distinctions in the context of assumed correlations between essentialist notions of female bodily value and profit. In the next chapter we will see why this is not so.

6 Profitable Bodies?

Every established order tends to produce (to very different
degrees and with very different means) the naturalization
of its arbitrariness.
　　—Pierre Bourdieu, *Outline of a Theory of Practice*
　　　(1977 [1972], 164)

If the girl is very pretty, she will be trafficked, one hundred
percent!
　　—Lao government official

It is early evening. Distant thunderclouds darken the horizon over
the Isaan plains. The sound of drumming raindrops fills the air. The
local market has just closed down for the day, and the streets are gradually emptied of people. The mechanical sound of mopeds and cars is less
intense. A barking dog and the squeaky noise of a *tuk tuk* interrupt the
monotonous rhythm of falling rain. Locals and visitors are gathering in
eateries along the river for supper and evening drinks.

Not too far away is a small house located along a back alley. Young
women sit around a television screen, watching soap operas. They wear
fashionable jeans and tops. Some of them wear slightly more evocative
attire, such as high heels and miniskirts. Their hair is neatly groomed,
and their nails are immaculately polished. Some of them have a trendy
handbag and habitually check the text messages on their mobile
phones. The women chitchat while watching TV. A middle-aged Thai
man enters. The *mamasan*, who is half-sleeping behind a desk, wakes
up and approaches the man. "Would you like a lady?" she asks. A pause
in conversation. Silence. Six more women appear from a back room.

They all line up. He stares. Some women stare back, while others avoid eye contact.

The silence surrounding this ritual does not last long. "Her!" the customer says, pointing at a woman wearing a miniskirt and a black top. While the customer pays the *mamasan*, the young woman goes behind the counter, gets two towels, a bar of soap, and a condom from a box. She escorts the customer to one of the back rooms. Some of the other sex workers remain sitting. Others disappear to the back room. The monotonous TV watching continues. Occasional small talk once again fills the air, accompanied by the sound of falling rain.

The Value of Bodies

The scene described above took place in the Bridge Hotel, a hotel-cum-brothel in Nong Kai. Its social script mirrors highly developed consumer culture, where the commoditization of female bodies involves a spectacle of surveillance, enticement, and subsequent choice of a commodity from a wider selection. It suggests an institutionalized form of sex commerce characterized by commodity fetishism, which is found throughout Thailand.[1] This is, however, only part of the story. The Bridge Hotel is not a high-end venue by Nong Kai standards. Nor is it part of the low end, such as the Boutique brothel discussed in chapter 5. Yet the Bridge Hotel and the Boutique are in subtle ways connected.

In the previous chapter we were introduced to Kham, who makes a living by providing customers to several off-site and on-site brothels in Nong Kai. At times Kham also takes part in recruiting Lao women for these venues. On occasion he goes to the Boutique, soliciting women there for employment in one of the venues he collaborates with, such as the Bridge Hotel. "Rich clients don't go to the Boutique," Kham says. "They think the place is dirty and that the girls are not clean. But the women there are not different from more up-scale places, such as the Bridge Hotel." Hence, although clients might project markers of symbolic and cultural capital onto female bodies in different venue settings ("dirty" girls at the Boutique; more upscale girls at the Bridge Hotel), such distinctions are in fact transgressed and malleable, with some Lao sex workers, for example, moving on from the Boutique to work in the Bridge Hotel. This raises larger questions of the relationship between client demand and the marketing of female bodies on the one hand, and the extent to which such constellations shape value, profit, and employment trajectories of sex workers on the other.

Human trafficking literature commonly assumes a congruence between market value of female bodies, profitability, and recruitment. In other words, the profitability of nonconsensual recruitment is read into essentialist notions of female bodies (the eroticization of the other, the value of "pretty girls," the commodification of virginity, and so on). Such assumptions are also evident within the Lao anti-trafficking sector. For instance, a UNICEF report states: "Sexual exploitation is a major aspect of trafficking. The physical appearance of the girls is a major factor in assessing their value as a commodity, the more beautiful the girl, the higher the price" (UNICEF and Ministry of Labour and Social Welfare 2004, 27). The same report also notes: "The underlying principle of trafficking is that the victims are bought and sold on the basis of their physical assets for the intended labour situation" (ibid., 41). But is "the physical appearance of the girls . . . a major factor in assessing their value as a commodity"? Is it true that "the more beautiful the girl, the higher the price" she will command? In what sense are victims "bought and sold on the basis of their physical assets"? More broadly, are there correlations between client demand, profit, price hierarchies, and deceptive recruitment?

This chapter problematizes such assumed correlations, and the introductory story from the Bridge Hotel and the Boutique introduces the argument at hand: that the sex industries of Nong Kai and Vientiane, as well as the recruitment practices within them, constitute a mixture of capitalist penetration and patron-client relationships. It is therefore not possible, as some anti-traffickers attempt to do, to extrapolate probabilities of trafficking from mechanical models of profitability and unilateral maximization of social actors.

Client Demand: Vientiane Beer Shops

The previous chapter introduced Gin, who for a short while worked with Nort in the Friendship Bar in Vientiane. During my research Gin's usual workplace was the Papaya Bar, which is located in a Vientiane suburb. The Papaya Bar is run by Sumalee, who is originally from Savannakhet, and is adjacent to the family house. As in many other venues, the *sao borigan* who work here, including Gin, reside at the premises.

The number of sex workers in the Papaya Bar fluctuates. The lowest number I witnessed was six, but at one point it reached thirteen. One might think such fluctuations have to do with variations in supply and demand for remunerated sex, but they are, rather, a reflection of the unpredictable and arbitrary policing by authorities who from time to time restrict the number of workers in entertainment venues. Such variation also reflects the employment trajectories of sex workers. They commonly work in a venue for a few weeks to several months, then move on to another in pursuit of more income and adventure, resulting in continuously fluctuating numbers of sex workers at each venue.

The clientele in the Papaya Bar is diverse. The predominant group consists of Lao men from a range of socioeconomic backgrounds (students, manual laborers, farmers, government officials, soldiers, and white-collar workers). Some visitors are local, but many come from other provinces and visit the bar while in Vientiane for business or recreation. The Papaya Bar also gets its fair share of Chinese, Vietnamese, and Indian men who are permanent or semipermanent migrants to Laos, as well as (to a lesser extent) foreign tourists (predominantly Western) and expatriates (Western, Korean, and Japanese). Juxtaposed with this variety in clientele are the several ways by which women debut working in the Papaya Bar.

Gin, for example, is Khmu and comes from Luang Prabang Province. She explained her bar work by saying, "I have to admit that I don't really come from a poor family. My family has food and basic necessities." When Gin moved to Vientiane, she was amazed by all the wealth. "There are many nice houses and cars here. I wanted to earn money," she said. Gin has been in Vientiane for a while. In the beginning she worked in a series of *han foe* (noodle shops) around town. She did not like the work very much, and the pay was poor (300,000 kip per month). While she worked in a *han foe* close to the main market in Vientiane, she learned from a friend about work in a beer shop. Gin realized quickly that her friend earned much more than she herself could in a noodle shop. Subsequently her friend, who already worked at the Papaya Bar, introduced Gin to it.

Dtuk, another woman from Luang Prabang, started working in the

Papaya Bar by knocking at the door. Dtuk had for some time worked in a garment factory in Vientiane, and it was there she became acquainted with other women who moved on to work in entertainment clubs and beer shops. Dtuk was married to an unfaithful husband who was at times violent. It was a miserable marriage that resulted in divorce. Dtuk decided to go back to her parents in Luang Prabang. While she was waiting at the bus station, she reflected on her situation. "My life was a mess, and I had almost no money," Dtuk said. She spotted a beer shop across the street. She went there and started talking to the owner. The owner made no secret of how the women who were employed there were expected to entertain customers, including selling sex. Out of frustration, having no money and feeling at a loss, Dtuk thought, "Why not try? My life is a mess anyway."

Sometimes recruitment is intertwined with family ties. Noi is ethnically Lao and is the niece of the *mamasan*. She is twenty-one years old but has already a long career as a sex worker, debuting at age thirteen. Both Noi and her auntie (the *mamasan*) conceal the real nature of their work from Noi's parents, who still live in Savannakhet.

A fourth sex worker, Bpet, obtained work in the Papaya Bar through an agent in Luang Prabang. Bpet's family lives in Luang Prabang town, and she had come to Vientiane several years earlier to study. She did not do particularly well at school and started working in a garment factory. She began going out to nightclubs with friends, which she enjoyed very much. After a while she got a boyfriend. The relationship did not work out, and he eventually left her. After this incident, Bpet started working in a beer shop. For reasons Bpet never explained to me, she decided to return to Luang Prabang. There she met Angkham, a male agent who arranged a job for her in the Papaya Bar in Vientiane, where she now works.

Over time it appeared that several other sex workers had obtained work in the Papaya Bar through Angkham. Most of the women, like Bpet, knew what type of job they were expected to perform. However, there were also cases that were less than transparent.

One night when my research assistant and I visited the Papaya Bar, a group of newly recruited young women sat outside. They were all dressed up in alluring silk shorts and wore considerable makeup. It was a fairly obvious marketing strategy to signal the availability of new arrivals to potential customers passing the bar. It is tremendously difficult to judge whether "new ladies" in a bar indeed are new to working in a beer shop or if it is merely a marketing strategy. However, in this case, some of the women were notably inexperienced. For instance, I observed that one of the women sitting with a customer failed to pour more beer in his glass while he was drinking, in contrast to experienced sex workers, who always make sure to top up customers' drinks. I could also see that she avoided eye contact with the customer and generally appeared disinterested and nervous, in contrast to the way experienced sex workers usually behave in these sorts of situations. I was unable to make any inquiries about the newcomers then and there.

We visited the Papaya Bar a few days later, and the new girls from Luang Prabang were gone. I asked Nok, a sex worker from Luang Prabang, what had happened. She told me that the women had returned to Luang Prabang. I asked, "But why did they come in the first place then? They only stayed a few days?" Nok responded, "An agent had recruited them from Luang Prabang. They did not know they were supposed to work in a bar." Nok told me that the recruiter got a commission from the *mamasan*.[2] At another visit this was confirmed by Gin.

The Demand-Recruitment Nexus

As we have seen, within an individual beer shop there is a range of different ways women obtain employment. Most cases are voluntary (in the sense that no third party forces or deceives them), yet in some cases women are not told the real nature of the type of job they are supposed to perform. Given that—if we follow what the anti-trafficking sector professes—trafficking therefore exists in the Papaya Bar, we should then be able to deductively account for the "demand side." Here I will focus on the notion of "client demand," or, in other words, whether particular preferences among customers influence recruitment practices.

The suggestion that trafficking is induced by a general difficulty in recruiting voluntary women to meet customer demand must be treated with caution. I visited the Papaya Bar frequently for more than a year, and I never witnessed any lack of sex workers relative to customers. As has been noted, the majority of sex workers debut in the Papaya Bar voluntarily, and in the cases where deceptive recruitment practices have been used, there is nothing to suggest that this tactic is a direct response to a lack of women in the bar. At the time when the group of women came down from Luang Prabang, there were already more than ten women working in the Papaya Bar, which is a relatively high number for a beer shop. Indeed, shortly after this incident, Sumalee had to lay off several of the girls when authorities clamped down on over-staffed beer shops. That being said, the anti-trafficking sector implicitly emphasizes the relevance of niche markets in the sex industry. This is not surprising. An intrinsic feature of capitalism is its seriality (Giddens 1994), and Linda Singer (1993) has pointed out that, within a capitalist logic, sex becomes doubly enacted through erotic desire and commodity fetish. In other words there is a perpetual displacement of erotic investment (ibid.). Thus sex industries tend to move toward diversification. Does diversification in the form of niche preferences then fashion recruitment practices in the Papaya Bar?

Diversification raises questions about both the institutionalization of monetized sexual services and the marketing of those services (via posters, flyers with photos, newspaper ads, and so forth), and here we must note that the Papaya Bar does not advertise, partly because of the restrictive political climate in which it operates. As in the Lao sex industry generally, new customers come to the Papaya Bar after hearing about it from others or through random visitation. Customers commonly enter the bar and sit down with whichever *sao borigan* approaches them, as is commonplace in Lao beer shops (Lyttleton 1999a; Lyttleton and Amarapibal 2002). Hence there is no explicit selection of sex workers by the customers. In the case of tourists (mostly Westerners) usually a *tuk tuk* driver takes them to the Papaya Bar. Although the *tuk tuk* driver will charge the client for transport and the procurement of a sex worker, there is no formalized commission arrangement between the bar and the *tuk tuk* driver (although the driver might demand an extra fee from the sex worker for "helping out" in soliciting customers). Hence, visitation in the Papaya Bar does not reflect in any way a response to advertisements or a deliberate marketing strategy.

I have earlier drawn attention to the dual social script that is enacted in Lao beer shops: the prelude of socialization and flirtatious drinking within the bar, with subsequent remunerated sexual liaisons in a nearby guesthouse. Not all customers, however, take *sao borigan* out for sex after socializing in the Papaya Bar. Conversely, the preceding drinking sessions with sex workers might be short and even nonexistent. As Chris Lyttleton (1999a) has observed, the effect of this double script is that customers' assessment of the desirability of women is far more extensive than in classic brothel settings. It is not only physical beauty and a perceived sexual repertoire that are factored in (which in any case can be shaped by dress, makeup, and body posture) but also the sex workers' charm (exchanges of jokes, smiles, laughter), personality (attentiveness, listening skills, friendliness), and flirtation (eye contact, hugs, touching). Furthermore, the consumer is never a passive spectator: "The consumption of goods no doubt always presupposes a labour of appropriation, to different degrees depending on the goods [or embodied services, in the case of sex commerce] and the consumers; or, more precisely, that the consumer helps to produce the product he consumes, . . . which requires time and dispositions acquired over time" (Bourdieu 1984, 100). In Lao beer shops (as well as elsewhere in the world), the perceived relationship itself between the customers and the *sao borigan* becomes part of clients' preferences. As one customer told me, "I don't want ladies who are only after money. They have to like me!" Hence, the register of what might be preferential for a customer is open-ended and can be almost limitless, which makes a customer's selection highly multifaceted and opaque. Because social interaction between customers and sex workers often involves a semicontrolled trajectory of inebriation (helped along by groovy karaoke tunes and a freewheeling party atmosphere), a customer's "preferences" can be met by many sex workers who can manipulate the situation with their style of dress and makeup (aided by dimmed lighting). Hence the move from customers' erotic desires to actual selection of a partner for the night has a particularly fluid and even drifting character in the Papaya Bar. There is however, one aspect of the Papaya Bar that could play a role as an "objective" marker for the selection of sex workers, and that is ethnicity.

ETHNICITY

It was earlier noted that the majority of the sex workers in the Papaya Bar come from Luang Prabang and that many of them belong to the ethnic minority Khmu. Does the dominance of Khmu sex workers have anything to do with customers' preferences? It has been highlighted elsewhere that the lowland Lao, who are the dominant ethnic group in Laos, commonly project both erotic and exotic meanings onto certain minority groups, such as the Akha.

> Local Akha sexuality and customs are highly sensationalized in lowland understandings and the exotic "primitiveness" of the minority groups is heavily eroticized. Lowland Lao talk in glowing terms of the cultural stipulations that require young Akha women to massage visitors; those visiting the mountains often wish to experience local sexuality beyond just the massage, and the money, status and increasing familiarity they carry often allows such liaisons. (Lyttleton et al. 2004, 84)

However, a parallel eroticism is not attached to Khmu ethnic identity. I once asked Bpet whether customers particularly liked Khmu women. "I don't know," she responded. "I have never heard anyone say they prefer Khmu girls to Lao." Sumalee, the *mamasan,* told me, "There are simply a lot of Khmu girls, and they come through friends who already work here. I have never heard men asking for Khmu." These views are further supported by another recent study in northern Laos (Lyttleton 2008).

Khmu women appear to be overrepresented in some sections of the Lao sex industry,[3] a point noted by several aid organizations that work with HIV/AIDS prevention. I have earlier pointed to the historical asymmetrical relationship between the dominant ethnic Lao and various minorities. In contrast to many other marginalized ethnic groups, Khmu has been relatively more exposed to lowland Lao culture because trade and wage labor have them in more direct, asymmetrical interactions with the dominant lowland Lao (Lyttleton 2008). As Carol Ireson-Doolittle and Geraldine Moreno-Black note: "Weak state control, combined with a lack of Khmu political organization, historically left villagers at the mercy of better-organized Lao in-migrants, who may have uprooted entire Khmu villages, taking the most fertile agricultural lands—a historical development which disadvantages Khmu" (2004, 151). In addition, as we saw in chapter 4, there is less social policing of female sexuality outside village settings (Lyttleton 2008). Considering that sex work brings in far higher income than does other wage labor available to marginalized, uneducated Khmu women, there are few normative barriers to entering sex work and from an income-generating point of view, it makes good sense to do so.

Another factor is undoubtedly the self-perpetuating informal recruitment within Khmu communities that appears to alter village perceptions of young women's role as material providers: "Young women are increasingly being seen as a direct and more reliable means increasing family wealth, particularly as they are seemingly able to enter into the lowland Lao service economy more readily than men" (Lyttleton 2008, 55). Hence, although Khmu women predominate among the sex workers at the Papaya Bar, this has more to do with a complex process of socioeconomic change altering local perceptions of the role of young women in Khmu villages than with a response to preferences among the bar's clientele.

TYPES OF SERVICES

Nonconsensual recruitment might also be a response to a desire to offer different types of services. Lyttleton has documented the complaints of men in Isaan villages about their spouses' sexual passivity, consequently projecting value onto sex workers who provide sexual services "being on top": "Given that Thai women are taught it is inappropriate for a woman to be above a man there are inhibitions to making love this way. Men told me that many CSWs [commercial sex workers] will do this with no qualms and the repeated quote 'just lie back and let me take care of you' is used as a glowing accolade describing certain prostitutes' practices" (2000, 173–174). In my own research the acrobatics of sex workers seem to vary. Nok, who was working in the Papaya Bar, said, "I just lay down and let them do the work." In contrast, Gop, who was introduced in chapter 4, boasted about her ability to do "twelve different positions," accompanied by a public demonstration in the bar (with her clothes on, one might add), to much laughter and applause among her fellow workers and the customers. Undoubtedly, porn movies (Thai, Western, and Japanese) play a role in shaping sexual repertoires, and it is common for sex workers to watch them. It is also usual for venue owners, clients, and coworkers to verbally teach other sexual skills.

When trying to come to terms with whether customers have a direct bearing on how women are recruited into a beer shop like the Papaya Bar, the way services and prices become institutionalized is of particular interest. It is unusual for customers to make explicit preferences known when entering beer shops, which in part has to do with the aforementioned open-ended and opaque social script enacted in such venue settings. However, on occasion some customers request oral and (much more rarely) anal sex. These services are semi-institutionalized in the sense that they have an added price tag. I was not able to confirm whether anal sex was practiced in small beer shops such as the Papaya Bar, but Nhut, the *mamasan* at the more upscale Naga Club, informed me that some of her sex workers offered anal sex. Although oral sex appears to be more common than anal sex, this does not mean that it is an easily obtainable sexual service. Only some sex workers provide oral sex, and many do it selectively, limiting it to customers with whom they have developed some level of intimacy, such as regulars or their boyfriends. Many sex workers express unease about oral sex and think it is, in Bpet's own words, "disgusting." This attitude appears not to be well recognized by health programs that operate in Laos, where eroticization of condom use (i.e., teaching sex workers how to put on a condom using their mouth) is becoming an acceptable and common project activity. Nonetheless, as only a limited number of sex workers provide oral sex, this service is scarce. It must be emphasized that it is rare that customers make explicit requests for such services, and during my regular visits to the Papaya Bar over the course of a year, I never personally witnessed a customer doing this. However, I was told that on occasion this happens. How is such scarcity mediated in beer shops such as the Papaya Bar?

A customer who has specific preferences he wishes to insist upon usually approaches the *mamasan* or one of the sex workers in the venue. If no sex workers in the beer shop offer such services, the *mamasan* or the *sao borigan* might ask colleagues in other venues. Most sex workers have access to a mobile phone, and as it is common to move on to work in new bars from time to time, they become acquainted with a large number of other sex workers. This network is then consulted to find a suitable person who provides what the client is requesting. The person who arranges this connection gets a commission from the earnings of the sex worker who provides the sexual service. In this way, the specific operationalization of supply to meet demand relies on extended informal networks and is not a mechanical response to market laws.

The assumption of direct linkages between client demand and recruitment is therefore problematic. In the previous chapter we saw that recruitment of women into entertainment venues is primarily driven by informal networks of extended kin and acquaintances, and the same logic applies to provision of niche services. However, one can easily critique this conclusion as being empirically overtly selective because it is based on only one particular venue setting. Therefore our discussion will move across the border to brothel-style venues in Nong Kai.

Nong Kai: Profitability and Bodies

In the previous chapter, I pointed out the overwhelming presence of Lao sex workers in Nong Kai, which might lead us to think that this reflects a particular preference for Lao women among Thai customers. There is no doubt that many Thai men project erotic value onto Lao sex workers, in part because of their simultaneous sociocultural similarity and difference (Lyttleton and Amarapibal 2002). This distinction is particularly pertinent in several Nong Kai venues, as the majority of Thai sex workers tend to be older and to have had several years of working experience. They are not only visibly older but also project a more jaded demeanor than that of younger Lao sex workers. In Nong Kai venues, I have myself observed Lao *sao borigan* sitting at tables with customers, pampering them by elegantly pouring whiskey and refilling their plates with snacks, while an older Thai sex worker will sit indifferently at another table, drinking beer and smoking cigarettes, habits undoubtedly acquired after working in Western-oriented bars. However, it must be emphasized that this co-presence of younger Lao and older Thai sex workers in the same venue is not common. Although some Thai students sell sex through some of the off-site brothels, they constitute only a small number of sex workers. Most Thai sex workers in Nong Kai tend to be older and either work in more upscale restaurants with female singers (*sao nakrong*)[4] or work (often freelance) in a few Western-oriented bars. Lao sex workers tend to dominate other venues, such as off-site brothels, brothels, restaurants, and mid- to low-market karaoke clubs.[5] It would, however, be a mistake to singularly attribute the overwhelming presence of Lao sex workers to client demand. I was repeatedly told by both customers and venue managers that the reason customers in Nong Kai chose Lao sex workers had nothing to do with preferences for them as such. Lao women were simply omnipresent and were cheaper than younger Thai women who sell sex locally. I will therefore shift our analysis slightly by focusing more directly on the presumption that there are direct correlations between profit, bodily value, and recruitment practices (Molland 2010b).

In the previous chapter, we became familiar with Kham, Rattana, and their involvement with a mobile phone–operated brothel network in Nong Kai. We saw that this network includes both Lao sex workers who have been recruited on a voluntary basis and Lao women who have been deceived (i.e., they can be considered trafficked). Given that this brothel business has both voluntary and nonvoluntary workers, can this be explained by profit maximization strategies? In other words, do deceptive recruitment practices stem from a demand for specific bodies that result in more profit for venue owners and recruiters? In exploring the nexus of profit, bodily value, and recruitment, we will first need to consider how this network generates income.

PROFIT MAXIMIZATION: OFF-SITE BROTHELS

Kham was one of the most open of my informants when it came to discussing brothel economics. He would often tell me that running these off-site brothels was "good business," and he boasted that a given venue could easily make more than 100,000 baht per month. As mentioned in the previous chapter, the standard price for purchasing "short term" sex[6] in these venues is 700 baht, of which 250 baht goes to the sex worker, 250 to the venue manager, and 200 to the agent who provides the client. Thus the venue earns 250 baht per customer. Kham also several times stated that it was common for a venue to have approximately ten sex workers averaging about two customers per day, which amounts to a total monthly income of 125,000 baht.

At the same time, Kham emphasized that some women are more popular than others and can get as many as five customers per night. Yet despite Kham's noting differences in beauty among sex workers, these venues operate with very limited price stratification. Higher prices occur only in three types of cases: the sale of virginity, prostitution of high-class Thai students, and extra charges for special services (anal sex, oral sex, etc.). However, the overwhelming service provision adheres to standardized prices for "short term" and "long term" sex. Sex workers who are considered more beautiful or more popular receive exactly the same retail payment as "average" sex workers. In other words, different subjective notions of beauty are not mirrored in a retail pricing hierarchy.[7] Consequently, if differences in "bodily value" have any bearing on profit, it must then be reflected in differentiations in customer turnover.

I repeatedly asked informants whether popular sex workers generated larger profits for venues, and to my astonishment no informant could provide a clear answer to this. Instead, they often stressed that "it depends" and that "sometimes some girls get many, sometimes not." Proprietors articulated their knowledge of their own venue according to their "feel" for their business. In addition, customers are more likely to take a particularly beautiful sex worker for long-term sex rather than short term, thereby limiting her possibility of getting repeat customers, which in turn decreases the amount of profit she will generate for the venue. It is also important to note the combination of low prices relative to high turnover of customers. Hence it is the total volume of customer turnover and not the appropriation of particular types of bodies that is important for profit in such venue settings. The reason for this has to do with the way customers choose sex workers.

First, it is not only different notions of beauty but also customers' desire for "newness" that inform preferences. And the way sex workers are marketed is open to considerable manipulation. In the off-site brothels, selection of sex workers is usually done over the phone. It is common for customers to make their preferences known (such as "pretty," "white skin," "short," "skinny," "big breasts," and "young"), but such preferences are very general and can fit many different sex workers. In interviews with agents (such as Kham) who provide sex workers for customers, they make no secret of how they present sex workers who have worked for longer periods of time as "new, fresh girls" to new customers, whereas they are more careful in providing newer sex workers to regular clients. Although "freshness" plays a role in the selection of sex workers for regular customers, it must be noted that, in contrast to notions of a hierarchy of beauty, freshness is a temporal status that all sex workers embody at one point, or several points, in time. In this sense, freshness does not refer to particular types of female bodies. In addition, the exact selection of sex workers depends on the availability of workers then and there. To assume a clear-cut causal relationship between customer demand, price, and desire for particular bodies is problematic, because the operationalization of sex commerce entangles such direct correlations, which operate in a heavily subjectivized arena of eroticism and desire.

RECRUITMENT COMMISSION

Within entertainment venues in Nong Kai the notion persists that some sex workers are more popular than others, based on variations in feminine beauty. This idea is reflected in the way recruitment is carried out. We have earlier seen several examples, from both sides of the border, of Lao sex workers who go back to their home communities and recruit other women for a commission. Venue owners in Nong Kai typically pay 1,000 baht to sex workers who are able to recruit a friend from home. It is also common that family members receive an advance, up to 4,000 baht, on the sex workers' earnings, which increases the amount of debt the new recruit will need to work off. In some cases a higher commission is paid if the new recruit is considered to be particularly beautiful. At one point twins were recruited into one of the off-site brothels for 3,000 baht each, and the higher commission fee was justified because the women were *soey mak* (very pretty). Hence, in contrast to standardized retail pricing of Lao sex workers, recruitment has a differential pricing hierarchy. What does this then tell us about correlations between bodily value, profit, and recruitment?

It is noteworthy that the amount of the recruitment commission is decided only after the new recruits arrive in Nong Kai. Thus the recruiter does not know for sure the exact commission when she (it is usually a she) recruits. Although there is a given range for commission fees (1,000 to 3,000 baht), the recruiter is in fact trading in unstable currency. Thai and Lao culture put great emphasis on bodily display, appearance, and surfaces (Phillips 1974; Van Esterik 2000), and recruiters are often women who already work in these off-site brothels themselves. Because the recruiter and the brothel owner know each other, a certain level of shared understandings of beauty no doubt exists. The fact that no recruits have been rejected (according to Kham) is telling. Hence, some degree of predictability for the recruiter in terms of evalu-

ating beauty and price is present. Nonetheless, commission price generation and notions of value are here subject to a network-based form
of negotiation, not a desocialized market transaction with standardized
prices. Nor is there a clear correlation between commission prices and
deceptive recruitment practices. Kham admitted that deceptive recruitment occurred among some women who were valued at only the normal commission fee of 1,000 baht and that women who were valued
at a higher commission fee were not necessarily deceived. In fact, the
distinction between "voluntary" and "deceptive" recruitment appeared
to not make much difference when I spoke to Kham.

If beauty, profit, and niche sexual services do not account in any
clear way for the specificity of deceptive recruitment, what then? One
dimension I have not yet analyzed explicitly is age. Human trafficking
programs and the media often point to underage prostitution in reference to both demand and the legal-technical implication of consent.
Simultaneously, in contrast to the lack of price hierarchies discussed
above, one niche market that exhibits considerable variation in prices
is that of virgins. In order to explore whether commodification of virginity might give us some answers regarding the congruence between
recruitment and the market value of female bodies, we will cross the
river again and return to Vientiane.

Commodification of Virginity

Trafficking literature often makes mention of underage prostitution,
with pedophilia and the sale of virginity described as particularly appall-
ing sites for both profitability and enactment of client demand (Hughes
2002; ILO 2006; Lynellyn 2004). Pedophilia and the sale of virginity can of course overlap, but they also have important differences.
Whereas pedophilia refers to sexual attraction to prepubescent children, the sale of virginity along the Thai-Lao border primarily involves
young, yet postpubertal virgins. In discussions of how human trafficking
discourse assumes correlations between bodily value, profitability, and
client demand, the sale of virginity is of particular analytical interest,
as it appears to insist on one specific unambiguous and objective physiological marker: that the woman or girl in question is indeed a virgin.
Furthermore, virginity plays important symbolic roles in many cultures

and is often a site where prestige is invested. As Sherry Ortner observes: "Virginity is a symbol of exclusiveness and inaccessibility, nonavailability to the general masses, something, in short that is elite. A virgin is an elite female among females, withheld, untouched, exclusive" (1978, 32). Part of the reason for the symbolic exclusiveness attached to female virginity no doubt has to do with the irreversible physiological transformation a woman or girl goes through. In this sense virginity is a transcultural scarcity, something that needs to be either protected or conquered (Ortner 1978, 1981). When this power logic is translated into sex commerce, one finds that virgins are considered scarce elite commodities. And here legal age becomes of interest, because one can expect that demand for virgins overlaps considerably with demand for underage girls. Because trafficking legislation defines children as incapable of exercising consent, underage prostitution equals trafficking. Here we see a resurfacing of the notion of "hot spots"—certain segments within the sex industry that are imagined as more trafficking-prone than others.

At times the media and some anti-trafficking activists tell sensationalist stories of the sale of virginity ("Demand for Virgins" 2007; Thomas and Pasnik 2002). During my time working on a UN trafficking program in Laos, I remained skeptical of such claims, and no organization had substantiated the existence of the sale of virginity on a large scale in Laos. Although I did not rule out its occurrence, I anticipated that it would be rare and therefore difficult to uncover. When I started my research along the Thai-Lao border, I did therefore not anticipate or actively seek information on the sale of virginity. However, over time it became clear that this practice was not uncommon. One of my first encounters with the sale of virginity was through Souksavan, the *mamasan* at the Mekong Lounge, who was introduced in the previous chapter.

I met Souksavan for the first time at her house, which is located on the outskirts of Vientiane city. Phut, my research assistant, happened to know her husband. At the time, Souksavan had left the job at the Mekong Lounge and had instead started a small restaurant in their family home together with her husband, Dtoi. She complained that it was too far to travel to the Mekong Lounge and involved inconvenient working hours. Given that she was married and had a ten-year-old daughter, it must have been difficult to combine work at the lounge with family life.

Before I met Souksavan, I was aware that the sale of virginity occurred in various places, but the extent to which it operated within the mainstream sex industry (in beer shops, karaoke venues, and so forth in the Lao case) or constituted a separate niche market operating from other places was unclear to me. The topic came up during one of the visits Phut and I made to Souksavan and Dtoi's house-cum-restaurant.

We arrived at their house around four o'clock in the afternoon. We were standing in the courtyard, where their home-style restaurant was situated. All the tables and chairs were gone. Dtoi was not home, but Souksavan welcomed us in. It was a hot day. Souksavan offered to go buy some beer and food. We gave her 60,000 kip.

Souksavan returned and sat down with us. She told us that the restaurant business hadn't worked out and she and Dtoi had to close it. A lot of friends and acquaintances had come there to eat but ran up huge tabs without settling them. At the moment, the outstanding tabs amounted to approximately $US600, and Souksavan was still trying to get the money back.

After a little while, Dtoi came home. We sat down and drank beer. Dtoi and Souksavan's daughter Loi was home. A fifteen-year-old neighborhood girl named Saeng was hanging around the house as well, playing with Loi. Souksavan jokingly asked me, "Perhaps you could find a *farang* boyfriend [*faen*] for her?" We all laughed, including Saeng. I did not think any more about the comment.

Not long after, other friends of Souksavan and Dtoi's came into the house, and the gathering evolved into a small party. Later on, we noticed that Souksavan was in the kitchen by herself, and we started talking to her. She told us that she might go back to work at the Mekong Lounge. She also had a possible job offer at a hotel not too far from their house.

In the context of the mundane domesticity of dinner preparation, Souksavan said that Saeng wanted to sell her virginity but hadn't found any customers yet. We were not able to continue this discussion at that moment, because other people came into the kitchen. Souksavan and the wife of one of the other men cooked a stir-fry and a soup (*tom yam*). We all sat down, including Souksavan's daughter and Saeng.

While we ate dinner, I realized that when Souksavan had asked me if I could help find Saeng a "boyfriend," she was possibly only half-joking, something I later confirmed. While we ate and talked, I thought about the various trafficking reports I had read. Viewed through the trafficking prism, I was in fact having dinner with a member of the dark forces of commercial sex: the ruthless and cunning professional mafia that preys on the enormous profit of young girls' virginity. Yet anyone who passed by and looked through the window that night would have seen a completely ordinary and modest Vientiane suburban family having supper with friends. The only unusual thing about our group was me—a *farang* who for some reason knew this family.

A few weeks later, Souksavan was working at the Mekong Lounge again, and Phut and I visited her there several times. The Mekong Lounge is by Lao standards a relatively large entertainment venue, and on any given night about twenty to thirty women are working there. However, the total number of women is about eighty, several of them working part-time. In addition, fifteen waiters and waitresses are employed, as well as a band that performs. I asked Souksavan about Saeng. She said that some potential customers had met her but thought she was "too ugly" because "her skin is too dark," Souksavan explained. Earlier on, Souksavan had told me that she was not involved in arranging the sale of virgins, because she felt sorry for them. However, over time it turned out that it was difficult to find a customer for Saeng, and Souksavan's involvement became more and more obvious. When two months had elapsed and no customer had been found, Souksavan told me that Saeng wanted to start working at the Mekong Lounge, but, Souksavan continued, "I advised her to sell her virginity first, because she would get much more money."

Souksavan said that sometimes customers ask for virgins at the Mekong Lounge. "There are a lot of girls [*phusaw*] who come and want to sell their virginity," she told me. Prices usually range from 15,000 to 50,000 baht and occasionally even more. "Once we had an incredibly pretty girl here," Souksavan recalled. "I helped her get a customer. She got 80,000 baht. She was very beautiful—she could be a movie star." It is common that young women and girls who know other women who work at the Mekong Lounge approach Souksavan for assistance with finding a customer. Souksavan claimed she did not get any set amount of money, but the girls usually gave her 300 to 400 baht afterward. In addition, customers usually give her 2,000 to 3,000 baht for arranging a girl for them. In some cases when the price for the sale was higher, Souksavan's cut could be as high as 4,000 baht. It is noteworthy that Souksavan described this payment not as a "commission" but as a "gift."

Although it would be an exaggeration to say that the sale of virginity runs rampant, Souksavan's involvement is by no means anomalous. Nor is the sale of virginity limited to high-end venues such as the Mekong Lounge. Over time it became clear that several of my informants had initially sold their own virginity. Daeng, Sei, and Thia, who were introduced in chapter 4, debuted by selling their virginity at a bar called the Factory. Nort, also introduced in chapter 4, was helped by "a friend" to sell her virginity at the Friendship Bar to a Thai man for 10,000 baht and 100,000 kip in tips. Within walking distance of Nort's bar is a larger entertainment venue called Sunrise Bar. Fai, one of the sex workers employed there, sold her virginity when she was nineteen for 20,000 baht. An agent made the arrangements and charged a commission of 5,000 baht. As at the Mekong Lounge, customers can approach the *mamasan* in the Sunrise Bar if they want virgins. The *mamasan* recruits young girls from one of the colleges in Vientiane. The girls are usually seventeen or eighteen years old, according to Fai.[8] Prices vary, ranging from 10,000 to 50,000 baht.

A little farther up the same road, a woman named Phan is working in a smaller beer shop. An older sister of one of Phan's friends asked her if she wanted to work as a *sao borigan*. This older sister happened to know the owner of the bar where Phan is now working. There, when she was sixteen years old, Phan sold her virginity for 30,000 baht plus a mobile phone.

VIRGINITY: SELLING IT, OR LOSING IT TO A BOYFRIEND?

The sale of virginity, along with pedophilia, is often symbolic of some of the worst aspects of trafficking and prostitution. Without denying that this practice involves enormous asymmetries in power and can indeed be traumatic for many young women and girls, it is worthwhile to consider some aspects of the sociocultural context, not so much to assess "rights and wrongs" of the commodification of virginity but to better understand its economic functioning within the commercial sex industry.

One aspect to consider is that the sale of virginity straddles the legal age of consent, which is eighteen. Souksavan admitted to me that most of the girls who sell their virginity through the Mekong Lounge are fifteen or sixteen years old. Nort and Phan were both underage when they sold their virginity (ages seventeen and sixteen, respectively), whereas Daeng, Sei, Thia, and Fai were all of legal age. Furthermore, the sale of virginity occurs around the time when Lao girls and young women start to come of age and begin to engage in romances, get boyfriends, experiment sexually, and—at least in rural areas of Laos—get married. Indeed, it is common for informants to explain their decision to sell their virginity in the context of noncommercial alternatives—that is, sleeping with boyfriends. A conversation I had with Daeng on this topic is telling:

> DAENG: We were lucky. Instead of losing virginity to a boyfriend whom you might not end up marrying, it is better to get money for it.
> SVERRE: But what about later in life, when you are going to get married? Would it not be more difficult to marry?
> DAENG: No, perhaps a hundred years ago, but now it is accepted to have sex before marriage.
> SVERRE: Do you know girls who have done this and gotten married afterward?
> DAENG: Yes.

The perception that it was a "better deal" to sell one's virginity instead of "wasting it" on an unfaithful boyfriend was not uncommon among informants. And sometimes the same feeling was uttered, albeit from a different viewpoint. For example, Bpet, who works in the Papaya Bar, said: "I regret I did not sell my virginity. Instead I lost it to my ex-boyfriend—it was such a waste." She half-jokingly added that these days it is difficult to find virgins, because the girls are as young as thirteen or fourteen when they debut sexually. I have earlier drawn attention to how norms regarding female sexuality have increasingly become commoditized due to the practice of fining sexual transgression. This monetized attitude to sex meshes with new modern identities enabled in the liberalizing environment that Laos is currently experiencing.

A similar association between sexual transgression, value, and virginity is documented in ethnographic accounts from northern Thailand in the mid-1980s: "Today parents often take girls of twelve for sale to Chiang Mai brothels. A frequent comment is that their value has to be realized before they lose their virginity to some village lad" (Paul Cohen and Wijeyewardene 1984, 258). Relating to this, Graham Fordham (2004) has provided a detailed account of the commonality of premarital and multipartner sexual experimentation among Thai teens, despite public norms among older generations that insist on female chastity. Although one must be careful to draw conclusions based on cross-border data (albeit sociocultural similarities), there is no doubt that premarital sex is now more common in Laos (Lyttleton 1999a), in part evidenced by sexual experimentation among young (unmarried) Lao women in local garment factories (Sene-Asa 2007). Hence Bpet and Daeng's comments reflect the simple fact that young Lao women and girls make decisions about losing their virginity in a social context where there is a simultaneous liberalization of norms regarding premarital sex and an increasing commodification of female sexuality. It must be emphasized that such comments are made in a context where sex is heavily monetized, and a degree of retrospective rationalization of conduct is undoubtedly taking place. Yet although many young Lao women with no experience of selling sex are unlikely to think along these lines, this sort of reasoning can—and does— enter the equation if their peers have previously taken such a step. Ambivalent attitudes toward their male peers, combined with the huge amounts of money involved for young women with few employment opportunities available to them, make the sale of virginity in a sense alluring. This is not to ignore the obvious fact that selling one's virginity, as well as debuting in the sex industry, can be traumatic (see Askew 2002), and no informants described their debut as a smooth process.

However, when we are trying to come to terms with presumed correlations between client demand, bodily value, and recruitment, we need to keep in mind that, as with recruitment into sex commerce more generally, we are talking here about a continuum from deception and sweet talk on the one hand, to cases of unfortunate circumstance and outright entrepreneurial voluntarism on the other.

Nevertheless, there are important differences in the way the sale of virginity operates as a market in comparison with the sex industry more generally.

QUANTA COSTA? HOW TO MEET IN A MARKETPLACE

Through conversations with Souksavan, I learned that—perhaps surprisingly—it can take considerable time to arrange a virginity sale. Souksavan's efforts in helping Saeng sell her virginity took months, and when I finished my fieldwork, she was still unsuccessful in finding a customer. Within this same period eight other girls had approached the Mekong Lounge to sell their virginity, but only four customers had been located. This pattern does not appear to be unique to the Mekong Lounge. Nort did not sell her virginity until she had worked for four months in the Friendship Bar. Similarly, Daeng, who was working in the Factory, told me, "I was here in the bar for a month before a customer came." It was an agent, a regular client, who solicited virginity clients for girls in the Factory, and he charged a 10 percent commission. No condoms were used when Daeng sold her virginity, but she was reassured because "he [the agent] checks if the customer has any diseases." Daeng explained to me that the agent examines the potential client's penis, by looking at it, to make sure he is "clean." That this nefarious practice occurs despite the presence of a peer educator who works for an HIV/AIDS project is indeed unfortunate and puts the efficiency of such health programs in question.

It is not always easy to match customers with girls who sell their virginity. Souksavan said that as long as she had worked at the Mekong Lounge, only one Western customer had requested a virgin. He wanted a girl who was dark and small, but the staff at the bar were unable to find a suitable girl. Several informants stressed that reasons for price differentiation have to do with differences in beauty, particularly skin color. But that alone does not account for the huge variation in prices. Both customers and the girls and women who sell their virginity find some difficulty in meeting in the marketplace, and this too has a bearing on price variation. I once asked Souksavan about price differentiation and beauty. "It doesn't work like that," she said. "There are no set prices." She explained, "It is up to the customer. It depends on his offer and whether the girl accepts it." In contrast to the more standardized pricing of more mainstream sexual services in both beer shops and high-end venues (although the prices are often negotiated), no corresponding institutionalization of retail pricing for the sale of virgins exists.

This disjointed relationship between bodies, value, and recruitment is further muddled by the fact that at times sex workers pretend to be virgins. Nhut, who was the *mamasan* at the Naga Club and had debuted as a sex worker herself several years earlier by selling her virginity, made no secret that some of her employees faked virginity in order to get higher prices from customers. Souksavan confirmed this phenomenon. The way the girls do this is by putting blood capsules up in their vagina before they go to bed with the customers, in order to simulate blood resulting from vaginal penetration. Kham informed me of the same trend in Nong Kai: Lao girls and young women would cross the border to sell their virginity, but some of them were in fact experienced sex workers with a talent for behaving as young and inexperienced virgins.

If no clear correlation exists between trafficking as a recruitment practice and essentialized notions of bodily value, how then can we account for the co-presence of deceptive and voluntary recruitment practice along the Thai-Lao border? The answer lies in the fact that the neat distinction between "deceptive" and "voluntary" recruitment is one that few informants recognize.

Explaining Deception

I did not come across a single informant who gave importance to the distinction between deceptive and voluntary recruitment, which is so important to trafficking definitions. A conversation that I had with Souksavan is significant. Given the obvious potential for profit from arranging virgins for customers, I wondered if that would make recruiters more prone to deceiving girls. "Does it happen that girls who come to work in the bar are surprised to find out what type of place they are supposed to work in?" I asked. Souksavan responded, "No, that doesn't happen here. This is not Thailand!" I then asked, "Do you prepare girls for when they sell their virginity?" "Yes, I tell them not to be afraid," Souksavan said, "and that they must take it easy [*sabai*]." She added that she also reminded the girls how much money they would be earning. Thus Souksavan quickly rebuffed the suggestion of deceit as something that happened only in Thailand, although she had no qualms in revealing that she persuaded and sweet-talked young women and girls, sometimes as young as fourteen, into selling their virginity.

A similar disassociation is also evident among sex workers who have been subject to deceptive recruitment. Bpet insisted that her debut of selling sex was due to a combination of family problems, loss of her virginity to a boyfriend who left her, and the desire to earn money. One night, while we shared a Beer Lao, I asked her how she was introduced to working in a beer shop. She reconfirmed that she got the job through a friend. Then I asked, "What did your friend actually tell you when she introduced you? What words did she use?" Bpet replied, "She told me that she could get me a job in a convenience store [*han kay houy*]." "So your friend did not tell you that the job involved going out with customers?" I asked. "No," Bpet said. Another sex worker in a beer shop not far from the Papaya Bar, where Bpet worked, expressed a similar sentiment; she denied "being sold" (*tuuk kai*), despite admitting that her friend lied about the true work she was supposed to perform. Why is it that informants are in apparent denial regarding deceptive recruitment practices?

In allowing an economy of bad faith, several euphemizing processes are at play that obfuscate the binary distinction between trafficking and "voluntary" recruitment. These include sociocultural aspects of entrepreneurial practices along the Thai-Lao border and the reproduction of pseudo-familial ties among sex workers in their everyday life.

Entrepreneurialism

Historically subjugation in mainland Southeast Asia has not been a primary function of production. As Andrew Turton has observed: "Slave labour was used on almost all tasks, but more especially in the less productive, in a way which contributed above all to the conspicuous consumption of the ruling stratum, serving to develop the fetters rather than the forces of production" (1980, 282). Furthermore, as James Scott (1976) famously argued, peasant societies that have a marginal buffer of subsistence tend to seek security and do not engage in profit-maximizing behavior. Although this view is based on historical ethnographic records, it resonates with many contemporary peasant communities, particularly those in Laos (Rehbein 2007). Even among contemporaneous Lao traders and businesspeople, it is far too simplistic to presume production and calculative profitability to be the central logic behind trade and business practices. A recent study on Lao entrepreneurialism gives the following depiction of Lao traders:

> Trade in Laos has mostly been conducted on an ad hoc basis, directed to obtaining what is necessary or desired at the moment and to ensuring that one's competitors behave in the same way. A trader might sit in the market for hours trying to sell a couple of bananas worth a ten-minute wage because she needs the money to buy some aspirin for her father. Lao trade is almost entirely devoid of the "spirit of capitalism" and "rational accounting". . . . Although one might suppose that exposure to foreign capital would encourage people to adapt to the market economy, and although on the surface profit-orientation appears rampant in Laos, profit is very rarely considered as something to invest. (Rehbein 2007, 66–67)[9]

This description can be applied to the sex industry, where employment and recruitment are commonly based on informal or extended kin networks. I have earlier pointed to the importance of patron-client relationships in both Thailand and Laos (Scott 1977). The patrimonial and personal character of Lao business and organization practice is obvious to anyone who works in Laos (Ireson-Doolittle and Moreno-Black 2004). Employment and promotions are based on personal alliances, without reference to any particular performance or skill. Even today it is, for example, commonplace in Laos to demand a commission (monetary or in kind) for helping others (friends and kin alike) with employment, whether this is in government or private business, such as securing a job as a maid for an expatriate. In other words the common practice among sex workers of taking a commission for recruiting others fits within larger cultural business practices based on patronage. The dual commodification of friendships and extended kin relations has clear euphemizing effects on the power relationships evident in the everyday-life reproduction of a fictive family sociality within entertainment clubs.

RECIPROCITY AND THE REPRODUCTION OF FAMILY ETHICS

We have earlier seen that young women enter sex work in a variety of ways, ranging from subjugation and deception on the one hand, to cases of circumstance (poverty, family problems, desire for modern lifestyles) on the other. And along this continuum we have cases in which the method of entry involves sweet talk, persuasion, and a process of socialization within the bar environment that entices women to remain. In chapter 4, I illuminated the difficulties in reading trafficking definitions in relation to temporality, given that women who are deceived into sex work often debut into selling sex only after being socialized into a bar environment. This not only allows for a normalization process for the new recruits but also facilitates venue owners' and recruiters' denial regarding their own complicity. In this process a social reproduction of a fictive family ethic is significant.

Within venues catering to sex commerce, fictive kin terms are evoked in everyday speech. Female managers or owners of venues are commonly referred to as "Mother" (Mae), and male managers as "Father" (Pho). Mamasans and papasans often talk about sex workers in an empathetic way, referring to them as their own children (luk). Sex workers often reside on the premises, which in many cases are adjacent to the owners' family home. Here venue owners and sex workers live together over extended periods of time. At times sex workers take part in household chores that extend beyond the bar environment, such as assisting with the harvest. A fictive family ethic is further reinforced by the incorporation of venue owners' own families into daily interactions and socialization within the bar environment (see also Lyttleton 2008). I have many times seen children of bar owners playing on the floor inside a bar, while sex workers who are not at the time entertaining customers take on the role of nanny. Sex workers are also incorporated into the household's religious practices. Both the Papaya Bar and the Factory held Bacci ceremonies[10] during the Lao New Year celebrations, and I once witnessed Nort and other sex workers sitting outside the bar with the mamasan preparing flower decorations for Boun Visakhabousa, a candlelight procession to the local temple to be held the next day in celebration of the birth of the Buddha.

We have earlier seen that sometimes the mamasan pays a commission for recruitment. However, often no monetary transaction takes place between the *mamasan* and the recruiter. While at times sex workers simply bring other friends along, it is also common that the *mamasan* entices sex workers to recruit acquaintances from their village upon their visits home as a way of enacting reciprocal moral obligations. This trend is also found in a recent study from northern Laos (Lyttleton 2008, 51).

Venue owners in Vientiane and Nong Kai also take part in helping sex workers, most notably with access to health services. For example, the *mamasan* at the Papaya Bar has on several occasions assisted sex workers with difficult clients. Once, one of the women had a violent drunk customer. The *mamasan* contacted the local village security, who came to her assistance and physically restrained the customer. On another occasion, Bpet had a Vietnamese customer who stole her mobile phone while she was showering in a local guesthouse they shared for the night. The *mamasan* assisted Bpet in reporting the theft to the police, which resulted in the customer's arrest and the return of the phone to Bpet. And when Daeng sold her virginity, she started to bleed badly. The *mamasan* subsequently took her to a private health clinic, where clinic staff were able to stop the bleeding.

All these everyday practices simulate family sociality. It is therefore not surprising that sex workers often express positive views of the *mamasan*. Trafficking literature tends to interpret such solidarity in pathological terms, often referring to post-traumatic stress disorder.

> Some women have loyal relationships with agents or employers who may also be boyfriends, husbands or family members. To an outsider, these feelings may appear inexplicable unless one understands the systematic isolation and dependency that are key components of the coercion used by perpetrators. In many cases violent or cruel acts alternate with gestures of kindness and mercy. These relationships can be confusing. A woman may feel taken care of, and the power imbalance may persuade her that her best hope for the future—for her survival— lies in the hands of those who are also abusing or exploiting her. (Zimmerman 2003, 8)

I am not here disputing the possibility of trauma among sex workers. We have seen that sex workers in Nong Kai are at times locked up in some venues. Earlier in this book we have also seen cases where managers have withheld the earnings of sex workers. Once when Phut and I visited Nort, she told us of a violent customer who had been very rough with her, as evidenced by her bruised chin. Sumalee and another venue owner told us of cases of drunk and violent customers (one involving a police officer). And Bpet and Gin told us of co-workers who had experienced attempted gang rape. One evening when I visited their bar, one of the girls had injured her leg and could not walk properly. It turned out that she had accompanied a customer on his bike, believing they were going to a local guesthouse, but the customer drove in the wrong direction. She told him to turn, but he sped up. She was horrified, believing he was taking her to his friend to be gang-raped (she had heard rumors that this had happened to other sex workers). She jumped off the bike, causing the injury to her leg. Bpet and Gin claimed to know other women who had been gang-raped.

However, throughout my research I did not come across evidence suggesting that physical violence was a direct result of, or a deliberate strategy among, recruiters and venue managers. Given that informants volunteer information that points to both the existence of deceptive recruitment practices as well as occasional experiences of violent customers, it is noteworthy that not a single informant claimed that physical coercion occurred as a deliberate strategy among venue owners (or recruiters) in order to entice women to work. This of course does not mean that its occurrence can be categorically ruled out.

The main problem with the anti-trafficking literature's emphasis on post-traumatic stress disorder is that it portrays trafficking as a pure form of power expressed in a victim-perpetrator dyad. This allows a particular calculative subjectivity to infiltrate the depiction of traffickers and exploiters. But the presumption that the "perpetrator" engages in subjugating practices in a reflexive and calculating manner is substantively wanting. As Horace Patterson (1982, 18) has pointed out: "Human beings have always found naked force or coercion a rather messy, if not downright ugly, business, however necessary. As Niccolò Machiavelli observed, it is the 'beastly' part of power. The problem has always been to find some way to clothe its beastliness, some idiom through which it can be made immediately palatable to those who exercise it" (see also Anderson and Davidson 2004, 37). Indeed, applying extreme violence to sex workers involves clear logistical dilemmas from the point of view of a venue owner: "Given that psychological responses to the trauma of being either sold or kidnapped or held hostage, then serially raped[,] include extreme forms of anxiety and withdrawal, thoughts of suicide, and so on, it is reasonable to assume that brothel owners use economic sanctions and 'incentives' partly because of the normalizing and legitimizing effect they can have upon abuse" (Davidson 1998, 36). Antonio Gramsci, Foucault, and many others have observed that domination is in a sense more powerful when not only does subjugation constitute overt coercion but the subjugated person also takes part in his or her own domination. In chapter 4, I described how venue owners facilitate sex work in a milieu that does not necessitate brute force but instead allows them to "free ride" on the disciplining effects of uneven market penetration and consumerism that entice women to seek high-earning work. Several reports point to a notable stigma attached to migrants who return to their hometown empty-handed (IOM 2004a; UNIAP et al. 2004). Hence, even in cases where new recruits are deceived, there are important disincentives for leaving the venue, regardless of the direct conduct of a venue manager.

This feeds in with broader cultural power relationships and the patrimonial character of social relations in both Laos and Thailand. Grant Evans writes: "In the Lao cultural world there is an ambiguous relationship between power and righteousness, one which often veers strongly in the direction of 'might is right.' People with power and wealth have maybe acquired them because of their Buddhist merit, or *boun*" (2002, 105). Indeed, a venue owner or a sex worker who is recruiting an acquaintance is in a superior position due to her accumulation of both economic capital (income, material wealth) and social capital (exposure to life outside village life). Heather Montgomery points to similar dynamics in Thailand, explaining how a child prostitute can gain high social status by starting to pimp other children: "A [child] pimp, with his or her control of other people, and distance from actual prostitution, is inevitably seen as having moved up the social ladder, because it is a movement away from controlled prostitution, which is the lowest form of sex work. For the children, their place in the hierarchy is determined by the number of people they can directly or indirectly control" (2001b, 95). Hence, recruiting acquaintances and friends into sex work does not necessarily entail negative moral sanctioning. On the contrary, it can both be a way of fulfilling reciprocal obligations through patron-client relationships and a strategy for climbing the social ladder. Such hierarchical relationships no doubt encourage fatalism in the recruit. As one sex worker in the Papaya Bar said, "When I arrived and realized it was a beer shop, I knew it was *too late*." She pointed out that without money for food or a return ticket home, she had no other choice than to start working. At the same time, a new recruit working among more experienced sex workers is continuously reminded of the possibility of acquiring modern status symbols such as nice clothes. Hence it is not merely that a recruiter or a manager may hold a higher social status. In Bourdieuian terms, the recruiter both possesses the cultural capital that is sought after and holds the key to it.

The social reproduction of a family ethos, the lack of a need for overt coercion strategies in most cases, and a recruiter's both possessing and providing access to material wealth have the important effect of giving recruitment a connotation of helping (*soi*). Souksavan repeatedly said she "pitied" many of the girls she employed "because they are poor." One night she told me that a fourteen-year-old girl, who she alleged was "very pretty" (*ngam lai*), had asked her for work. Souksavan hired her, reasoning, "I felt so sorry for her, I had to employ her." Similarly, Kham rationalized the occasional deception of new recruits by referring to the final outcome of their employment: "These girls are poor, but after they have worked for a while, they get used to it, and they can earn much more money than staying home."

It is not uncommon for sex workers who themselves take part in recruiting others to portray recruitment as an altruistic act. One night when we visited the Papaya Bar, Nort had brought a friend from her village. Nort explained that the girl's mother had encouraged her daughter to come along to the bar to sell her virginity and that the mother wanted at least 20,000 baht. Nort denied she was getting a commission for this but later said, "I think I will get some money for it, but I do not want any." Similarly, Souksavan referred to the commission gained from arranging the sale of virginity as a gift.

Daeng and Thia also occasionally brought acquaintances from their home community to the Factory for the purpose of selling their virginity. As was noted in an earlier chapter, Daeng, Thia, and Sei introduced each other to sex work, and all of them debuted by selling their virginity. Daeng told me that one of the motivating factors for her, besides earning a lot of money, was that she knew that many of her friends had done so previously. Sometimes younger girls in the village would ask them about selling their virginity. Daeng claimed that she advised them to "think carefully" about doing this. Yet one night Phut and I found that Daeng had brought a young girl to the bar.

Thia and Sei were sitting in one corner, drinking with an older man and a younger one. Phut and I sat with Daeng and a newly arrived girl. She looked young. It turned out that she was fourteen. She had come to the bar a few days earlier. Daeng told us that she had come with a friend to the bar and that she was not going to sell sex. Daeng said that she hadn't started menstruating yet. The impression was clearly that the intention—at the very least—was to expose the girl to a round of socialization in the bar environment in preparation for a possible debut selling her virginity in the future. Because of the girl's obvious young age, we did not pursue this topic.

On another occasion, Daeng brought three girls to the bar to "help" them sell their virginity. None of the girls liked being in the bar and subsequently returned to the village. Later on I asked Daeng why she had brought the girls to the bar if they did not want to be there in the first place. Daeng explained: "In the village it is difficult to imagine what a job like this is like. Many girls are scared. When I am home, I am also scared when I think about working in the bar. But when I get back here, then it is OK again. It is so different, and you get used to it." Daeng added that young women in her village see the nice clothes and material wealth she possesses, so they want to try. But when they arrive at the bar, they do not like it and return home. The relative physical proximity between Daeng's bar and her village makes this plausible, though difficult to verify. It is only a three-hour bus ride away, which makes the investment in migrating only a matter of a bus ticket. In other cases—such as in the Papaya Bar, where most women come from Luang Prabang—claims of "tagging along to see what it is like" are less plausible due to the considerable distance traveled and the necessary investment required for such movement. We see that Daeng's explanation of her involvement in bringing other women and girls to the bar references her own trajectory as a sex worker, which further obfuscates binary distinctions between "trafficked" and "consensual" recruitment methods.

In regard to "shame" and "guilt" cultures, Millie Creighton (1990) has argued that guilt primarily refers to the transgression of norms, whereas shame is related to the performing capacity of an individual in the social domain (see also Giddens 1991). In contrast to guilt, which involves the sanctioning of transgressing moral boundaries, "shame involves the awareness of inadequacy or failure to achieve a wished-for self-image" (Creighton 1990, 285). Some of the toughest aspects of debuting selling sex, according to several informants, were articulated, not in terms of transgressing norms (i.e., guilt), but in terms of being looked down upon by others (i.e., shame). As Gop and Daeng said, "It is really hard when people call you a whore."

As well as the difficult and sometimes traumatic adjustment of getting used to the bar environment, many women express this adjustment in terms of their ability to appropriate status symbols and alter their appearance—that is, their acquisition of cultural and economic capital. It is not uncommon for newly recruited sex workers to have old, faded clothes, revealing an impoverished rural background, in stark contrast to the trendy clothes worn by more experienced sex workers. With regard to adapting to selling sex, one of the things that often surfaces in conversations is the increasing ability to earn money and possess nice clothes and makeup. Informants articulate their acceptance of sex work in terms of gaining a sense of material adequacy in the eyes of the wider community. The body becomes a site where agency can be rebuilt, worked upon, and mediated by the ability to display visual markers of material wealth (High 2004; Van Esterik 2000). In other words, agency takes on here an embodied form where "self-esteem is redeemable through material gain" (Lyttleton 2000, 158). The importance of this is that a recruiter who is less than transparent about her "invitations" can engage in a self-deception by imagining her actions as reciprocating favor with fellow young villagers.

Here, agency needs to be understood in two ways. On the one hand, there is a socialization process within the bar environment, where repetitive tasks and interactions become the habitus for social actors. On the other hand, social actors' orientation is geared not only toward the past (social reproduction) but also toward the future (see Emirbayer and Mische 1998)—that is, in Bourdieu's terms, toward the acquisition of capital. Staying on in the sex industry becomes part of social agents' projection through material gain and bodily status markers. Because a recruiter has been subject to the same trajectory that she is "inviting" her peers into, it is not difficult to see the rationalization process taking place. Paradoxically, entry into prostitution becomes both the cause and the remedy of one's social inadequacy. It is therefore no surprise that informants refer to the final outcome of recruitment as a trope of helping. And by pointing to the end outcome of recruiting someone into the sex industry, recruiters euphemize their own personal involvement. It is notable that "helping" is not unique to the Lao-Thai context. Bridget Anderson (2008b), for example, observes that employers of domestic workers in Europe commonly articulate this relationship as one of helping. Consequently, "power is clothed in the language of obligation, support and responsibility, rather than power and exploitation" (ibid., 255).

In a classical existential analysis of bad faith, Jean-Paul Sartre (1957) calls attention to how social actors deny to themselves their complicity in their own actions. He contrasts this with a lie thus:

> The essence of the lie implies in fact that the liar actually is in complete possession of the truth which he is hiding. A man does not lie about what he is ignorant of; he does not lie when he spreads an error of which he himself is the dupe; he does not lie when he is mistaken. The ideal description of the liar would be a cynical consciousness, affirming truth within himself, denying it in his words, and denying that negation as such. (Ibid., 48)

Following Sartre, a liar is consequently acting in a highly self-conscious and calculative fashion. Although such a depiction might resonate with the way trafficking definitions tacitly presume that deception occurs, we see from the discussion above that trafficking along the Thai-Lao border does not fit neatly with this picture. Instead, the deceptive forms of recruitment that at times occur along the Thai-Lao border are best understood as bad faith.[11] As we have seen, social actors seek ways to rationalize their behavior, and they do so within an environment that allows for the reorientation—and therefore camouflaging—of sub-jective action into objective final outcomes of recruitment. A com-bination of several factors—an environment where social actors take advantage of the opportunities modernization has made available to them (the commoditization of friendships), the social reproduction of a family ethos, and the recruiter's embodiment of what she introduces to her friend or acquaintance—allows subtle differences between decep-tion, sweet talk, persuasion, and information to take a back stage in the recruitment process. In other words, both the trajectory of sex work as well as the social environment in which it operates enable social actors not to personalize their own complicity.

This does not mean that venue owners and recruiters are unaware of their own complicity, but it does suggest that deception is rarely a result of a calculated lie but rather constitutes circumstantial and opportunis-tic behavior. This renders the trafficking-voluntary dichotomy semi-coincidental and is the reason why one cannot simply account for traf-ficking by referring to ideal models of profitability and demand. Just as the previous chapter pointed to a discursive ignorance toward social relationships, we have seen in this chapter that not only are social rela-tions the key to understanding recruitment into entertainment venues on both sides of the border, but they also disturb the binary logic of traf-ficking definitions, because the victim and the perpetrator often know each other and sometimes are even embodied in the same person. Such glaring discrepancies between discourse articulation of trafficking and the sociality of sex commerce along the Thai-Lao border raise the obvi-ous question of how local anti-traffickers marry these two realities. Part III explores this question.

PART III

BETWIXT AND BETWEEN

The Anti-traffickers

7 Combating Trafficking, Mekong Style
Tales of Fishponds and Mushrooms

> To render a set of processes technical and improvable an arena
> of intervention must be bounded, mapped, characterized, and
> documented; the relevant forces and relations must be identi-
> fied; and a narrative must be devised connecting the proposed
> intervention to the problem it will solve.
> —Tanya Murray Li, *The Will to Improve* (2007, 126)

IN 2004 a trafficking project held a meeting in Vientiane with its stakeholders to carry out a mapping exercise. UNIAP had in its first phase
implemented several anti-trafficking programs, such as income generation and awareness raising in rural areas of Laos. However, due to the
increasing numbers of anti-trafficking programs, the project wanted to
play a stronger role in coordinating the anti-trafficking effort in the
Mekong region. An important part of this strategy was called Program
1 in its project document: building the knowledge base on trafficking.
The project had previously collected various information on all the
trafficking projects, such as their activities and geographical locations.
This was deemed an essential task in order to avoid duplication of program activities as well as to identify possible gaps in project implementation. The meeting in Vientiane was taking this mapping one step further. In addition to knowledge of project activities, the anti-trafficking
community had over time produced several reports, collected cases, and
developed a "working knowledge" of trafficking. The aim of the meeting was to collate all this information into a spatial presentation of data
on trafficking in order to illuminate trafficking hot spots.

Such visualized representation was not new. Both the United

Nations Educational, Scientific and Cultural Organization (UNESCO) and the International Labour Organization (ILO) had used global positioning system (GPS) data in their work to monitor trafficking trends and routes. However, to combine these data with the locations of anti-trafficking projects was novel. With the use of GPS maps, the combat between traffickers and anti-traffickers would come to light. In the meeting we sat around the table discussing the trafficking situation in Laos. Through the dream of high modernist planning (Scott 1998b), we attempted to re-create a miniature world of trafficking and anti-trafficking—a world we ultimately wanted to alter and control. Like generals fleshing out their next strategy for attack, we discussed the best ways forward in our combat against trafficking.

From Silences to Compulsion

Cross-border migration in Laos is highly politically sensitive. Like the governments of other nation-states, the Lao government is concerned with controlling its population and borders. Two important historical precursors link cross-border mobility directly with the political identity of Laos and give cross-border migration a particular political connotation. The first is the sacking of Vientiane by Siamese forces in 1828, when huge numbers of residents of Vientiane were taken as slaves and brought across the border to what is today Thailand (Stuart-Fox 1997; Turton 1980). The second is the exodus of Lao citizens in the 1970s following the communist takeover in the aftermath of the Vietnam War, when more than 10 percent of the total population of Laos fled (Evans 2002; Stuart-Fox 1997). The latter migration was a rejection of the communist government and its socialist project, whereas the former was a bitter reminder of the precarious inferior status Laos has relative to Thailand. The two incidents have caused the ethnic Lao population in Thailand to be larger than the whole population of Lao PDR itself, a sore historical point of which the Lao government is of course well aware. Hence, even to this day uncontrolled cross-border migration transgresses moral-political boundaries in a dual sense. It is a rejection of both national identity and political-civic belonging. At the same time, because Laos is a one-party state that adheres to the principles of Stalinist governance, internal movement has until recently been restricted. Before the year 2000, Lao citizens required official travel documents to cross provincial boundaries, and exit visas were abolished only in 2006 (Phouthonesy 2007c; *Vientiane Times* 2007b). It is within this political-historical context I started working for the Lao office of the United Nations Inter-Agency Project on Human Trafficking in the Greater Mekong Sub-region (UNIAP) in May 2001.

At that time the project was located within the Ministry of Labour and Social Welfare, and only a few other trafficking projects were operating in Laos. I remember the first few months, when even the term *gan kha manut* ("people trade," or human trafficking) could not be uttered freely in government meetings. This was not a problem within the government office I worked in, where staff were used to collaborating with international aid programs. However, when meeting officials from other ministries or provinces, one could not assume that it was acceptable to speak freely about this particular topic. A partial acceptance that trafficking was a problem to be discussed, and possibly addressed, did exist however, evidenced by the Lao government's agreement to participate in two regional trafficking projects.

Gradual changes took place over the three years I worked with UNIAP. More and more trafficking projects were launched in Laos. Slowly but steadily the Lao media started to write about trafficking from Laos to Thailand. Just as international attention to trafficking had accelerated on a global scale within a relatively short period, the trafficking issue in Laos went from a state of silence and denials to a state of compulsive debate.

Within the three years I worked for UNIAP (2002–2005), the number of trafficking projects in the Lao aid sector increased from zero to twelve, and by the time of this writing, the anti-trafficking sector had ballooned to include more than thirty projects. In 2002 the Lao government signed a memorandum of understanding (MOU) with Thailand concerning the regulation of labor migration (Government of Lao PDR and Government of the Kingdom of Thailand 2002). In the following year the Lao government acceded to both the Transnational Organized Crime (TOC) Convention and its underlying protocol on trafficking and established the Lao Anti People Trafficking Unit (LAPTU)[1] within the immigration police.[2] In 2004 Laos became party both to the regional Coordinated Mekong Ministerial Initiative against Trafficking (COMMIT), which seeks to strengthen multilateral cooperation to combat trafficking, and to the amended Article 134 of the Lao penal code, which criminalizes human trafficking.[3] The Lao government also developed further legislation addressing violence against women and trafficking. Also in the same year, the government formed an inter-ministerial task force and a ministerial-level national trafficking com-mittee. In 2005 another MOU was signed between the Lao and Thai governments, focusing specifically on the repatriation of trafficked vic-tims. As of late 2011, the Lao government was developing a national plan of action to combat trafficking. Alongside all these developments, rarely a week passes without a trafficking meeting being held, a traffick-ing training workshop being conducted (for social workers, counselors, police officers, and the like), or stories about trafficking in one shape or form being covered in the local media.

There are several reasons behind this increased action and atten-tion. Anti-trafficking programming in Laos has emerged in tandem with the ascendancy of trafficking both globally and regionally. Laos joined ASEAN in 1997 and is eager to be on a par with its neighbors. It is therefore not surprising that the first anti-trafficking programs in Laos were regional ones.[4] Simultaneously, as with any aid program, a trafficking project brings fiscal and material resources to a govern-ment with underpaid officials and few resources. In the eyes of the government, combating trafficking fits with its overall poverty reduc-tion strategy (Lao PDR 2004). From the beginning of my work in Laos, it was—and still often is—common among government officials to equate the fight against trafficking with rural development under the rubric of "prevention"—that is, bringing development (*pattana*) to villages to deter migration to Thailand. In this way, agreeing to col-laborate with international organizations to combat trafficking suited two government objectives: curbing migration to Thailand and boost-ing rural development projects. Several aid organizations happily fol-lowed along these lines. After all, rural development is something many aid programs are already familiar with, and it allows a project to "combat trafficking" without becoming embroiled in the sensitive issues and possible dangers of dubious labor migration recruitment. A fact sheet from the ILO project entitled *Micro-finance Interventions: To Combat the Worst Forms of Child Labour, including Trafficking* (ILO-

IPEC 2002) illustrates this trend. Except for its mention of the word "trafficking" briefly in the introduction, the rest of the document is full of advice on "marketing research," "monitoring," and "enterprise development." The actual issues of trafficking, labor exploitation, and migration are silently ignored. If not for the project title, one would be at a loss to know that this was in fact a "trafficking intervention." ILO is far from alone in implementing such programs. Several aid organizations implement "trafficking projects" that in real terms consist of activities such as microcredit loans, vocational training (weaving, carpentry), or rural improvements (irrigation, fishponds), often with awareness raising (e.g., posters warning against dangers of trafficking). In short, such trafficking projects are rural development projects in disguise.

The global concern with organized crime undoubtedly had an impact on the increasing attention to trafficking in Laos. In my position as a project adviser—at the time located within the Lao government itself—I was able to see some of the political strategizing (or rather, the lack thereof) when the Lao government acceded to the TOC Convention and its underlying trafficking protocol. I recall the day I learned by chance of this agreement. I thought, "No, that's not possible—I would know." To my knowledge, the government had not yet discussed this in the National Assembly, nor could I recall any of our government counterparts mentioning that this was even on the agenda. No changes had been made to the penal code or other legal reforms as required prior to acceding to an international convention.

I went on UNODC's website, and there it was—the listing of Laos' status regarding the convention.[5] I was struck by surprise and embarrassment. After all, I was in an advisory role for a project that was supposed to coordinate and be on top of information about trafficking in Laos. "Why didn't any of our government counterparts—with whom we have a good working relationship—inform us?" I thought. "Did they know?" Throughout the day my coworkers and I made several phone calls to colleagues in UNICEF, UNODC, NGOs, and the government. Nobody knew! It turned out later—as we discovered through some informal queries—that the foreign minister had signed both the TOC Convention and the UN trafficking protocol in New York while attending a conference relating to terrorism, despite the apparent lack of discussion within the National Assembly (though the politburo must have been informed).

To this day it is unclear exactly what the prelude was for the Lao government's acceding to this convention. The initiative did not stem from lobbying by UN agencies or from any of the government's various task forces and committees on trafficking. Instead it is conceivable that the government sensed that organized crime and terrorism were high on the agenda in New York. In other words, it was not the immediate concern with trafficking per se that made the Lao government join in the convention and the trafficking protocol. That my colleagues in government were unaware of Laos' accession is a strong indicator of this. Instead it is plausible that a more general concern about appearing to be willing to fight international organized crime and terrorism provided a stronger motivation for the Lao government's action.

Hence the initial anti-trafficking programs, as well as the government's willingness to allowing them to operate, must be understood within a broader context where official government policy is shaped by stated aims of development (*pattana*) as well as a desire to be a responsible player in regional and international arenas. However, the broad framework of generic objectives of development and performativity of statehood within a context of regional and international integration does not explain exactly how anti-trafficking programs are shaped. The way human trafficking meshes with development and government practices raises broader epistemological questions that I will now explore.

Knowledge Production and Coherence

In order for an aid project to carry out its activities, it must possess certain kinds of knowledge about what to do. In other words, development aid always involves the articulation of its object, thereby not only legitimating the possibility of development but also enabling development to take place (Ferguson 1990; Murray Li 2007; Escobar 1994). As such, development aid entails a notable means-ends rationality (Olivier de Sardan 2005) whereby its object must be made legible (Scott 1998b), targets must be identified, and remedial action must be projected in order to fulfill the goal of development. This is of course also the case for trafficking projects, whose programs habitually frame activities in terms of "targeted interventions" (see ILO-IPEC 2002).[6] As the vignette presented at the beginning of this chapter shows, hot spots of trafficking must somehow be identified in order to plan, implement, and justify anti-trafficking projects. Such processes of objectification raise interesting challenges for anti-trafficking projects. As noted earlier, anti-trafficking programs within the development sector are traditionally defined in terms of demarcated space, yet they need to design their activities in relation to a phenomenon that is deterritorialized. In most cases, as we have seen, trafficking is presumably taking place away from where anti-trafficking programs operate. Hence aid programs must identify exactly where trafficking is a problem. However, providing a rationale for where trafficking is taking place is not the only necessity; a second layer or objectification is required to account for exactly why a given object can be considered to constitute trafficking. I elaborated in Part I how this second requirement is commonly gauged in terms of implicit notions of agglomeration within a marketplace. Given that it is widely acknowledged that within the Thai-Lao context numerous individuals migrate but only some of them end up in what may be considered a trafficked situation, anti-traffickers must come up with a rationale for how they distinguish what is a hot spot from what is not. Put simply, trafficking programs must identify hot spots. However, exactly what is hot, as well as where one may locate hot spots, is not self-evident, as is exemplified by two large trafficking studies that I will now explore in some detail.

The ILO and the "Three Nos"

In the early days of anti-trafficking programming in the Lao PDR there was widespread recognition that more data and research were needed in order to enhance project activities. Some reports did exist, but they tended to be small-scale and to relate only to areas that respective organizations worked in. The first large-scale anti-trafficking study was conducted by the ILO-IPEC in 2003, with the results published in a report titled *Labour Migration Survey in Khammuane, Savannakhet, and Champasack.* The study's survey questionnaire covered more than thirty-five thousand people and approximately six thousand households in three southern provinces bordering Thailand where the ILO-IPEC project already worked. According to the report, the study's objective was "to explore the benefits and risks of Lao migrant workers in Thailand": "The exercise is to identify those at risks and [those who] possibly have been trafficked for labour exploitation as well as to identify those migrant workers with decent jobs and sending remittances to support their families and themselves" (ILO-IPEC 2003, 42). After several pages presenting various socioeconomic data, the report emphasizes remittances as a key indicator for assessing "success" and "risk" of migration. Noting that approximately half of the migrants surveyed remit money, the report reasons:

> More than half of the migrant workers in Thailand may have decent jobs that allow them to have some savings that they could send back home to support their families, but 45.6% have never sent any remittances home. . . . Within this group, there are possibilities that they did not earn enough to make savings, were underpaid, underemployed, unemployed, and in the worst case may have been trafficked for labour exploitation, in particular children and young women. (Ibid.)

Thus remittances are taken as an indication of the well-being of a migrant.

Conversely, a lack of remittances is presumed to be a proxy for various risks, including trafficking. How the study assesses risk and trafficking is fleshed out later in the report, where it attempts to use the data gathered "to analyze and trace 'migrant workers at high risks of being victims of trafficking.'" The report then states, "The assumption used for the sake of this exercise is: 'Migrant workers who their head of households have no contacts, have no information about their livelihood and have never receive[d] remittance since they left the village at least a year ago'" (ibid., 47). In other words, the report suggests that, based on interviews with household heads, trafficking risk exists if the "three nos" apply to the migrant—that is, the household head has received no remittances, no contact, and no information from the migrant. However, it is not difficult to point out some of the problems with this approach. Anthropologists have for decades noted shortcomings in the reliability of survey data, and I do not need to repeat some of the common problems here. Suffice it to say that data collected on poor villagers' families by enumerators (many of whom are government officials) ought to be treated with extreme caution, given the sociopolitical context of Laos, where returning migrants have been routinely fined and even sent away for reeducation (*saminar*). What is more interesting than such methodological limitations, however, is the way the report determines hot spots through the prism of its "three nos."

At first glance, using the three nos as criteria gives the report an aura of positivist scientism, as the study seems to provide three variables validating an analysis of risk and thereby probability of trafficking among a migrant population. However, the three nos end up as a tautology, because possessing information about a migrant's livelihood and receiving remittances are both examples of contact between a migrant and his or her family. Hence the three nos boil down to a question of a connection between a migrant and a household. And here we run into a further problem: the assumption that the absence of contact (in the form of lack of remittances or knowledge of the migrant's livelihood) is an indicator of risk and trafficking. As several other studies have pointed out, migrants might have numerous reasons for avoiding contact with or remitting money to their families. For example, as academics and aid reports alike have observed (UNICEF 2001; Montgomery 2001b), a common reason for entry in sex work is to avoid difficult family situations and sometimes abusive relationships, particularly with stepparents. We have seen examples of this in this book. Conversely, the assumption that the presence of contact, such as a stream of remittances, is equally problematic for the identification of trafficking vulnerability. As has been pointed out in academic research (Lindquist 2009) and even another trafficking report from Laos (UNIAP et al. 2004), agents often facilitate the flow of remittances. Hence one cannot assume either that a migrant is in control of the flow of remittances or that this flow reflects a positive working environment. To be fair, the report acknowledges that more research is needed when it comes to the exact nature of both trafficking and the remittance process. However, this ILO report was published back in 2003, and at the time of this writing the ILO project has yet to follow through with additional research. But the most interesting problem with the three-nos approach is that ultimately it is logically self-destructive, because it by definition excludes the possibility of families having contact, knowledge of, or remittances from a family member who is in a trafficked situation.[7] As we have seen earlier in this book, anti-trafficking discourse has a tendency to turn absence of evidence into evidence of trafficking. Here this logic is taken to the point that any information about trafficking that is known within the village community is ironically excluded from the report's definition of trafficking risk!

Despite all these shortcomings, the report concludes that only 1.4 percent of the total number of migrants are considered at risk of trafficking. One would perhaps think that this would make the ILO reconsider whether their designated hot spots were actually hot enough to warrant a multimillion-dollar anti-trafficking program. Yet these findings did not stop the ILO from continuing its project. To the contrary, in the second phase of the project, the number of target villages expanded considerably with boosted funding from the United Kingdom's Department for International Development (DFID). I will later on consider what enables this seeming perpetuation of anti-trafficking programming in light of flimsy data and dubious project justification. But before doing so, it is worth considering another report, this one commissioned by UNICEF.

UNICEF and the Problem with Temporality

It is perhaps unsurprising that the 2003 ILO report was received with mixed reviews within the Lao anti-trafficking community. Although some appreciated its comprehensive data in terms of documenting migration and remittances, others thought the report fell well short of saying anything meaningful about human trafficking. The following year, two other significant reports were in the making. One report was relatively small in scale but included long-term ethnographic research (UNIAP et al. 2004). At the same time, UNICEF designed the first nationwide study on trafficking that included all provinces of Laos. Furthermore, in contrast to the survey methods employed by the ILO, UNICEF hired an anthropologist with respected research credentials within development aid circles in Laos to carry out the research.[8] Therefore the UNICEF report raised a great deal of interest within the Lao aid community.[9]

Prior to the publication of the UNICEF report, informal meetings about it were held among UN agencies. Apparently the study had found, in stark contrast to the ILO's estimation of 1.4 percent, that the level of trafficking in Laos was alarmingly high.[10] Predictably, UNICEF's findings were debated among individuals working for anti-trafficking programs in Laos. Other aid organizations were eager to get a copy of the report, but UNICEF was reluctant to share it beyond government counterparts. After several delays, the report was finally published. However, the draft report's initial estimate of one hundred thousand trafficked victims was notably absent. Furthermore, as with the ILO study, UNICEF's research findings had a number of problems.

The report used the definition of trafficking in the Palermo Protocol (which the report quoted in full) yet did not apply it consistently and at times appeared to conflate migration and trafficking.[11] However, more serious problems related to the methodology of the study. The report claimed: "In the majority of cases, this identification process [of informants] went smoothly and even though their experiences were painful and fraught with emotion, people were willing to recall their experiences" (UNICEF and Ministry of Labour and Social Welfare 2004, 15). This assertion is substantially wanting, considering that the research team spent only a short time (usually only one day) in each village studied, a factor that is not explicitly recognized in the report.[12] This raises questions about the reliability of responses. Although UNICEF states that "the report's case studies provide a vivid portrayal of the extreme vulnerability to exploitation of children" (ibid., 7), a closer reading suggests that the promise of revealing profiles of victims, traffickers, routes, and trends must be treated with caution. The report documented 253 cases of trafficking based on research in 149 villages. It is noteworthy that the report used purposive sampling, which suggests that the villages selected were thought to be at particular risk for trafficking. Hence, according to the report, the study found on average only 1.69 cases of trafficking per village. Furthermore, the majority of the case studies presented turned out to be several years old, in some cases as old as eleven years from the time the research took place. Just as with the hot spots in the ILO report, what is deemed hot becomes somewhat diluted when one recognizes that the trafficking cases occurred over a long time span. Thus it is unclear whether the report is a contemporary study of trafficking or a historical study of villagers' autobiographies regarding migration. The report offers no reflections regarding this serious methodological problem. For these reasons, some individuals within the aid community were a bit perplexed and perhaps disappointed over the report.

Notably, the lead author and some UNICEF officials distanced themselves from the report in the aftermath of its release. They emphasized that a draft version of the report apparently contained information that was considered too sensitive to be published. Here again we see that the absence of data becomes a justification for the existence of trafficking (and thereby for the existence of aid programs to combat it). Later, in informal conversations as well as in print, the lead author claimed that "UNICEF omitted the analytical portion of the research," (ADB 2009, 4), thereby discrediting the report yet at the same time maintaining that this omission entails one of the big secrets of the true nature of Lao trafficking.

Additionally, the charge of the omission of the "analytical part" may be an indication that the UNICEF report was strongly "donor driven," with unambiguous glossy knowledge production taking precedence over critical scholarship due to the need of aid organizations to create "authoritative knowledge" (Goldman 2001) in order to enable (and legitimize) development interventions. In the next chapter, we will see that although such knowledge production undoubtedly has to do with bureaucratic needs for legibility (Scott 1998b), it must also be understood in the context of aid workers, who after all are the vessels for the perpetuation of such knowledge. As will become evident, such reports do not merely reflect docile bureaucrats responding to institutional demands; rather, knowledge production is simultaneously a form of capital (Bourdieu 1977 [1972]) that is important in attempts to secure particular interpretations (Mosse 2004) of anti-trafficking work within the broader field of development.

Ascendancy of a Victim Focus

I have earlier shown that programs that do "income generation" projects in rural communities in order to deter migration (and hence "prevent" trafficking from taking place) imply a classical market logic by attempting to address a shortfall of labor "at home" in order to contribute to a labor market equilibrium. Many aid programs in Laos still operate according to this recipe in one shape or form. Yet this type of project implementation has come under considerable criticism within the anti-trafficking community itself. One of the first explicit criticisms surfaced in a field report by UNIAP (Ginzburg 2002a), which questioned the blurring of anti-migration and harm reduction strategies among trafficking projects. This critique was later followed by others (Haughton 2006) and myself (Molland 2005). There is now a growing realization within the trafficking community in Laos that by engaging in "community development," or what some anti-trafficking actors have caustically labeled as the "stay where you are approach" (Marshall and Thatun 2005), attention is drawn away from the "real" problem of migrants being exploited.

A village meeting in northwestern Laos that I participated in when I worked for UNIAP makes this point clear. By the time I and other UNIAP staff entered the village for the meeting, we had accumulated some eight government officials along the way. Besides my government colleagues from Vientiane, we could not escape preparatory "consultation meetings" with both provincial and district officials before going into the village (per diem allowances, as well control of aid programs, are obvious motivations for such participation by government officials). When we all arrived in the village, many adults (mostly men) had gathered. All participants were "concerned parents of youth in the village," we were told. Not a single person below the age of thirty was present. The meeting was obviously choreographed and rehearsed. In the presence of the attending government officials, we heard the village members plead for fishponds, weaving projects, skill training, and improved irrigation in order to strengthen the village's "fight" against trafficking. The villagers' remarks were suspiciously in line with the official government agenda on poverty reduction, and it was frustratingly difficult to discuss trafficking in a more specific way.

In recent years, several other trafficking and migration-related studies have been conducted in Laos.[13] These studies suggest that trafficking is taking place within the context of a much larger migration pattern that is often—at least in the eyes of village folks—beneficial both economically and socially. Nor is there much evidence to support the assumption that poverty or lack of jobs at home necessarily has much to do with why migrants leave in the first place (Haughton 2006; Rigg et al. 2004), let alone why some may end up in exploitative (i.e., trafficked) situations. Many anti-traffickers in Laos have gradually realized that it is perhaps somewhat far-fetched to think that by vaccinating chickens and pigs in a Lao village, they somehow prevent rape and physical abuse of Laotians in Bangkok sweatshops and brothels. To be fair, part of the reason aid programs have tended to focus on community development is the political sensitivities involved. Many aid workers (but not all) are keenly aware of this limitation and do what they can to lobby the government to change its perception of anti-trafficking work and focus more strongly on labor exploitation itself. Yet this is not to deny the role of aid programs' in promoting microfinance and vocational training as real efforts to combat trafficking. No doubt the spatial habitus of aid programs, the idea of having a defined geographic area—a project site—where one does something one already knows how to do (i.e., community development), contributes to this role.

Since mid-2000 the understanding of the focus of anti-trafficking work has gradually shifted from prevention to harm reduction, or "safe migration"—in other words, from considering annihilation of movement as a "success" to concentrating on factors that may make a migrant vulnerable to exploitation. Consequently, the message presented in awareness-raising material has changed from one of preventing movement ("Don't go!") to one of making departure safer ("Go safely!"), and increased interest has been paid to the ways in which projects can meaningfully empower migrants. In parallel to all this, the Thai and Lao governments have been slowly but gradually implementing the 2002 MOU to legalize labor migration (Government of Lao PDR and Government of the Kingdom of Thailand 2002).

In addition to this shift in approach, internal trafficking in Laos has received growing attention, in terms of both the participation of Laotians in a trafficking network and the possibility of end destinations being within the Lao jurisdiction. This shift has no doubt been sensitive for the Lao government because it seems to legitimate out-migration, and at the time of writing it is still politically difficult to initiate projects explicitly targeting "end destinations" within Laos' borders. The aforementioned UNICEF report (2004), however, did document internal trafficking for the purpose of prostitution and factory work.

Given that this report was published in cooperation with the Ministry of Labour and Social Welfare, it constitutes an official partial admission of trafficking "at home."[14]

The consideration given to internal trafficking has not diverted attention from cross-border trafficking. In many respects the focus on cross-border trafficking has been strengthened. At the time of my research, there were no fewer than six regional trafficking projects in the Mekong region—all of which were operating in Laos.[15] and the Asia Regional Cooperation to Prevent People Trafficking (ARCPPT) project (which focuses on law enforcement), the regional COMMIT MOU, and the UN protocol itself reinforce the perceived need for cross-border cooperation.[16]

The combination of cross-border cooperation, a slow move toward realization and admission of the existence of internal trafficking, and the questionable efficiency of the "stay where you are" approach has created somewhat of an identity crisis for aid projects. Although many programs still practice "prevention" under the rubric of rural development, many seek new activities such as services for victims.

Until 2005 only the International Organization for Migration (IOM) worked on the repatriation and reintegration of victims between Laos and Thailand. In 2006, Acting for Women in Distressing Situations (AFESIP) signed an MOU with the Lao government (Human-Trafficking.org 2006a). This project works specifically with the sex industry and operates a shelter for trafficked victims. The Lao Women's Union also operates a shelter and provides counseling services for victims of domestic violence and trafficking victims. Currently several other NGOs are exploring ways they can work with repatriation and reintegration of victims into village communities in Laos.

In 2004 the Australian government launched a trafficking program targeting the criminal justice process and reinforcing a focus on both victims and traffickers. More recently UNODC, in cooperation with the Ministry of Justice, also initiated a program targeting the criminal justice system. By acceding to the TOC Convention and the UN trafficking protocol, as well as signing the regional COMMIT MOU, which includes specific provisions for prosecution as well as victim support and identification, the Lao anti-trafficking community was clearly moving toward a stronger concentration on both victims and traffick-

ers. This shift was reflected at the first meeting of the national trafficking committee, held in May 2007, where it was asserted that "law
enforcement needs to guarantee that human traffickers are duly punished for the crimes they have committed and to make a clear distinction between a victim, an illegal immigrant, and a human trafficker"
(*Vientiane Times* 2007a).

Who is a trafficker? Who is a trafficked victim? And who is merely
a "migrant"? These become central questions. We will shortly look at
how some of my anti-trafficking informants responded to such challenges in their everyday work, but first I will discuss how victim identification is dealt with in training programs delivered by aid organizations
in Laos and Thailand.

Victim Identification

Victim identification poses several challenges for anti-traffickers. It is
during this process that ideal types of trafficking meet real cases in a
constructed space. In this precarious activity, victim guidelines become
the main heuristic device assisting anti-traffickers in identifying trafficked victims. A PowerPoint presentation produced by the IOM and
used in training within the Mekong countries, including Thailand and
Laos, is representative of such guidelines. It outlines victim identification thus:

Element 1: Process
Ask yourself, was the person:
    Recruited? OR
    Transported? OR
    Transferred? OR
    Harbor[ed]? OR
    Received?
If the answer is yes, go to Element 2.
If the answer is no, this NOT a victim of trafficking.

Element 2: Means
Ask yourself, was the person:
    Forced? OR

Threatened? OR

Coerced? OR

Abducted? OR

Subjected to fraud? OR

Deceived? OR

Subjected to abuse of power?

If the answer is yes, go to Element 3.

If the answer is no and the victim is a child, go to Element 3.

If answer is no and the victim is an adult, this is NOT a victim of trafficking.

Element 3: Exploitation

Ask yourself, was the person exploited OR was there an intention exploit?

Exploitation may include:

Prostitution, OR

Other forms of sexual exploitation, OR

Forced labor, OR

Slavery, OR

Other practices similar to slavery (i.e., forced military service), OR

Servitude, OR

Removal of organs.

If answer is yes, the person is a victim of trafficking.

If the answer is no, the person is NOT a victim of trafficking.

We see that these guidelines are simply a reproduction of the trafficking definition from the Palermo Protocol. Identifying a victim is articulated as a straightforward and unproblematic linear checklist that operates according to a binary, either-or logic. None of the terms are problematized, and how one ought to interpret terms such as "coerced," "forced," and "exploited"—or how one ought to ask about them in an interview setting—is not addressed. At the same time, representing victim identification as a checklist has the effect of externalizing the act of victim identification away from the social worker onto objectified guidelines. In this way it is up to the guidelines, not the caseworker, to determine whether someone is deemed a trafficked victim, and the potential need for interpretation of cases is not directly addressed. In addition, the PowerPoint presentation suggests "cues" for detecting trafficking cases. For instance, social workers are advised to look for "trafficking symptoms," which may include the following:

> Psychosomatic reactions (headaches, neck pain, backaches, stomachaches, trembling, sweating, sleeping problems, immunosuppression, etc.)
>
> Psychological reactions (hopelessness, despair, suicidal thinking, self-harm, aggressiveness, violent [behavior], isolation, withdrawal, distrust, memory problems, chronic fatigue, frequent crying, etc.)
>
> Psychoactive substance abuse and dependence (overdose, addiction, physical damage, needle-introduced infections, dependence on drugs, alcoholism, participation in high-risk behaviours such as promiscuous unprotected sexual acts, violence, crime, etc.)

We see here that identification of a victim of trafficking includes two intersecting scripts: a mechanical, objectifying checklist that is copied straight from the UN protocol's definition of trafficking, and cues that include a range of symptoms. After these other cues are combined with the guidelines, it is hard to imagine what might not be considered an indication of trafficking.

Not all programs use trafficking definitions in such an explicit way, however. When AFESIP, an NGO working to combat trafficking and sexual exploitation in Laos, does outreach work in the sex industry, it uses a questionnaire that focuses on socioeconomic data and some details of the women's experience working in the sex industry. It is noteworthy that the questionnaire seeks no information about recruitment in general or about the use of deception or force in the recruitment process. The only question touching on the direct issue of trafficking is "Did you ever meet [with] violence?" Thus it is far from clear exactly how trafficking cases are determined from responses to the questionnaire. One informant who had previously collaborated with an outreach team using this questionnaire told me that it was difficult to draw conclusions from the information gathered in this way. He also pointed out that sex workers commonly changed their stories, which further complicated the identification process. As with the IOM's PowerPoint presentation, we see here a difficulty in translating the concept of trafficking into reliable means of identifying victims. This problem is also inherent in police investigations.

Many anti-traffickers consider law enforcement to be the flagship of agencies in the war on trafficking. After all, if anti-traffickers indeed want to reduce demand—as the market logic of trafficking suggests— one way of doing so would be to investigate, arrest, and prosecute traffickers. This is one of the main rationales behind the AusAID-funded trafficking program in Laos (ARCPPT 2002). The focus on law enforcement was reinforced when the US State Department ranked Laos at tier three in its 2006 trafficking report, due to a lack of arrests and prosecutions of traffickers.

From a law enforcement perspective, identifying a victim as such is important in two ways. First, identification is necessary in order to grant victims of trafficking their rights (see Gallagher 2001). We have seen that the TOC Convention is weak when it comes to specifying state parties' obligations to provide various rights to trafficked victims (Gallagher 2001; Kempadoo 2005). Academics have gotten mileage out of making this point in their critiques of the trafficking industry, and several aid agencies and other groups working within a human rights framework actively lobby to strengthen rights and protection of trafficked victims. This is also reflected in the UN Guidelines on Trafficking, whose first clause states: "The human rights of trafficked persons shall be at the centre of all efforts to prevent and combat trafficking and to protect, assist and provide redress to victims" (ECOSOC 2002, 3). And it has been reinforced in police training manuals used in both Thailand and Laos (ARCPPT 2004).

Second, from a policing perspective, there are two principal ways trafficking investigations are carried out. In Thailand, proactive investigations (i.e., surveillance) have been applied both in training programs and in operational police investigations when Thai nationals were suspected of having been trafficked to another country.[17] However, such surveillance methods are technically complex, requiring a high level of investigative capacity and expertise, as well as considerable cordial cross-border cooperation between respective law enforcement agencies. The far more common mode of police operation is reactive investigation. Commonly, a response to a trafficking case arises when a victim who has escaped an exploitative labor situation approaches a law enforcement authority, a victim is discovered by law enforcement officials through their work, a victim is rescued, or a victim is reported by a third party (i.e., a family member, an anti-trafficking project, etc.) (ARCPPT 2004, 9). Reactive investigation is the only operational mode of police investigation being applied in trafficking cases in Laos.

Reactive investigations have important implications for the role of victims because witness testimony in many cases is the main source of evidence that can be used in court cases. A trafficked victim is almost always the only person who has witnessed all three aspects of trafficking: movement, deceit/coercion, and exploitation. Hence the victim of trafficking is deemed a vital witness. It is therefore not surprising that training manuals for Thai and Lao police forces place great emphasis on the importance of victims as potential witnesses. A slogan for a police training workshop on trafficking that I once attended in Vientiane stated, "The victim is the witness." So just how are Lao and Thai police officers trained to identify a trafficked victim?

Training manuals for police officers follow a logic similar to that of the IOM guidelines mentioned above. The three elements of trafficking (movement, force/deceit, and exploitation) inform both interview question used to identify victims (in order to grant them their rights) and procedures for gathering evidence (in order to arrest and prosecute traffickers). The following excerpt from a training manual exemplifies this:

> The recruitment phase: (questions include: if force was not involved, how was contact made between the victims and the recruiter? What did the victim believe she or he was going to be engaged in following arrival at the final destination? Has the victim paid any money to the recruiter etc.?)
>
> Transport phase: (questions cover: false documentation? Where are documents now?)
>
> Exploitation phase: (questions include: what activity has the victim been engaged in and when did it begin? What were the working conditions? What degree of freedom of choice and movement did the

victim have? Why didn't the victim escape sooner?) (ARCPPT 2004, 20–24)

This type of training manual is far more detailed and methodical than the PowerPoint presentation issued by IOM, as it includes numerous suggested interview questions for the police to ask. Nevertheless, although asking numerous questions may build a basis for a more thorough analysis, the need for interpretation by the interviewing police officer remains.

Like the IOM training material, police training manuals also emphasize cues to who may be a potential trafficked victim, as in this example:

> *Age*—in general terms and in most cases, the older the victim is, the less likely it is that the case involves trafficking. All available indicators point to growth in the trafficking of children and young adults. . . .Trafficking for labour exploitation will normally centre on younger victims, as traffickers know that arduous physical labour in slavery[-]like conditions demands younger and fitter victims. The same point can be made in relation to trafficking for sexual exploitation as client preference is for younger and younger victims who are more profitable than older victims. In most cases of sexual exploitation, traffickers will not normally traffic victims over the age of thirty years because there is little client demand for them. (Ibid., 9)

We see here once again the imagined congruence between probability of trafficking on the one hand, and profit and bodily attributes on the other—that is, victims are profitable because they are young. The relevance of gender is also highlighted:

> Sex trafficking predominantly affects females because heterosexual prostitution remains the most profitable and visible form of exploitation. Nevertheless, male trafficking for the purposes of prostitution, particularly of teenage and younger boys, is beginning to increase and should not be excluded. . . .
>
> Latest intelligence assessments point to a new trend in the internal and external trafficking of children for the purpose of paedophile abuse

and the commercial and non-commercial production of paedophile pornography and this trend can afflict girls and boys equally. (Ibid.)

Thus girls are considered to be more profitable than boys, and certain niche markets such as pedophilia are noted. I question this assumed economism elsewhere in this book. What I want to draw attention to here is that such training manuals engage in a process of objectification of social categories and that they canvass a typology (see also Salt 2000, 45). However, their descriptions of such cues are so general that they barely provide any guidance at all. After all, how helpful is it for a police officer to know that a victim of sex trafficking *might* be a woman or girl under thirty years of age? In other words, a trafficked victim could be practically anyone. However, such obvious challenges are not addressed in these training manuals. Instead other challenges are emphasized. For instance, the investigative police officer is warned:

> The interview will be a challenging task for law enforcement officers because victims are likely to be hostile, suspicious, distrustful, reticent. Reluctance on the part of an individual to provide detailed responses may be a manifestation of a genuine victim's fear of the trafficker, fear of exposure, or suspicion and mistrust of any official figure or, in severe cases, reluctance to provide any form of detailed response may be because the individual is simply too traumatised to speak about the subject. (ARCPPT 2004, 11)

Indeed, much literature (discussion papers, training manuals, and so on) emphasizes the reluctance of victims to cooperate with law enforcement authorities. I have earlier in this book mentioned that the anti-trafficking community gives importance to post-traumatic stress disorder, and this training manual follows that trend:

> In simple terms, the condition occurs when a victim lives through an experience or series of experiences that are so extreme that she/he is unable to comprehend the nature of it or accept that it has happened to her/him. In most cases, the trigger for the condition involves the use of violence that is so extreme that it falls outside of the victim's own system of values of human behaviour to such an extent that she/

he cannot rationalise it and may even deny that it ever happened to her/him.

As an example, to cite evidence from recent case histories involving South Eastern European victims, incidences of abuse have been inflicted by traffickers upon victims that have involved acts of extreme violence or abuse such as multiple or "gang" rape, the severing of fingers as punishment for disobedience or the removal of teeth to improve a victim's ability to provide sexual services.

For the victims that suffer the abusive and traumatic experience, the extremity of it is not only beyond their ability to rationalise and accept that it has happened to them, but will often lead to their denial of it—which is a psychological condition known as "dissociation." (Ibid., 11–12)

In addition to these challenges, Lao and Thai police officers are told in their training courses that trafficking trajectories themselves are another source of cues for determining victim status:

The chronology is also a key indicator; in genuine trafficking cases, the exploitation phase will begin immediately or very soon after the illegal entry because the trafficker wants to gain profits or services from the victim as soon as possible.

If there is a significant time gap between the illegal entry and the beginning of the exploitative purpose, it is more likely to indicate a case of simple illegal entry—followed subsequently by un-related coercion or a deliberate decision to engage in exploitative work. (Ibid., 22)

The significance of exploitation is reemphasized:

Continuous exploitation is achieved through continuous coercion. To put it simply, the working conditions and exploitation are such that any rational human being would escape from them—if they could—at the first opportunity. (Ibid., 22)

I do not wish to argue against the assertion that victims of trafficking may suffer from post-traumatic stress disorder, or against the possibility that trafficked victims may show empathy and support for their captors, known as the Stockholm syndrome, which are described in both this training manual (ARCPPT 2004) and other trafficking literature (UNODC 2006b). But I do want to question the premise that these possibilities constitute a central and indeed a typical reality that Lao and Thai police officers will encounter in their trafficking work. Without denying the horrific experiences to which women and girls (as well as men and boys) in the sex industry might be subject, the effect of such training manuals is that identification of a victim of trafficking can easily become a self-fulfilling prophecy. According to such manuals, if the alleged victim of trafficking claims to be just that, then the police officer should take this as a strong indication that she or he is a trafficked victim, but if the person in question denies being a victim of trafficking, then this is equally a reason to suspect that she or he is a trafficked victim. Consequently any female who has any alleged association with the local entertainment industry can be a potential victim of trafficking. To be fair, the manual does stress the need for involving psychologists. Yet such advice is unlikely to translate into operational programming. My former colleagues in the Ministry of Labour and Social Welfare who worked directly with trafficked victims knew of only one psychologist in all of Laos. The problem here is that the identification of post-traumatic stress disorder, which is usually the domain of clinical psychology, enters a wider discourse of anti-trafficking programming, where it serves the purpose of making meaning within a wider anti-trafficking audience. Here again, we see that trafficking takes on a ubiquitous and mystical character that tends to make counterevidence into evidence ("Watch out! Her denial of trafficking means she is traumatized!" "The traffickers have made her deny it—this is just one of the trafficker's smart tricks." "She must definitely be trafficked!").

Furthermore, such training manuals insist on clear-cut, polarized cases where the statuses of the victims and the perpetrators are beyond question. Anything that points to ambiguity is not addressed, and little consideration is given to the social relationships in which the alleged trafficked victim is involved. In fact, the greater the emphasis on the horrific situation to which trafficked victims are subjected, the less possible it becomes to imagine any forms of social relationship between a trafficker and a trafficked victim. In other words, the types of trafficking cases that I came across in the field are incomprehensible within the pedagogical narrative produced by these trafficking training manuals. Just as the market metaphor of trafficking desocializes both traffickers and trafficked victims, the law enforcement regime within the anti-trafficking sector reinforces this trend. This raises the obvious question of how the trafficking cases (if we can call them that) I came across in my own research fit into the pedagogy proclaimed by trafficking manuals, workshops, and training on victim identification? And how do trafficking actors in Laos engage with such cases? The next chapter explores these questions in detail.

8 The Drifters

Anti-traffickers in Practice

> Knowledge and action mobilize extremely dissimilar registers
> of legitimation.
> —Jean-Pierre Olivier de Sardan, *Anthropology and Development:*
> *Understanding Contemporary Social Change* (2005, 199)

"Hmmm . . . hmmm. This is interesting." John is sitting behind his office desk, rereading a story about Nort:

> A girl called Nort was introduced by a friend to sell her virginity in a bar when she was seventeen. She got 25,000 baht for this and has been able to help her family with income. After selling her virginity, she continued to work in the bar selling sex. Nort is now eighteen, and she has assisted other girls arriving at the bar, some of them under eighteen, with selling their virginity. She receives a commission from the girls' earnings for doing this.

"Are all these cases from your research?" John asks. John is a lawyer and works for an anti-trafficking program in Vientiane. Throughout the course of my research, I met with anti-traffickers such as John to discuss the trafficking situation in Laos. I had brought several case studies from my own research to seek his opinion as to whether he believed they constituted cases of trafficking, as well as how they should be dealt with by anti-trafficking programs.

The case study of Nort is the fourth one John reads. Nort has been a recurrent informant in this book and exemplifies one of the main paradoxes of recruitment into the sex industry along the Thai-Lao border: that is, the trafficker embodies the very exploitative situation she leads others into. Furthermore Nort was underage, not only when she began selling sex, but also when she started recruiting others who often were underage themselves. Hence Nort does not make herself an easy read in light of legal trafficking definitions, and for this very reason I was particularly eager to hear John's opinions about her situation, due to his legal background.

But John reveals a marked hesitance in responding to my case studies. As he leans back in his chair, I realize that my aim of collecting material on his views on my "trafficking cases" is only partly materializing. At times John's responses are touching on what I am after: "Do you think this case constitutes human trafficking? And how do you think authorities should deal with it?" But for the most part he instead comments on his plans for his up-and-coming trafficking project and offers other general reflections. Rather than giving his expert legal opinion on my case studies, John is drifting into his own thoughts and falls silent. Then he says, "You know, I think these cases would be excellent for training purposes." John told me earlier that he is writing a book about the legal aspects of trafficking. He now expresses excitement about the novelty of my case studies and offers to make a more thorough legal analysis of them later on—in his own time—and then he could share it with me. He asks me if it would be OK to use this analysis in his book, as an appendix perhaps. I agree.

Managing Ambiguity

When I met with John, I was hoping to get a better understanding of how anti-traffickers would deal with some of my own case studies. He is after all a legal expert involved with trafficking programming in Laos and, one would have thought, well acquainted with the local trafficking situation. I was therefore surprised to learn that cases such as Nort's were not only new to him but also, in John's view, worth including in training material for local officials in the legal sector. I had entered John's office hoping to extract information from him, but it was he who ended up extracting information from me.

John's ambivalent response is characteristic of a tendency among anti-traffickers in Laos. They struggle to reconcile the legal-economic metalanguage of trafficking with field realities, and in their everyday anti-trafficking work, they commonly drift between different models of knowledge. This drifting back to idealized models maintains the currency of the models because they become meaningful entities in a discursive sense and hence are useful to anti-traffickers in dealing with ambiguity. Indeed, as we will see, the way trafficking programs operate makes ambiguities discursively unacceptable. Yet this drifting must not be understood as trafficking discourse merely recited through docile subjects. The way trafficking programming is shaped is also a product of anti-traffickers' own strategizing for achieving recognition within the broader development sector. As such, similarly to how anti-traffickers act in bad faith, the way they drift between different idealized models of trafficking requires externalization of complicity in the form of deliberate ignorance in order to sustain anti-trafficking programs.

Case Studies

In chapter 4 we were introduced to Da, who alleged that her stepmother forced her (by beating her up) to work in a Lao beer shop. This is how I presented Da's story to several anti-traffickers:

> A mother has debt and asks her daughter to begin working in a beer shop to sell sex in order to pay back the money. The daughter refuses, but the mother forces her against her will and takes her to a bar. The mother complains that her daughter is lazy and contributes nothing to her family. The bar owner feels sorry for the girl and allows her to work, although she is not very pretty. The girl leaves after a few days without selling any sex. No one knows where she is now, but it is believed that she is hiding and fears retribution from her mother. The mother has called the bar several times, and at least once she came to the bar to look for the daughter.

As a researcher, I am of course guilty of framing such cases in a certain way. It is, for example, unclear whose voice is present in this story, and it is not clear where the information originates. I also use certain words that can be questioned (e.g., what does "force" mean in a given context?). However, framed narratives like this are precisely what anti-trafficking programs have to deal with in their everyday work, whether it is information coming from a distressed mother reporting her missing daughter, information from a victim who was able to escape, or suspicious information a police officer came across while carrying out other duties. During the interviews I carried out during my research, participants were explicitly asked to assess such cases based on the information provided, as well as to indicate what additional information would be useful in making their assessment. Hence these interviews were not only a heuristic device prompting anti-traffickers to comment directly on my own case studies but also a way to tease out what information they saw as relevant to the victim identification process. One anti-trafficking informant, Renee, for example, did not believe that Da was a victim of trafficking:

RENEE: How far away is the village from the bar?
SVERRE: About sixty kilometers.
RENEE: It [Da's case] can technically fall into the definition [of trafficking]. From a police perspective it will not be seen as trafficking, but perhaps as a prostitution offense. It is, for example, illegal to pimp others.
SVERRE: What about the owner?
RENEE: You have to determine her knowledge, [as to] why is the girl there?

Two other informants saw Da's case differently. Charlotte asked, "The age of the girl might be relevant here, no?" adding that it would be suitable to try to collect more information about the case by sending a social worker to the bar. Thou concluded, "It's trafficking." He noted that it was a bit unclear how much the bar owner knew, but he believed that "the mother should be prosecuted and the daughter separated from the family." Whereas Renee, Charlotte, and Thou all disagreed as to whether Da's case constituted trafficking, a fourth group of anti-traffickers hesitated to commit themselves to a particular position, repeatedly saying, "We need more information." When assessing whether Da was a trafficked victim, informants sometimes emphasized the importance of whether exploitation had taken place. For instance, one informant said, "No[, it is not trafficking], because no exploitation has taken place yet." Another asked, "What level of force are we talking about?," then added that the girl appeared to have left the bar by her own will. Nevertheless, he thought the bar owner was guilty of doing something illegal but not of trafficking.

At the beginning of this chapter, I introduced the case study of Nort, as well as John's reluctance to give his opinion about the case. "Based on the information given here, I do not think you can say she is a victim of trafficking," Renee observed. On the other hand, she thought that Nort could be a trafficker because "the girls who are recruited are underage." Renee suggested that in cases like these the police could use disruptive techniques (maintaining a police presence, scrutinizing licenses, and so on) to make it harder for the bar to sell sex.

Another informant was far more vague: "She's an agent, but this is a child rights issue. . . . The girls are under eighteen? Hmmm, no. Difficult. The girls are voluntary? I am unsure." A third informant saw this case—based on the information given—as an instance of trafficking: "Nort is a trafficked victim and a trafficker. I do not think she should be arrested." This informant pointed out that because Nort herself was a trafficked victim, her situation needed to be considered more carefully, and that the police could give her a warning or some sort of counseling. This informant said that she had heard of similar stories. A fourth informant was less certain. "It is not clear what has happened," he said. "On the one hand it appears to be voluntary, but she is 'introduced.'" Then he said, "It is a process—she becomes a trafficked victim." I asked him to elaborate: "How can you tell it is trafficking?" He replied, "It is because of the commission [for recruitment]."

Considerable variety, inconsistency, and ambiguity exist in these responses. Interviews I conducted with anti-traffickers usually took well over an hour each to complete. I asked the anti-traffickers to assess a total of nine case studies, and during the course of the interview, their opinions changed frequently. As the two case studies presented above demonstrate, Da was considered both a victim and a nonvictim, and Nort was perceived as being a possible victim, trafficker, and nonvictim/nontrafficker. Indeed, it is telling that in eight of my nine case studies, interviewees gave varying responses as they attempted to determine victim status.

Not only are there considerable differences among informants regarding whether someone was deemed a trafficker or a trafficked victim, but sometimes the same informant appeared inconsistent in commenting on the same case study. For example, Renee's response to Nort's case study seems to apply the relevance of legal age to the girls Nort recruits, but not to Nort herself. Although Nort was underage when she was recruited, this does not count as trafficking, whereas the underage girls Nort recruited appear to qualify as trafficked victims. This apparent lingering ambivalence toward legal age may reflect the fact that many anti-traffickers in Laos are well aware that although the legal age is technically eighteen, in practice older children (fifteen to seventeen years of age) are often treated as adults (domestic responsibilities, marriage, etc.). This is evident in the questionnaire used by AFESIP (discussed in chapter 7), as it gives particular attention to the number of sex workers under sixteen. Thus, when it comes to practical programming, projects show considerable ambivalence in regard to the legal age of trafficked victims. Also there is no indication in Nort's case study that the person who recruited Nort received a commission or other form of benefits, and this may have led Renee to consider Nort's debut in prostitution as outside the scope of trafficking definitions.

Hence, the way anti-traffickers in actual practice make decisions about victim identification differs from the recommendations in training manuals such as the IOM guidelines. Anti-traffickers do not merely take a "check box" approach. Instead, anti-traffickers interpret trafficking with reference to a range of parameters, such as the following:

- Whether exploitation has already taken place (the significance of temporality)
- Whether the intent of the trafficker was to exploit
- Whether any "benefit" was provided to the trafficker (e.g., a commission)
- Whether deception/force was used (regardless of benefit, profit, or outcome)
- Whether debt bondage or debt was part of the transaction
- Whether exploitation was in one way or another present in the case study (regardless of its connection to anything else)

Despite these ambiguities, no informants reflected on their own multivalent assessment of victim identification. Instead, several informants appeared to have internalized an essentialized understanding of trafficking, assuming there was one correct answer to each case study. One informant even asked if it was possible to obtain the right answers to the case studies after the interview. This should come as no surprise, for victim identification refers to both legal rights (of the victim) and criminal law (in terms of prosecution). And as Cowan et al. (2001, 6) have aptly pointed out, "[because] it is usually grounded in a positivist view of truth, law essentializes social categories and identities." The effect is that informants tended to immerse themselves in the case studies, perceiving them as riddles with real ontological answers rather than stepping back and questioning the very act of projecting trafficking onto the social reality of migration and sex commerce.

There is a stark difference between the rigid and clear-cut style in which training manuals depict trafficking on the one hand and how anti-trafficking actors respond to my case studies on the other. Whether someone is deemed a victim of trafficking appears to be nebulous. Therefore, when the Lao anti-trafficking sector becomes more involved with police investigations and victim support, it is likely that the way social categories of victimhood and perpetrator translate into actual program implementation will be highly random. This is not to deny that some cases may conform more clearly with instances depicted in such training manuals. For example, during my time working for UNIAP, there was a trafficking case (for domestic labor) that was particularly serious in terms of its exploitative aspects. This case received considerable media coverage and is discussed in two trafficking reports (UNIAP et al. 2004; UNICEF and Ministry of Labour and Social Welfare 2004). The torture-like working conditions and the ability of the recruiter, who was an influential person, to pay off the victim's family to stop legal proceedings suggest a labor recruitment process that conforms closely with stereotypical depictions of trafficking. However, I do question the premise that such cases are typical of trafficking in the context of the Thai-Lao border.

I highlighted the various spatial dimensions of trafficking discourse in an earlier chapter. We see that space also comes up in relation to these case studies. In determining whether trafficking occurred, some informants placed relevance on the location of the venue (how far away is the bar?) and whether a border crossing was involved. We also see that some informants habitually associated trafficking work with "source communities." They simply assumed that the bar was either out of reach for the project and/or across the border and therefore anti-trafficking action ought to focus on the victim's village community. Such assumptions have to do with a broader insider-outsider dichotomy of how trafficking is imagined to operate, including the role of traffickers.

Insider-Outsider Dichotomy

While I discussed my case studies with anti-traffickers, a former colleague forwarded the following e-mail to me:[1]

> Subject: trafficking in Chinese children
> To: United Nations Inter-Agency Project on Human Trafficking in the
>   Greater Mekong Sub-Region (UNIAP)
> From: Dr. Xxxxx
>
> Dear Sir, dear Madam,
>   During my investigations on TIP [trafficking in persons] in SEA [Southeast Asia], I have been recently informed, from a quite reliable source, that there has been being a slave market held each year in Houeissai [Houaxay], Laos, concerning Chinese women, under age, specially trained as domestic employee[s] (including sex slave), bought or rent[ed] (?) by rich Chinese families from Chinese diasporas, coming from anywhere in the world. The given price for one girl would be 15,000 US$. This information has to be confirmed anyway.
>   I suggest that, if it is possible, somebody qualified could undertake a deeper investigation around there (Houeissai and Chiang Kong) on that question.
>   Thank you for attention.
>
> Best regards,
> Dr. Xxxxx
> Social Anthropologist
> Member of the Xxxxx
> Former Scientific Director of Xxxxx

Here the claim is not only that transnational organized trafficking is occurring in Laos, but that actual slave markets exist. I happened to have conducted some research in Houaxay's local sex industry some months earlier. I did not, however, pursue what this e-mail was suggesting—an investigation of the claim of a transnational organized slave market. I cannot of course dispute this claim (as we have seen before, sweeping claims about trafficking have a tendency to make themselves immune to falsification), but one may wonder what motivates "rich Chinese families from Chinese diasporas, coming from anywhere in the world," to travel as far as Houaxay, of all places, to pay US$15,000 for a maid? Domestic work is after all a type of labor that in most places is available locally and is affordable for the rich. The logistics of arranging such a slave market also raises obvious questions. The town center of Houaxay is very small, comparable in size to the university campus where I am writing this book. How on earth Chinese diaspora—who would stand out locally due to their ethnicity—could arrange a slave market in such a place without drawing attention from local government, international aid workers, and city folk alike, as well as how such slaves would be transported out of Houaxay back to "anywhere in the world," warrants considerable explanation, to say the least.

Such a claim is not by any means representative of anti-traffickers in Laos. Indeed, many of them doubted and even ridiculed this e-mail. Nevertheless, the claim might have some roots in actual observations of migratory labor practices in the Mekong region. Some trafficking reports from Laos have—through interviews with returned migrants—come across evidence of "holding houses" in Thailand where Lao labor migrants are brought and employers come to select workers (IOM 2004a; UNIAP et al. 2004). Indeed, a movie, produced jointly by UNICEF and the Lao government (Sirisackda 2006), dramatizes this (based on actual interviews with returned migrants) and includes scenes in which an agent sells two Lao girls to such a house and exploitative employers subsequently buy them. However, when one reads the fragmented information about such houses in trafficking reports, it is far from clear whether this enterprise exemplifies "slave trade" or is merely an employment service for migrant laborers. The extent to which agents who bring migrants to such places are aware of the actual working conditions to which various employers subject their employees also remains nebulous, and that uncertainty is acknowledged in several trafficking reports (IOM 2004a; UNIAP et al. 2004). Nor is it clear whether employers who solicit workers from such holding houses typically "enslave" them, let alone whether such enslavement, if it exists, is systematic.

I am not attempting here to demonstrate one way or another what the real situation of such houses is. What is notable is the subtle transformation of fragmented information about migrant labor practices to imageries perpetuated through trafficking discourse—that is, transnational organized crime operating in a frictionless marketplace. Indeed, my own research can be read through this lens. For example, it is a short step from noting Kham's opportunistic involvement with a string of Nong Kai brothels in Nong Kai to interpreting this as an indication of a network of brothels being "organized." That some sex workers obtain local work permits makes it easy to presume official government complicity and thus reinforces the notion of organized crime. Furthermore, because many Lao sex workers frequently cross an international border, it is easy to read the complicity of immigration officials into such cross-border oscillations. On top of all this, that some Lao women are subject to restriction on their movements makes it fully possible to gather these different pieces together to create a picture of the border zone between Laos and Thailand as an organized slave market, something I have been at pains to show is not the case. Hence I suggest that it might be such fragmentary information that has led to the impression, at least for one particular anti-trafficker, that slave markets indeed occur in northern Laos.

The effect of all this is that just as anti-traffickers are ambivalent about determining who ought to be considered to be a trafficked victim, the way trafficking is imagined is elastic and allows anti-traffickers to drift between different views of both traffickers and how trafficking presumably operates. This sort of vacillation was evident during a conversation with Thou.

I was sitting in Thou's office, and we had just gone through my case studies. She reacted to the cases with a mixture of excitement, surprise, and yet familiarity. At one point in the interview she mentioned that she had heard of cases from Vietnam that were similar to mine, such as the story about Nort. In contrast to many other informants, Thou immediately saw the implication for law enforcement.

How can we deal with this? The perpetrator might be a young woman from the same village, even underage. And given that both the victim and the perpetrator may come from the same community or even the same village, what does this mean for anti-trafficking programming? Yet, parallel to such reflections, in this same interview with Thou, the notion of traffickers being outside of social relations was evident in her responses. Commenting on current trafficking trends in Laos, Thou said: "Because of the growing number of anti-trafficking projects in the south, we now believe that the traffickers have relocated and now target the north."

Thou's remark reflects a double narrative that is common among anti-traffickers in Laos. On the one hand, they recognize that traffickers can be community members and that trafficking can be an informal affair. Indeed, Tom (the project manager introduced in chapter 1) told me once that some of my case studies were "classic Lao trafficking cases." Yet traffickers can simultaneously be faceless creatures possessing fluid properties and the mystical ability to adapt to new situations, whether due to changes in the market or interventions from trafficking programs. This drifting in the thinking of anti-traffickers produces a notable outsider-insider dichotomy that is clear in several trafficking reports.

One report suggests that traffickers are external and exist predominantly across the border in Thailand:

> While evidence from other parts of the region (Bangladesh and Myanmar, for example) indicates that many people are trafficked by friends or relatives, this does not appear to be the case in Laos. It is people who are not guided by those who have already been that appear most at risk, and the potential to be trafficked on the Thai side of the border for these people is high. (ARCPPT 2006 [2003], iv)

Another report, by UNIAP et al. (2004), draws attention to how trafficking and migration from Laos to Thailand can at times involve a string of agents, although it recognizes that it is difficult to distinguish "agents" from "traffickers" and to determine the extent to which these networks are organized. While providing considerable details about agents, the report also states, "Very few trafficking cases were the deed of a totally unknown, out-of-nowhere trafficker" (UNIAP et al. 2004, 55). In other words, the traffickers are known to the community. The report then highlights "trusted networks" stressing the importance of informal and existing connections among co-villagers for safe migration because "these [migration] channels are in reality mechanisms for information sharing and support, a way to make knowledge held by some members of the community available to all" (UNIAP et al. 2004, 48). The report recommends the creation of "protection networks" at the community level to ensure that "traffickers are not allowed to operate in the village" (UNIAP et al. 2004, 43). Now the suggestion is made that the traffickers are external to the community, and it is the community that can provide safeguards against traffickers.[2] Hence we are told that traffickers are from both within and without. Despite relatively detailed descriptions of migration routes, different brokers, and migrant experiences, the report fails to unravel how such agents (whether they traffic or not) are embedded in village communities, resulting in agents being portrayed as desocialized subjectivities[3] who exist outside social relationships. In this way, the report gives the impression that the existence of external agents equals "risk" of trafficking, whereas informal networks (friends and extended kin) are presumed "safe."

This report is far from unique in making this assumption. I myself am a prime example of this lingering conceptualization of trafficking in Laos. While I worked for UNIAP, I wrote an article reviewing trafficking research in Laos that was published in UNDP's *Juth Pakai*. Although this article primarily critiqued assumptions being made about the connections between poverty reduction and trafficking, I also touched on the question of "safe" networks and their relation to trafficking: "Knowledge of potential dangers is internalised in the village community, and informal networks, often helped by cross-border family links, provide latent support networks that migrants can draw support from should they face challenges. . . . [I]t is the social relations that migrants are equipped with that are the key to protection against trafficking" (Molland 2005, 32). Here I was assuming that "informal networks" and "family links" are safe, implying that what is external to the community is dubious. To be fair, some reports do note "family involvement" in trafficking (see UNICEF and Ministry of Labour and Social Welfare 2004). Yet it remains implicit that it is not family members per se who traffic but rather some parents who "sell" their children to agents. That young Lao women who work in the sex industry can in some cases deceive other peers into prostitution is overlooked. Furthermore, if one explores the way anti-trafficking programming is designed in Laos, it is clearly the assumption that "traffickers are external" that dominates. This is evident in the policy shift I mentioned earlier in this chapter—a move from attempting to discourage all migration to encouraging safe migration. Relying on the informal connections among friends and village folks with migration experience is now becoming one of the main approaches in anti-trafficking programs. A recent World Vision report makes the following recommendation: "It seems therefore appropriate to use this existing network to pass on information about migration to Thailand. Returnees hold knowledge about life as a migrant that should [could?] be exploited [i.e., used productively]. Workshops could be organized with returnees as peer-educators transmitting their experiences to other Lao villagers" (Doussantousse and Keovonghit 2006, 7). Hence the insider-outside dichotomy has clear ramifications for how anti-trafficking programs now reshape their approaches to combating trafficking. Before considering the reasons for this dichotomy and what this means for the circulation of discourses of trafficking, I will discuss the direct policy implications of anti-traffickers' vacillation.

Blind Spots and Dangers

Development programs have a legacy of projecting romanticized notions of egalitarianism onto village communities (Olivier de Sardan 2005), and the Lao anti-trafficking sector's assumption that communities, informal networks, and extended kin relations are safe can be seen as an extension of this view.[4] This assumption is far too simplistic. On the contrary, the "trafficking cases" I have come across can be perceived as informal and originating within communities. The dual boundary-making within social categories (friend versus external agent) and space (borders) is also evident in new awareness-raising material in Laos.

The considerable increase in donor assistance to combat human trafficking in Laos has in some areas filtered down to the bar environment. This is not (yet) the case in Vientiane but is evident in entertainment clubs in Houaxay, where some aid programs have provided several bars with a UNICEF trafficking poster.

When my research assistant and I visited such clubs, we were able to discuss with some sex workers what they thought of this poster. Some were able to paraphrase fairly accurately what the poster suggested. One young woman summarized the poster in this way: "Trafficking is, for example, when an agent comes and lies to another person about work across the border, and the job turns out to be bad." Although "exploitation" was part of their understanding, they always related it to "moving across the border." On another occasion, while drinking Beer Lao with Nhut, I noticed the UNICEF trafficking poster on the wall behind her back. Nhut (introduced in chapter 4) had been deceived by a friend into working in a beer shop in Houaxay. When I asked what she thought of the poster, she responded that she thought it was useful, and it was good they were warned how to avoid ending up in trouble in Thailand. Whereas several of my anti-trafficking informants would consider Nhut to have been, perhaps even still to be, in a trafficking situation, Nut herself did not associate the poster with her own situation.

I suspect that there are at least two reasons that these sex workers did not relate the poster to themselves. First, the poster creates an imagery of traffickers as evil outsiders. The poster caricatures this with an image of three adults who project icy looks. Notably, the traffickers are portrayed as older people, from outside village communities. The man on one side is wearing a collared shirt and carrying a briefcase, the woman in the middle is wearing a necklace, and the man on her other side wears an apron, indicating that he works in some form of trade. Juxtaposed with this image of traffickers are the victims, who all look like teenagers. This depiction of traffickers resonates with village understandings of trafficking. A recent ILO survey exploring village attitudes to trafficking reports: "The young people interviewed in this survey thought that a trafficker was more likely to be a stranger who is unknown to the victims. Less than 2 in 10 people surveyed thought the perpetrators were likely to be friends or neighbours and even less (1 in 10) thought they were likely to be a relative" (O'Connor 2006, xviii). Although the poster does not in itself suggest that trafficking is exclusively cross-border, this is nonetheless what is commonly implied in awareness raising, particularly among government officials (humantrafficking.org 2006b). Hence the poster is indicative of a general trend within Lao anti-trafficking programming—that is, reinforcing the perception that a trafficker is doubly external to the village in both a social and a spatial sense. My research, however, is suggesting something different, as far as the sex industry along the Thai-Lao border is concerned. Although bar owners and even agents at times carry out recruitment, the common trafficker is a young woman coming from, or being acquainted with, the village community.

I am not suggesting that ruthless betrayal is daily fare among fellow villagers. Nor am I arguing that no agents or traffickers are external to communities or are part of organized networks. What I am saying is that although many Lao communities represent cases of generalized reciprocal obligations, it is nonetheless within such social relations that deceptive recruitment occurs. And this has clearly not been thought through in anti-trafficking programming. Several trafficking projects are now using peer education methods[5] that rely on experienced migrants, and these projects appear to be completely ignorant of the fact that they might empower the very individuals they are ultimately attempting to thwart.

This ignorance is also evident in the way the anti-trafficking sector is providing technical capacity in the law enforcement sector. As we have seen, one of the main strategies behind law enforcement relies on witness testimony from victims. Although such an approach recognizes the challenge of making victims collaborate with police investigations, it does so primarily with reference to the pathology of post-traumatic stress disorder. There is no recognition that the victim and the perpetrator may well be acquainted and may come from the same village community. As I have shown, sex commerce and migration need to be seen in light of a social order governed by patron-client and reciprocal relationships among extended social networks. It is therefore problematic to project a Western-style legal-civic system of justice that presupposes neat distinctions between victim and perpetrator. Not only are identified trafficked victims unlikely to testify against members of their own community, but doing so can even be dangerous for them, given that these young women are often at the bottom of asymmetrical patron-client relationships within village settings.

But there is a far greater danger here. In the US State Department's 2007 *Trafficking in Persons Report*, Laos was back in tier two after the previous year's bottom ranking. Why had the State Department modified its position on Laos' anti-trafficking efforts? The report states:

In 2006, the government reported 27 trafficking investigations that resulted in the arrests of 15 suspected traffickers, 12 of whom were prosecuted. The remaining three suspects were not prosecuted, but were "re-educated" and released. Among the 12 prosecutions, three traffickers were convicted and sentenced to an average of six years' imprisonment, five remain incarcerated pending court action, and four are in pretrial detention pending the results of investigations. Two convictions involved investigative cooperation between Lao and Thai police. The government was not as active in investigating some internal trafficking cases. There are reports that some local government and law enforcement officials profit from trafficking, but there were no reported investigations or prosecutions of officials for complicity in trafficking. (US State Department 2007, 133)

That the State Department places emphasis on law enforcement in combating trafficking is well known and is explicit in its reports on trafficking (US State Department 2007, 2008). Indeed one of my informants, Thomas, was an American diplomat serving in Vientiane, and he confirmed that "one of the reasons they [Laos] were ranked in tier two again had to do with better information sharing on such [trafficking] cases." Despite the improvement in information sharing, however, Thomas admitted to me that the US government had information on only "some" cases. Later on, I asked a range of informants, many of them my former colleagues, if they had any details about these prosecution cases. It turned out that nobody had specific information on the alleged trafficking cases that were mentioned in the State Department's report.

Preceding the State Department's 2007 report, there were important legislative developments relating to trafficking in Laos. Article 134 of the penal code was amended, and a new Law on Development and Protection of Women was adopted by the assembly. The latter not only defines trafficking but stipulates strengthened sentencing: "In cases where offenders cause the victim lifetime incapacity, or [cause the victim to be] infected with HIV/AIDS, or cause death, the offender in trafficking in women and children shall be punished with life imprisonment and shall be fined from 500,000,000 Kip to 1,000,000,000 Kip[,] and shall be subject to confiscation of property as provided under Article 32 of the Penal Law, or shall be subject to capital punishment" (National Assembly of the Lao PDR 2004). Determining human trafficking in light of recruitment into the sex industry along the Thai border is notoriously difficult, as evidenced throughout this book. At the same time we see that, at least for the sex industry along the border, the common trafficker is herself a young (in some cases, even underage) sex worker whose means of recruitment range from outright honesty to sweet talk, persuasion, and deception. Furthermore, to single out a recruiter in this way is also problematic, as venue owners are often clearly complicit. To be fair, some anti-traffickers I interviewed commented on what action ought to be taken against venue owners. However, as we have seen in several examples, their focus remained on the recruiter.

Lobbying for an increase in the arrest and prosecution of traffickers, as well as introducing the death penalty, is of course much easier when human trafficking is pictured as constituting clear-cut binaries of victim and perpetrator and when traffickers are imagined as faceless members of organized crime syndicates. The legal-economistic metalanguage of trafficking facilitates such policy directives. I am unable to predict exactly how the Lao police and courts will actually deal with trafficking cases, but I can only note that Laos is an authoritarian one-party state with no tradition of the rule of law and where both the police and the legal establishment are just starting to become acquainted with the principles of criminal justice (Evans 2004; Stuart-Fox 2005; Warning 2003). Highly random prosecutions are a possibility, which has also been a concern in drug trafficking cases. One would have thought that juxtaposing my case studies with the more stereotypically clear-cut imagery of traffickers and victims (something the US State Department's actions are presuming) would raise several concerns among my anti-trafficking informants and perhaps give them pause for thought. Yet to the contrary, these two worlds appear to live happily in coexistence. I will now consider why this is so.

The Necessity of a Legal-Economistic Metalanguage

The reader might be left with the impression that I am suggesting anti-traffickers are not worried by the Lao government's introduction of the death penalty for trafficking. On the contrary, many of them are keenly aware of the dangers involved. Yet ironically it is precisely this attentiveness that fuels the notion of transnational organized crime and in turn encourages the introduction of the death penalty. During one workshop I attended, attempts were made to develop indicators for a national plan on trafficking. On the question of law enforcement measures, one international adviser suggested that it was not a good idea to measure the impact of law enforcement by counting the number of arrests, prosecutions, and convictions. Instead it was suggested that the impact of law enforcement should be measured by how many victims each prosecution covers. The reasoning here is in a sense well taken, for it is indeed understandable that aid programs and international advisers are worried that Laos—being an authoritarian one-party state—will target "small fish" in its law enforcement efforts to demonstrate high numbers of convictions. Indeed, this suggestion can be read as a way of preventing what many think the US *Trafficking in Persons Report* will do, and might already have done—that is, push the government to obtain many prosecutions, with the result that arbitrary arrests are carried out among people who live along the border. The effect of expressing concern in this way, however, is that the notion that traffickers belong to sophisticated mafia-style operations reenters through the back door. Concern about "small fish" implies that "big fish" not only exist but are indeed central to effective anti-trafficking measures, thereby drawing attention away from ambiguous trafficking cases.

Similarly, a recent donor checklist provided by UNIAP reinforces this trend by suggesting that donors evaluate anti-trafficking projects by asking: "Does the [anti-trafficking] activity focus on the most egregious exploitation, the most threatening emergent criminal activities, or the most vulnerable populations, using the most effective interventions?" (UNIAP 2008c, 7). Although such criteria can be applauded for alerting donors to rethink their funding of vague and indirect projects (such as the poverty reduction program discussed in the previous chapter), another process is at play here. The suggestions to focus on big fish and "the most threatening emergent criminal activities" are made, not primarily with reference to a solid body of empirical data, but to a discursive necessity. And this brings us to one of the main reasons why anti-traffickers tend to vacillate between different models of knowledge in the way they imagine Lao trafficking.

James Ferguson (1990) has drawn attention to how development programs are shaped by internal discursive logic rather than by reference to the empirical reality they attempt to address. In a similar vein, the metalanguage of trafficking maintains its acceptance—alongside a far more contradictory picture on the ground—because it gives anti-traffickers something to hold on to. It becomes a meaning-carrying vessel. And the nexus of a legalistic binary and a market metaphor is particularly useful because it removes ambiguities, rationalizes anomalies, and brings stability to categories, whether in terms of imageries that are subjective (victim, perpetrator), spatial (hot spots), or bodily (risk groups).

The anti-trafficking sector shares a context in common with that of a larger development sector. They have a common epistemology, demanding identifiable cause-effect relationships (Edelman and Haugerud 2005; Olivier de Sardan 2005). Trafficking programs depend on a coherent narrative and need to justify their projects in light of their anticipated impact. If human trafficking is perceived as being polycentric and carried out in a quasi-coincidental manner among peers, it becomes extremely difficult to design interventions. In contrast, catchy phrases such as "the demand side" and "the push-down, pop-up phenomenon" provide a sense of coherence. And when one articulates trafficking in terms of supply and demand, it becomes possible to imagine agglomerations (hot spots, trends), cause-effect correlations, and targets for social engineering.

Metaphors such as the push-down, pop-up phenomenon and the imagery of the all-knowing, well-organized traffickers who operate in a cross-border marketplace justify why the impact of anti-trafficking programs cannot be easily demonstrated.[6] In this way trafficking programs find themselves chasing horizons. Without any obvious, demonstrable impact on trafficking, the notion of agglomeration, made possible by the market metaphor, allows programs to reinvest in new projects that fit this logic. To put it crudely, the goal of trafficking programs is not to find answers to the challenges of trafficking, but the reverse: they seek problems that fit their solutions, in the form of their own development programs (Ferguson 1990). The way "safe migration" is understood in the anti-trafficking sector, the focus on big fish, and Steinfatt et al.'s enumeration method (2002) involving taxi drivers are all examples of this.

Such discursive slippages are not merely a result of a deterministic and automated process whereby anti-traffickers reproduce officially sanctioned knowledge regarding trafficking. To the contrary, anti-traffickers are very active agents in this process. The UNICEF report discussed in the previous chapter (UNICEF and Ministry of Labour and Social Welfare 2004) exemplifies this. It presents an imperative of objectification that answers institutional demands of development programming: problems must be identified, profiles must be made, remedial action must (at least implicitly) be anticipated, and—in the case of anti-trafficking—hot spots must, somehow, be domesticated, making them receptive to development programming. At the same time, the UNICEF report speaks not merely to donors but to a wider community of other anti-trafficking projects and the aid community at large.

As such, aid reports are important sources of "symbolic capital" (Bourdieu 1977 [1972]), for their recognition within the broader field of development provides prestige, furnishes interpretations of "success" of activities (Mosse 2004; van Ufford 1993), and strengthens the ability to set the agenda for aid activities.[7] Analytic credentials are a valuable resource. In this sense there are limits to how banal a report can be, for poor quality can undermine its status as an authoritative text. In the case of the UNICEF report (UNICEF and Ministry of Labour and Social Welfare 2004), the reason why an anthropologist was hired to do the research was precisely—at least according to some UNICEF officials—that they wanted to avoid a donor-driven report. For them, the significance of academic recognition (by hiring a respected anthropologist) was important.

Perhaps the best example of this intertwining of recognition and bureaucratic demands is the rearticulation of UNIAP during the conception of its second phase. I have referred to the push-down, pop-up phenomenon several times in this book. To my knowledge, the first expression of this idea surfaced in some field reports by UNIAP while assessing the impact of various anti-trafficking programs in Laos, Cambodia, and Thailand (Ginzburg 2002a, 2002b). It is notable that this was around the same time UNIAP was starting to seek funding for its second phase. A draft project proposal articulated the very same principle thus:

> There is now growing acknowledgement of the "displacement" or "push-down pop-up" phenomenon. Trafficking is a dynamic phenomenon and traffickers can quickly adjust to changing environments. Research from several countries has indicated that some community-level trafficking interventions which appear successful on the surface may simply be moving the problem from one community to another— that pushing the issue down somewhere may lead to it "popping up" somewhere else. (UNIAP 2003, 8)

It is not difficult to see how this idea carries a distinct cause-effect logic, making it receptive to development programming (and hence donor funding). We also see that the market metaphor resurfaces in explaining trafficking trends. Yet, at the same time, the metaphor also carries an analytical allure, as it after all offers a form of abstract explanation of how trafficking takes place. This has resulted in the concept being smuggled into peer-reviewed academic texts. An observant reader will notice that the aforementioned quotation is very similar to a paragraph in chapter 3 that I quoted from Marshall and Thatun's chapter of Kamala Kempadoo et al.'s influential book *Trafficking and Prostitution Reconsidered* (2005).[8] In other words, the push-down, pop-up phenomenon has become a trope within the anti-trafficking sector that sits comfortably with both academic and donor audiences and reaffirms the omnipresent adherence to a marketplace where "insufficient measures to reduce demand" both explain why trafficking takes place and points to how new programs must improve remedial action. Although there are important institutional differences between aid workers and academics in terms of knowledge production, the boundary between the two are not necessarily always clear-cut. Trafficking discourse does not merely dictate the activities of anti-traffickers but is at the same time a form of symbolic capital that is actively sought after, reappropriated, and reproduced (see William F. Hanks 2005, 73).

The twin forces of institutional demands and anti-traffickers' pursuit of recognition mean that anti-traffickers must actively navigate between means-ends rationality characterized by aid programs and the local complexity of migration, sex work, and other labor practices. Thus, what anti-traffickers say and do is structurally contingent on modes of deliberate ignorance. In other words, like the traffickers and venue owners discussed in part II, anti-trafficking programs too can be considered to be participating in economies of bad faith. Does not, for instance, the repeated call for clear guidelines to identify trafficked victims constitute a Sartrean anguish of choice (Sartre 1957) whereby anti-traffickers are seeking to externalize the act of victim identification away from their own subjective engagement with this process? Thus, anti-traffickers actively attempt to camouflage to themselves what is by necessity a subjective and ambiguous decision they need to make, by giving it an aura of objectivity and due process. Bad faith is precisely what allows anti-traffickers to seamlessly drift between different modes of knowledge.

At the time of this writing, the anti-trafficking sector is paying increasing attention to infrastructure programs, and concerns have also been expressed about the booming tourism industry in Laos. I am not saying that road projects and tourism necessarily have nothing to do with trafficking. I merely highlight that such concerns are driven, not by the empirical reality that anti-trafficking programs attempt to address,[9] but by a logic made possible by a trafficking discourse. Nor are such new projects guided by "success stories" by which programs can confidently demonstrate actual reductions in trafficking elsewhere in order to move on to similar new projects. Rather, such new approaches are a result of a fumbling search for an ideal type model that allows itself to be explained in the categories that have become part of anti-traffickers' operational habitus, thus creating "areas of opacity, in which a carefully constructed ignorance [is] allowed to prevail" (van Ufford 1993, 149).

It is, however, not only aid organizations that have adopted these understandings and remolded them. During my research a political crisis emerged between the Thai and Lao governments, as well as the United Nations and several bilateral donors to Laos. Hmong refugees had crossed the border from Laos into Thailand, claiming that they were fleeing persecution (*Nation* 2006; *Vientiane Times* 2007d). Both the Thai and Lao governments portrayed the incident as a "problem of human trafficking."

At the time of this incident there was speculation among some diplomats and aid workers that agents making false promises of US visas had in part triggered the Hmong's movement to Thailand. Lao government officials also publicly alleged this (Ismail Wolff 2006). However, given the legacy of political conflict between the Hmong and the Lao government, the actual reasons for labeling this as trafficking probably have more to do with political concerns than with an attempt to convey an accurate description of what was taking place. The Hmong could not be labeled "refugees," as that would have been politically unacceptable to the Lao government. The two sides therefore needed to find a common language, and "trafficking in persons" fit the bill. Furthermore, by drawing attention to the "transnational" and "organized" aspects of this so-called trafficking, both governments could in a sense distance themselves from the issue. The following statement from a Lao government spokesman is telling: "It's time to solve the Hmong problem. We have no hidden agenda because neither of us [the Thai and Lao governments] caused this migration but we, as well as the Hmong refugees, *are the victims of human trafficking*" (*Nation* 2006, emphasis added). Just as a national border could allow either government to say that "the problem is over there," focusing on professional and organized trafficking syndicates was a way of externalizing the problem—a way of saying, "It is out of our hands." Thus it was not only the Hmong who were victims of traffickers but also the Thai and Lao governments! At the same time, labeling the problem as trafficking was a way to rebuff suggestions that this was a "refugee issue" and even to imply that Western governments were the "cause" of trafficking: "The Hmong in Phetchabun and elsewhere are only the effect, but we have to look into the cause, and the cause is that some third countries propose to take the Hmong to their countries. That is why they create the gap for traffickers" (Ismail Wolff 2006). Both the Thai and Lao governments insisted on the need for repatriation and rejected the involvement of international organizations or other counties: "We [Thailand and Laos] agreed together that this is human trafficking, so we will find a solution to deal with this problem in our own territories" (ibid.). This had the additional effect of saving face for the Lao government. On the one hand, the departure of Hmong did not reflect political problems in Laos because they had been "misled" into leaving. On the other hand, labeling the Hmong's flight as a trafficking problem was also an attempt to legitimize the repatriation of the Hmong back to Laos. Designating migrants as trafficked victims rather than as refugees not only suggests that repatriation is appropriate but also humanizes such a policy response.

Later, the Lao government again portrayed an incident as trafficking—this time it was North Korean refugees who attempted to travel through Laos on their way to Thailand (BBC World 2007). In this case the Lao government was in a unique and delicate position, for it is one of the very few countries that has diplomatic relations with (and receives aid from) both North and South Korea. Once again, explaining the incident as trafficking externalized the problem. In this sense, not only has trafficking become a trope where migration and prostitution agendas can be played out, but in the case of Laos, it has moved one more closer to becoming a tool for discussing (and avoiding) problems of geopolitical dimensions.

These incidents might at first glance seem indicative of how trafficking discourse penetrates new spheres for increased control and regulation of migration. Whether this is the case or not is a question I address in the conclusion of this book.

Conclusion

The Tenacity of the Market Metaphor

> His elevation transfigures him into a voyeur. It puts him at a
> distance. It transforms the bewitching world by which one was
> "possessed" into a text that lies before one's eyes. It allows one
> to read it, to be a solar Eye, looking down like a god. The exal-
> tation of a scopic and gnostic drive: the fiction of knowledge is
> related to this lust to be a viewpoint and nothing more.
> —Michel de Certeau, *The Practice of Everyday Life* (1988, 92)

I AM ON THE TOP FLOOR of one of the most expensive hotels in Vientiane—it is situated on the bank of the Mekong River. I am nearing the
end of my fieldwork, and an anti-trafficking organization has invited
me to attend a large planning workshop. I am sitting with many other
anti-traffickers, some of them former colleagues, as well as friends and
acquaintances. The Lao government is developing its first national
plan of action to combat trafficking in persons, and in this meeting we
will provide input, with particular focus on monitoring and evaluation.
In front of me is a draft logframe (short for "logical framework"). It is
the classical tool used in development planning, containing goals, supporting objectives, activities, expected outcomes, and indicators. The
government has developed most of this plan, with the exception of the
latter two components. Hence the meeting today to gather government officials, donors, UN agencies, and international NGOs together
to brainstorm how to monitor and evaluate the national plan of action.

After a formal keynote speech by a senior government official and
an overview of the plan by two expatriate consultants from Bangkok,
the workshop splits into smaller groups. The atmosphere is now more

informal. One group discusses monitoring and evaluation in relation to policy and cooperation, a second group explores prevention, a third examines law enforcement, and a fourth group handles monitoring and evaluation. I happen to sit with the fifth group, which is exploring protection. Together, these five areas of policy comprise fairly standard policy responses to trafficking.

Our group starts to examine the draft logframe, which will become the grand framework for combating trafficking in persons in Laos. A logframe is a trueborn child of Enlightenment thought. It attempts to colonize the future by identifying case-effect relationships articulated as development problems and corresponding programmatic remedies. The promise of Weberian technical-rational clarity is somewhat contradicted by our group's hesitant and rambling discussions. "Develop clear guidelines for the identification of trafficking victims" is one of the activities. "Establish an anti-trafficking hotline" is another. "What's the difference between an expected outcome and indicators in this instance?" one participant asks. And what would an indicator be for "Develop guidelines for care [management] of shelters"? Some participants are frustrated. We are trying to work out where activities, outputs, indicators, and outcomes belong on a piece of paper. That the activities and outputs have already been set by the government frustrates some participants. Does not activity "4.2.1—Strengthen existing transit centre for victims who have been sent by official channel" overlap with activity "4.2.4—Build and strengthen capacity of stakeholders regularly"? One participant wonders, "Do we need separate indicators for that?" Isn't the outcome the same? We go back to the question of identifying victims. "We need to have clear guidelines for victim identification," one person says. "Yes," agrees another. I ask, "Has anyone seen such guidelines?" Silence. I ask again. Nobody gives an answer. But guidelines we need. Our discussion remains disjointed. While this goes on, I am drifting off—daydreaming. I look outside the window. Through the hazy tropical sun, I see Si Chiangmai—a small Thai town directly opposite Vientiane. During both my research and my time working for the United Nations, I have never heard anyone mention the possibility of trafficking to Si Chiangmai. Yet earlier I paid a visit there to explore whether it would be a suitable place in which to conduct research.

I started to think of Lek, a twenty-three-year-old Lao woman who works in one of Si Chiangmai's clubs. After a stint of working in a garment factory in Vientiane, a friend introduced Lek to selling sex in a small bar in Si Chiangmai. In addition to being a sex worker, Lek has recently taken on the role of a part-time *mamasan* in the bar in which she is working. She lodges with the owner, who is married to a local policeman. Although Lek has a passport, she often crosses the border illegally from Si Chiangmai directly to Vientiane to shop at the main market. "Ironic," I thought. "A Lao woman who crosses legally to Thailand to work doubly illegally as an employer and an employee but crosses illegally back to Laos for mundane recreational shopping trips." Lek told me that sometimes she uses an agent, a Lao woman, to recruit young girls back in Laos for work in the bar. From time to time sex workers from the bar also go back home and recruit. "Sometimes they lie to their friends and relatives," Lek told me. But then she added that the *mamasan* "does not like employing girls who were lured," claiming that the *mamasan* turned down newly recruited girls when the recruiter had not told them what type of work they were supposed to perform. "Was she speaking the truth?" I was thinking to myself. Or perhaps it makes sense. It must be difficult to employ unwilling girls. Perhaps it is an example of "failed trafficking," when the recruiter does not receive a commission, I was wondering what my colleagues would respond to Lek's story.

"What do you think, Sverre?" a participant asks me. "Uh, what?" I say. My group is discussing "Supporting Objective 4.3—Provide complete assistance to victims after they are freed from the control of traffickers with consideration of their human rights." Four activities are listed under this "supporting objective." The first one is "Establish referral systems with relevant authorities internally and in destination countries to provide assistance to victims of trafficking and other forms of exploitation and to ensure victims' safety, their confidentiality and their human rights." I am thinking to myself, "'Internally'? It seems that 'internal trafficking' has sneaked into the plan." We do not finish discussing supporting objective 4.3—it's time for a coffee break.

We all stand up to stretch our legs. I go over to the window. There it is. Si Chiangmai. I could spot Lek's bar. In fact, standing on the top floor of the highest building in Vientiane, one gets a very good view of large parts of Vientiane and Nong Kai provinces. If I had binoculars, I would be able to spot most of the places in which I conducted research. Standing in this panopticon (Foucault 1975) of anti-traffickers, I wonder in what light the Lao anti-trafficking programs would consider the bars, the sex workers, and the recruiters that I know from these places. Yet their gaze is focused elsewhere—on the logframe of the draft national plan of action. While staring at Lek's bar, I too feel far away from the "victims" and "traffickers" I have spent so much time trying to understand. I move away from the window and join the others as we walk toward a nearby restaurant for our break.

Interconnections?

This vignette encapsulates the main conclusion of this book: instead of witnessing a Foucauldian governmentality play out in the Thai-Lao sex industry, anti-traffickers have a tendency to draw attention away from the social world in which they are attempting to intervene, even when it is literally right under their own noses. In other words, the circulation of forms of knowledge between trafficking discourse, the local context of Thai-Lao sex commerce, and the anti-traffickers are in strange ways disconnected, albeit only partially so.

There is hence considerable divergence between the metalanguage produced discursively by the anti-trafficking sector and the actual unfolding of sex commerce and recruitment on the ground. The key common thread here is that whereas trafficking discourse tends to insist on a legal-economistic language, attention is perpetually driven away from what is essential for understanding trafficking along the Thai-Lao border—that is, social relationships and the social embeddedness of practice.

This raises the question of how local anti-traffickers mediate between the two worlds of a metalanguage of trafficking on the one hand, and the local reality of sex commerce and migration along the Thai-Lao border on the other. We have seen that they rarely reconcile these two worlds. Instead a notable vacillation is evident, and an astonishing ambiguity regarding victim identification coexists with mechanical binary notions of trafficking. Indeed, market metaphors and terminology such as "supply" and "demand" become meaning-carrying vessels that anti-traffickers use to deal with ambiguity in their anti-trafficking work.

This brings me to some of the more theoretical points of this book. In some respects, I have drawn on discourse analysis, which has in recent years been fashionable in anthropological research on development. However, one of the major shortcomings of this approach is its lack of attention to empirical detail regarding social actors. The way discourse is internalized, resisted, or avoided is an empirical question that needs to place its focus on social actors. What insights can we draw from this book?

Governing and Avoidance

In a celebrated (and critiqued) discursive analysis of development aid in Lesotho, James Ferguson (1990) has argued that development programs are driven more by their own internal logic than by the actual development problems they seek to address, and that a side effect of such programs is an increasing penetration of government power. Although my book resonates with Ferguson's first point, it diverges with regard to the latter. Despite Ferguson's emphasis on the decentralized nature of power, his conclusions retrospectively reintroduce a monolithic take on power, as pointed out by Morgan Brigg: "Linking power with the failure of development in this way builds an association between the operation of power and the failure of development (and introduces a conspiratorial tone into Ferguson's analysis)" (2002, 426). This relates to one of the broader shortcomings of discourse analysis—that is, neglect of attention to social practice. In contrast, this book, by focusing on both social actors within sex commerce as well as individuals and institutions that seek to combat trafficking along the Thai-Lao border, has provided a more nuanced picture of how ideal types circulate.

This does not mean that the (re)production of trafficking discourse is entirely devoid of the processes of governmentality or expanded state power. I have noted the introduction of the death penalty, the existence of repatriation programs and shelter services for trafficked victims,[1] and the practice of fining and reeducating returning migrants by Lao authorities. And the example of Jai (chapter 4) might be a precursor of anti-trafficking programs' creation of, rather than response to, the social category of "trafficked victim." These examples can be perceived as producing subject positions and an encroaching social control, enabled by disciplining instruments articulated through a discourse of trafficking. However, we must be careful not to overstate the importance of this. The number of Laotians who go through repatriation programs is after all a tiny minority relative to the number of Lao migrants.[2] Although the death penalty has been introduced, it applies only in egregious cases, and we must keep in mind that legal statutes in Laos are poorly disseminated and often ignored, even by government bodies themselves (Evans 2004; Stuart-Fox 2005, 2006). Although it has been alleged that traffickers have been arrested and even convicted in Laos (*Vientiane Times* 2006), this does not mean that trafficking legislation is disseminated evenly throughout the Lao political body. Moreover, the practice of fining returning migrants predates anti-trafficking programming and needs to be understood within a larger political anxiety about sociopolitical control. In fact, anti-trafficking programs can probably take some of the credit for advocating for the abolition of this practice, and there are some indications that it is now being phased out as a result.[3] Although human trafficking is certainly manipulated politically in various ways, it does not—at least at the time of when research for this book was carried out—constitute a large-scale disciplining apparatus that permeates Lao society.

At the same time, something else is evident as well—a form of avoidance. I am not here pointing to subaltern "resistance" or individuating ways people internalize, appropriate, and utilize discursive forms of knowledge (de Certeau 1988; Scott 1986). As opposed to reproducing subject positions "on the ground," trafficking discourse produces a peculiar navel-gazing effect. What is astonishing is that despite the considerable efforts being put toward the fight against trafficking, the social world in which anti-traffickers are trying to intervene is in many respects untouched. To be fair, this might be different in village communities where most Lao anti-trafficking activities have been carried out, but where trafficking into the sex industry on both sides of the border is concerned, there is a notable disjuncture. None of the sites in which I conducted research had been subject to, or in contact with, trafficking programs (with the exception of some bars in Houaxay), nor did informants see their social world in terms of trafficking, victims, and traffickers. The trafficking cases that I came across in my research were not particularly difficult to uncover, and many of them—as we have seen—are literally just outside the door of where anti-traffickers design their interventions. Hence, in a Foucauldian sense, we are not (yet) seeing the discursive reproduction of the regimes' self-government on a subject level within the sex industry. Of course, this has partly to do with political sensitivities and the reluctance of the government to admit that "trafficking at home" exists. However, there is a larger issue here: trafficking discourse has a particular ability to allow itself to circulate within its own sphere without necessarily governing mentalities on the ground.

On the one hand, articulating both the Hmong and North Korean refugee incidents in terms of trafficking can be interpreted as resulting in increased state power, as Ferguson (1990) similarly argued. Indeed, articulating such incidents as trafficking is suggestive of repatriation as the logical outcome, and there is no doubt that in these cases both the Thai and Lao governments manipulated the issue of trafficking to gain control over the destiny of the alleged refugees. Yet at the same time it is possible to see the Hmong and North Korean refugee incidents in a different light—as examples of running away from governing. Similarly, when aid programs advise donors to look at "clear-cut" trafficking cases, they are in effect insisting on ideal forms of knowledge (perfect traffickers, perfect victims), consequently denying their own engagement with the reality they are trying to address.

Although trafficking discourse has not yet reproduced regimes of self-governance on the ground, a more important point is that trafficking discourse actually allows for a degree of inertia due to its search for ideal types. As we have seen, labeling something as trafficking does not necessarily result in, or legitimize, surveillance control or self-governing but can effect quite the reverse; that is, it can rationalize inaction, since trafficking is assumed to be beyond the control of a single government.

And this brings me to some similarities between "traffickers" and "anti-traffickers." Just as traffickers tend not to personalize and thereby refigure their own complicity, anti-traffickers, by thinking and acting through perfectionist forms of knowledge, deny that they themselves are acting subjects. Yet both traffickers and anti-traffickers see themselves as helping. In essence, they are both actors of bad faith. Just as deliberate ignorance is instrumental for the reproduction of recruitment within the sex industry, anti-traffickers are dispositioned to act in bad faith, as willed avoidance of complexity is intrinsic to the perpetuation of program activities. Yet it is this very same reproduction of anti-trafficking activities that has the ironic effect of maintaining a disjuncture between the worlds of traffickers and anti-traffickers. Although anti-traffickers' agency is projective in the sense that they attempt to intervene and change a social world through an institutional apparatus, they nonetheless remain—like "victims"—constrained when it comes to practical implementation. What traffickers, victims, and anti-traffickers have in common is that they attempt to "flee in order not to know" (Sartre 1957, 43), thereby distancing their own lifeworlds from trafficking. This is so much the case that their identities can even merge, as in this passage recorded in my field notes:

The nights are cold in Houaxay in the early dry season. My research assistant and I join Dtoi—the *papasan* of a small beer shop—outside his bar, where he has lit a small fire. Inside, sex workers are drinking with a group of intoxicated Vietnamese men. We can see a magnificent sky, full of stars. Dtoi tells us that he feels cruel because he has to lay off at least two *sao borigan*. The local authorities have clamped down on the numbers of sex workers in local beer shops. "Who should I choose?" he asks himself. During our discussion, it becomes clear that Dtoi is also involved in other pursuits. He takes part in an anti-trafficking project! One of his specific tasks is developing an awareness-raising campaign. Realizing that we also work with anti-trafficking, Dtoi becomes excited. He tells us that there are many "hot spots" along the border, with lots of Laotians going to Thailand. To be fair, there was no indication—unless you define all sex work as trafficking—that any of his employees were coerced to work in his bar, but it was still interesting that just as the bar girls did not relate to trafficking "messages," the bar owner did not appear to see the trafficking issue as being related to his bar business. From the outside, I am sure some anti-trafficker would see Dtoi's involvement in an anti-trafficking project as "evidence" that traffickers have infiltrated anti-trafficking organizations. Unless one is particularly fond of conspiracy theories, I believe this is fanciful. Dtoi tells us that when the residents of his home village were asked by the anti-trafficking organization whether they wanted to become involved, none of them did, as they were busy with farming and other activities. Yet they had to send someone. Dtoi was chosen by his fellow villagers because he was one of the very few of the younger generation who was not working in Thailand (not that Dtoi, who is in his late thirties, is young). When discussing how he thinks the trafficking awareness-raising campaign is moving along, he is far more to the point than he himself realizes when he tells us, "Human trafficking is like a song. Everybody knows the song, but nobody listens to the lyrics."

Notes

Chapter 1: Introduction

1. All informants' names throughout the book are pseudonyms.

2. For some of the expositions on discourse and governmentality, see Foucault 1980, 1982, 1991.

3. For a study that relies on a Foucauldian view of power and provides detailed analysis of social agents, see Murray Li 2007.

4. Whether self-deception is possible has been subject to sustained debate. I follow Ronald Santoni, who argues that self-deception is possible in a qualified sense if one interprets bad faith to mean the acceptance of unpersuasive evidence, due to the translucent nature of consciousness. See Santoni 1995, 42–45.

5. For Sartre, bad faith is grounded in a particular view of agency that emphasizes human beings' freedom to pursue alternative courses of action. In this view, freedom becomes inherently anxiety provoking. In fact, bad faith is in this sense a response to freedom.

6. In their interviews of returning migrants or family members of migrants, most reports appear not to reflect on the significance of temporality. A UNICEF report from Laos, for example, is astonishing (UNICEF and Ministry of Labour and Social Welfare 2004). It attempts to portray an alarming picture of child trafficking in Laos, but a close reading reveals that nearly all the trafficking cases included in the report were dated four to eleven years before the interviews were conducted.

7. Researchers spent approximately six weeks in each village they visited. This contrasts with other reports on trafficking in Laos, which are based on research by teams that commonly spend only one day in each village.

8. Because the anti-trafficking sector is relatively small in Laos, I personally knew most officials who worked with trafficking at the time of my research. Of course, several staff, as well as expatriates, were aware of local venues in Laos that catered to the commercial sex trade. However, when it came to the specific question of trafficking within the sex industry, none of my informants could provide clear answers. One reason for such a gap in knowledge is the political sensitivity of researching trafficking "at home." Thus my

anti-trafficking informants had extremely limited knowledge of Lao sex workers (whether voluntary or trafficked) in Thailand, even in border towns that were near one another, such as Nong Kai and Si Chiangmai.

9. As clients are transitory within these venue settings, developing rapport with them constitutes a challenge. Hence the focus on clients in this research is limited.

Chapter 2: Do Traffickers Have Navels?

1. The *New York Times* online allows archive searches back to 1852. The search results described in this paragraph are derived from http://query.nytimes.com/search/query?query=%22human+trafficking%22&srchst=nyt.

2. The endemic regurgitation of trafficking estimates has led UNESCO's Bangkok-based trafficking project to trace quoted statistics on trafficking numbers. See http://www.unescobkk.org/index.php?id=1022.

3. I have borrowed this rhetorical metaphor from Ernest Gellner and his debate with Anthony Smith regarding the historical emergence of nationalism (Gellner 1996).

4. Arguably, there are expectations, such as the systematic use of forced labor by the Burmese military junta (ILO 1998).

5. Diana Wong (2005) makes a similar observation, pointing out that anxieties about refugee flows, not prostitution, explain why many governments take an interest in human trafficking and broader patterns of irregular migration.

6. Although there are two separate protocols for people smuggling and trafficking in persons respectively, neither the Palermo Protocol nor the TOC Convention provides any guidelines for victim identification. In practice this omission allows each nation-state to determine whether a case is one of people smuggling or of trafficking, as it sees fit. See Gallagher 2001.

7. A draft project document produced by the Australian Agency for International Development (AusAID 2002) is particularly telling. It proposed setting up an "early warning system" in Lao villages under the auspices of a regional anti-trafficking project. Although the document does not explain what such a warning system might consist of, several other anti-trafficking programs raised concerns that such a system would involve increasing surveillance of potential migrants and could have severe punitive consequences within the context of an authoritarian state such as Laos. How an "early warning system" would have eventually played out in light of political agendas of social control and discipline is unknown, because this part of the project document was eventually omitted before project execution.

8. Numerous "trafficking movies" have been made in recent years, including, but far from limited to, Jerry Allen Davis 2008; Duguay 2005; Moodysson 2002; Yang 2007; and Yates 2006.

Chapter 3: The Market Metaphor

1. Although some case studies in such reports stem from prosecution cases, the specific source of such cases is often unclear.

2. One of the main goals of the *Toolkit to Combat Trafficking in Persons*, from which this case study is taken, is "to increase awareness and to help policymakers in national Governments, criminal justice systems, law enforcement agencies, non-governmental organizations and intergovernmental organizations to understand and respond effectively to trafficking in persons" (UNODC 2006b, x).

3. For example, one training manual produced by UNODC (2006b) is exemplary of the way inconclusive information regarding recruitment is interpreted into a framework of organized crime. It is also notable that UNODC is unashamedly self-referential, as it relies heavily on another UNODC report (2006c) in its effort to make authoritative claims regarding organized crime. The referenced report is not a trafficking report but a global study of organized crime, which covers information on forty organized crime groups. The information is based on a survey sent out to selected member states, which raises a series of methodological problems, something the report partly recognizes. The report treats human trafficking as an unproblematic concept and does not reflect on the possible variation in responses due to the well-known blurring and confusion of distinctions between terms such as "illegal migration," "people smuggling," "organized prostitution," and "trafficking in persons." Nonetheless, the report documents six specific cases of organized criminal groups being involved with trafficking in persons. Despite the various shortcomings of this report and the fact that only six organized crime groups were identified as dealing in human trafficking, the subsequent UNODC report sees no problem in relying on this source to account for the omnipresent and gloomy danger of highly organized trafficking syndicates, stating in its introduction: "The traffickers' web spans the whole planet: people are moved from poor communities in the southern hemisphere to richer countries in the North." (UNODC 2006c, 11).

4. Statements such as "During the expansion of Thai prostitution in Japan in the 1980s, around 90 percent of the women were forced or tricked into the trade" lack referencing (Phongpaichit 1999, 93). In the cases where sources are revealed, it turns out that most of the information is derived from interviews with consular staff at Thai embassies, interviews with NGO staff, and other secondary literature.

5. Analyses with a political economic orientation rely more broadly on a notion of rationality to that of neoclassical models, where there is a tendency to replace the rational economic individual with the rational economic class (see Munck 2008; Tsing 2000; and Goss and Lindquist 1995). Within the trafficking sector, several organizations emphasize broader structural inequalities

in relation to migrant labor, yet they nonetheless end up with an individuated approach that focuses narrowly on victimhood.

6. Both academics and development reports also assert that decision making must be seen in the context of the household. Such analyses have been made of Thai prostitution by Lisa Rende Taylor (2005) and others. However, this genre of analysis does not evade rational choice models. As Jon Goss and Bruce Lindquist have pointed out, it "is the effective substitution of the rational, calculating individual with a rational, calculating household" (1995, 327).

7. One can, for instance, compare the views expressed in reports by Donna Hughes (2005) and the ILO (Pearson 2005). Hughes is a well-known advocate who seeks to abolish both prostitution and trafficking. Although the ILO report is less explicit in taking a stand on the relationship between prostitution and trafficking, it hardly advocates for the abolition of prostitution. Despite these differences, both reports identify clients and third parties (pimps, brothel owners, traffickers, corrupt government officials) as "causes" of demand.

8. The way a market metaphor is evoked in trafficking literature often relies on overlapping and competing theoretical legacies ranging from Marxist notions of surplus value (the emphasis on debt bondage and profiteering from marginalized labor), classical economic theory (the demand-supply nexus), and more recent scholarship on consumption and desire. It is important, however, to emphasize that the use of economic metaphors in the trafficking sector is more an issue of habitual expressions than one of explicit analysis.

Chapter 4: Teens Trading Teens

1. Female and male venue managers, or owners, are usually referred to as *mamasan* and *papasan*, accordingly.

2. A *tuk tuk* is a three-wheeled taxi that is common in Laos and other Asian countries.

3. This phrase translates directly as "Do it for me," but it takes on a few different meanings: "Have a drink for me"; "Raise a toast for me"; or "Enjoy it for me."

4. The only academic to my knowledge who has written specifically about prostitution is Chris Lyttleton. In addition, various aid programs write about prostitution. The quality of these aid reports is uneven.

5. For a detailed discussion of this topic, see Embree 1969 [1950]; Girling 1981; Kirsch 1969; Mulder 1969; and Punyodyana 1969.

6. For a similar analysis on Cambodia, see Derks 2008.

7. Marc Askew (1999) notes that the tendency to enter prostitution after a failed relationship may be more prominent among older sex workers who specialize in tourist-oriented prostitution. However, in my research, this was a

common theme even among younger Lao sex workers (in their late teens and early twenties).

8. I know both male and female expatriates with Lao partners who have been subject to fines, arrest, and extortion by local police due to this policy.

9. Previously, there were also streetwalkers close to the main market, Thalat Sao. What is new is the visibility of commercial sex along the main roads where one finds Vientiane's eateries that cater to tourists, expatriates, and the upper strata of Laotians.

10. *Tuk tuk* drivers facilitate transport, translation, and a venue by taking customers to one of the numerous beer shops in Vientiane where a sex worker can be obtained. Sex workers commonly complain about *tuk tuk* drivers' greediness and extortionist commission fees for providing customers in this way.

11. The Ministry of Information and Culture polices the number of *sao borigan* per venue, ensuring that each venue pays local taxes accordingly.

12. The government sets quotas and regulates the number of women who can work in such venues. In practice, quotas continually fluctuate.

13. Fordham (1998) argues that prostitution use is a common way of reconfirming Thai masculinity, and it often results from men frequenting beer shops in groups. In my research, it appeared to be far more common for older men to go to these shops alone and, conversely, for young men to go in groups. For the latter, there is no doubt that visiting beer shops involves the demonstration and reconsolidation of masculinity among peers.

14. The Transnational Organized Crime Convention and its underlying trafficking protocol primarily function as an instrument to facilitate cooperation between state parties. Whether there are any definitional requirements in terms of the scale of an organized group depends on national legislation as well as the source of law cited in prosecution cases. The Lao trafficking law, for example, does not include any definitional requirement that the crime must involve a certain number of people to qualify it as trafficking in persons.

15. One trafficking report from Laos provides relatively detailed accounts of how "successful" and "unsuccessful" migration can have a bearing on how returned migrants are perceived in their home villages (Gotehus 2006). See also IOM 2004a; and UNIAP et al. 2004).

16. One of the reasons some migrants prefer debt bondage arrangements is that the migrant does not have any up-front costs, hence reducing risk during migration if something goes wrong (e.g., being refused entry into the country or being deported).

Chapter 5: Hot Spots and Flows

1. For example, Save the Children Australia's trafficking program bears the name "Cross-border Project against Trafficking and Exploitation of Migrant and Vulnerability of Young People."

2. Currently there is another bridge between Laos and Thailand: the Savannakhet-Mukdahan bridge, which was completed in 2006. A third bridge, between Houaxay and Xiengkong, is in the planning stages.

3. Udon Thani, which is approximately an hour's drive from Nong Kai, also attracts many Laotians for labor, shopping, and leisure.

4. Similar dynamics can also be found at the border between Savannakhet and Mukdahan in the south, as well as between Houaxay and Xiengkong in the north. Lyttleton and Amarapibal (2002) have studied the former pair of cities with reference to mobility and sex commerce.

5. The ILO report, for instance, is completely silent in regard to the time dimension of migration: Would going to Thailand for a weekend trip count as "migrating"? A one-week visit to relatives in another province in Laos? A one-month visit to relatives across the border? Or crossing the border to work as a wage laborer on a farm for a week? Or simply leaving the village area? The report appears to count "migration" in whatever type of movement respondents in the survey interpreted as "migration."

6. 1,000 kip = $US0.10 or 3.7 baht, at the time of this research.

7. It must be noted that this is probably not the norm. Most high-end nightclubs are open only at night, which limits how many customers women can get. However, possessing a mobile phone is increasingly common among sex workers, and some workers get additional customers by freelancing outside working hours.

8. Several victim support agencies assist Lao trafficked victims, such as the Foundation for Women and the government-run shelter Ban Kradtakarn (Huguet and Ramangkura 2007; IOM 2004a). However, knowledge regarding the whereabouts of victims remains sketchy. It is not uncommon that these agencies come in contact with victims only after they have escaped or through a referral from a local police branch as a result of a police operation. Although rescues sometimes occur, to my knowledge no rescue operation during the time of my research targeted Lao trafficked victims per se within the sex industry in Thailand.

9. Askew (2006) refers to this style of operation as "booking" and the agent who solicits customers as "captain."

10. While exploring possible sites for research sites I made a visit to Si Chiangmai which is located directly opposite Vientiane.

11. I was able to observe such encounters over long periods of time in one particular venue that masqueraded as a hotel, which gave me a convenient excuse to reside there during my stays in Nong Kai. Throughout the numerous hours I have observed customers arriving and choosing sex workers, I have not seen a single incident of a sex worker rejecting a customer.

12. In these latter venues, the customer pays the additional *ka ok han* to the venue manager.

13. The situation might well be different in other parts of the country.

14. Most sex workers take a few days' rest due to menstruation, but some ignore this and keep working.

Chapter 6: Profitable Bodies?

1. In larger towns it is not uncommon for women to wear number tags, and in some massage parlors sex workers sit on display behind a glass wall, allowing customers to pick the woman of their choice. And as Ara Wilson (2004) has described, red-light districts, such as the infamous Patphong, are spatially organized as shopping malls.

2. I was never able to confirm in this particular instance whether the *mamasan* had to pay the commission or whether the girls were obliged to pay for their recruitment, given their early departure. Commission practices vary. In some cases considerable pressure is used to make recruits pay off debt bondage (i.e., the owner's investment), whereas in other cases a venue owner does not pay the recruiter a commission unless the recruits are willing to stay on working.

3. Local officials in northern parts of Laos estimate that approximately 80 percent of women in beer shops are Khmu (Lyttleton 2008).

4. One can even wonder whether *sao nakrong* in Nong Kai accord with a definition of prostitution. In the venues I visited, it was not possible to take women out (i.e., to pay *ka ok han*) during their working hours. Nor do these venues allow on-site sex. Several women might go out with customers after closing hours, however, in exchange for money, gifts, or more open-ended material support. The women in these venues earn a living from tips, sitting fees (*kha nang*), and a commission from drinks and the number of flower garlands customers buy for them. The purchase of flower garlands is common in *sao nakrong* venues throughout Thailand and is a way for customers to express their admiration for the singing skills (and beauty) of their favorite hostess.

5. There is of course variety. I have seen both younger Thai sex workers in some of these venues, as well as older Lao sex workers, including Lao transvestites (*khatoey*), in venues oriented toward older foreigners. But they are in the minority.

6. I will limit my analysis here to "short term" prices, which is the most common purchase among customers. However, in a minority of cases customers pay more to stay the night ("long term") with the sex worker. It is extremely difficult to make accurate calculations on how this affects the overall profit levels for a venue, and Kham and Rattana, with whom I spoke about this topic, were unable to provide a clear answer to this. Both sex workers and venue managers receive a higher price when a customer pays for long term, but this profit gain is somewhat nullified by the sex worker's loss of a chance of getting additional customers that night.

7. This contrasts to larger venues in Bangkok, which can employ approxi-

mately a hundred women and operate with a retail price strategy. One particular venue I visited had women retailing for 1,500, 2,000, 2,500, and 3,000 baht, according to ranked beauty. There is no doubt that the scale of an operation is an important factor in allowing such price hierarchies.

8. Her assertion about their age is most probably correct. Other sources (personal Lao friends and former colleagues of mine) confirmed to me that students at this college straddle the legal age. It is also noteworthy that these students come from predominantly urban middle-class families, which suggests that the sale of virginity is not merely a function of socioeconomic marginality.

9. One limitation with Rehbein's ethnography (2007) on trade in Laos is that it does not explore the role of Chinese and Vietnamese trade and business. His analysis is solely on ethnic Lao entrepreneurialism.

10. A Bacci ceremony is often held in order to celebrate a particular event ranging from a marriage, a birth, or an important event within the Buddhist calendar to the return or departure of a family member.

11. For a more theoretical and detailed analysis of bad faith in relation to human trafficking, see Molland 2010a. In anthropology, bad faith has been popularized by Pierre Bourdieu and Nancy Scheper-Hughes.

Chapter 7: Combating Trafficking, Mekong Style

1. LAPTU was initially established as a counterpart to the AusAID-funded Asia Regional Cooperation to Prevent People Trafficking (ARCPPT) project. The Australian government mistakenly advised the Lao government to locate LAPTU within the Lao immigration police, which—it later turned out—had limited investigative capacity (the investigative police are in another police department). In May–June 2007 it became clear to the trafficking community in Laos that LAPTU had been abolished. The trafficking focal point within the police force has now been moved to the general police department, but at the time of writing its exact official status remains unclear.

2. A full list of state parties to the convention and protocol can be accessed at http://www.unodc.org/unodc/en/treaties/CTOC/countrylist -traffickingprotocol.html.

3. Article 134 is clearly inspired by how trafficking is defined in the Palermo Protocol. The article states: "Human trafficking means the recruitment, moving, transfer, harbouring, or receipt of any person within or across national borders by means of deception, threats, use of force, debt bondage or any other means and using such person in forced labour, prostitution, pornography, or anything that is against the fine traditions of the nation, or removing various body organs [of such person], or for other unlawful purposes."

4. ILO-IPEC and UNIAP were the two first trafficking projects in Laos, both as part of regional programs. Save the Children UK and UNICEF soon followed with regional activities on trafficking.

5. http://www.unodc.org/unodc/en/treaties/CTOC/countrylist -traffickingprotocol.html.

6. The ILO is not unique in this. UNIAP had in its second phase a whole program portfolio titled "targeted interventions."

7. Another trafficking study (UNIAP et al. 2004) came across several cases where family members indeed had information about family members who found themselves in difficult and abusive working situations in Thailand. There were even several examples of family members attempting to cross the border to Thailand in order to locate their relative and provide assistance.

8. The research method was clearly influenced by another report on poverty in Laos, *Participatory Poverty Assessment* (ADB 2001), for a study commissioned by the Asian Development Bank. In brief, the selection of research sites included a mix of purposive sampling, but at the same time "participatory methodologies based on rapid appraisal methods" were used to collect data (UNICEF and Ministry of Labour and Social Welfare 2004, 14).

9. Also noteworthy is that the ethnographic flair of the report reinforced its credibility. Survey data are ubiquitously used in development programming, but partly because of the increasing importance of social impact assessments by institutions such as the World Bank, anthropologically oriented research, which provides a "view from within," is often considered more authentic within aid circles (Goldman 2001; Olivier de Sardan 2005). This is especially so when it comes to researching a topic such as trafficking, which is clouded in illegality and political sensitivity.

10. At one point when I worked for UNIAP, I had an informal conversation with the lead author of the report, who solemnly informed me that the number of trafficked victims was likely to exceed one hundred thousand.

11. The report equates migration and trafficking by suggesting that any movement of a child (UNICEF and Ministry of Labour and Social Welfare 2004, 16), for whatever purpose, constitutes trafficking in persons. This deviates from the trafficking protocol, which makes it clear that trafficking—even in the case of minors—is contingent on its purpose (i.e., exploitation).

12. I took part in several planning meetings for this study, and hence I am aware of aspects of its methodology that are not acknowledged in the report itself.

13. These include but are not limited to Caouette 1998; Doussantousse and Keovonghit 2006; ILO 2003; Phetsiriseng 2001; UNIAP and Ministry of Labour and Social Welfare 2001; UNIAP et al. 2004; UNICEF and Ministry of Labour and Social Welfare 2004; and Wille 2001.

14. The Lao government appears to be gradually accepting this reality. In an official country paper by the Lao government from 2004, there was no mention of internal trafficking (COMMIT 2004). Two years later, the subject of internal trafficking appeared in the draft national plan of action to combat human trafficking. Public statements referring to internal trafficking have also

been made repeatedly by the vice minister of justice, Ket Kiettisak, and by the deputy prime minister and minister of defense, Douangchay Phichit, who chairs the national trafficking committee.

15. The projects are United Nations Inter-Agency Project to Combat Trafficking in the Greater Mekong Sub-region (UNIAP); International Labour Organization's International Programme on the Elimination of Child Labour (ILO-IPEC); International Organization for Migration (IOM); Save the Children; Asia Regional Trafficking in Persons Project (ARTIP); United Nations Children's Fund (UNICEF).

16. All of these projects and instruments justify their existence by referencing the necessity for governments to cooperate across borders.

17. Personal communication with anonymous informant, 2006.

Chapter 8: The Drifters

1. I have slightly edited this e-mail to protect the sender's anonymity.

2. The tendency to presume village communities to be egalitarian, homogenous, and harmonious is ubiquitous within the development sector (see Olivier de Sardan 2005). For an ethnographic problematization of the concept of "community" in the context of Thai communities in mainland Southeast Asia, see Walker 2009.

3. The report chooses to describe agents using fictionlike metaphors such as "hyenas," "part-time hyenas," and "caring brokers" (UNIAP et al. 2004, 51).

4. Such views are echoed among the Lao as well. Lao informants, both within the sex industry and in the broader community, frequently express a belief in solidarity among relatives (*phee nong*). However, as Evans (2002) has pointed out, this ethos ignores the importance of patron-client relationships and often glosses over asymmetrical forms of power among extended kin networks.

5. For example, the Lao Red Cross' HIV/AIDS/STI, Drug and People Trafficking Awareness and Prevention Education Program, under the Northern Economic Corridor Project, employs peer education methods.

6. On the topic of measures against traffickers, an ILO official is on record as having said: "We don't quite know: we cannot distinguish between traffickers and brokers. Maybe brokers have good intentions but it goes wrong on the other side" (Ginsburg 2002a, 7). And with regard to the impact of their programs, the same official said: "There are different interventions and we don't know which one has impact: community building with village chiefs, income generating activities, awareness raising" (ibid., 11).

7. A couple of specific examples would be how the ILO (Phetsiriseng 2001; ILO 2003) attempted to prioritize income-generating activities and how the UNICEF report (UNICEF and Ministry of Labour and Social Welfare 2004) highlighted the need for social policy measures. During my time working for

UNIAP, there occasionally were heated exchanges between the staffs of various projects regarding such different approaches, and the legitimacy and status of knowledge (in the form of reports) played an important part in establishing recognition and thereby maneuvering space for particular sets of activities. This interplay reflects not only the institutional context of these projects but also a form of contestation for recognition and ability to set the agenda within the anti-trafficking community.

8. Two of the contributors to that volume played a central role in UNIAP.

9. Chamberlain (2006) has on behalf of the Asian Development Bank conducted a risk assessment that argues that road projects will increase trafficking. However, this report conflates migration and trafficking. Several arguments of the report are not reflected in the data provided. For example, most of the data focus on socioeconomic conditions of various ethnic groups, and there is a glaring lack of information about the migration process itself, let alone the outcome of migration trajectories.

Conclusion

1. I have been told about the first repatriation of trafficked victims, which preceded my time working for the UN in Laos, where all "victims" were dressed in identical coloured t-shirts with an accompanying "welcome home" ceremony at the Thai-Lao border, with the presence of local press. During my time working with trafficking in Laos, I several times listened to government officials who duly informed meetings of the "reintegration" ceremonies they held for trafficked victims upon their return to their villages. Such activities are very difficult to observe directly as they are subject to political control. I can only suspect that they contribute strongly to stigma, and hence have the effect of producing normative categories of "failed" and "success" migrants.

2. Between 2000 and 2006, the total number of officially identified trafficked victims from Laos was approximately 1,000. The total number of officially registered Lao migrants was almost 200,000, and the actual number of migrants was far higher than this. See Huguet and Ramangkura 2007; and UNIAP 2008a.

3. Throughout my time working for UNIAP as well as during my research, anti-trafficking projects lobbied the government continuously to change the practice of fining returning migrants. It appears that their lobbying has had some impact, with the governor of Savannakhet Province being one of the first senior government officials to take steps against this practice. Some of the background research that was done for UNDP's 2006 Human Development Report for Laos also indicates that this practice is being phased out, at least in some places (Chanthavysouk 2006; UNDP and NSC 2006). This is not to say that it has stopped completely.

BIBLIOGRAPHY

ABC News Online. 2007. *Australia to take 200 Lao refugees from Thailand.* ABC News Online. http://www.abc.net.au/news/2007-02-14/australia-to -take-200-lao-refugees-from-thailand/2194092.

Abolafia, Mitchel Y. 1998. "Markets as cultures: An ethnographic approach." In Callon et al. 1998, 69–85.

ADB (Asian Development Bank). 2001. *Participatory poverty assessment: Lao People's Democratic Republic.* Manila: Asian Development Bank.

———. 2009. *Broken lives: Trafficking in human beings in the Lao People's Democratic Republic.* Manila: Asian Development Bank.

Agustín, Laura María. 2007. *Sex at the margins: Migration, labour markets and the rescue industry.* New York: Zed Books.

Allen, Denise Roth, James W. Carey, Wat Uthaivoravit, Peter H. Kilmarx, and Fritz van Griensven. 2003. "Sexual health risks among young Thai women: Implications for HIV/STD prevention and contraception." *AIDS and Behavior* 7 (1): 9–21.

Amnesty International. 2005. "Thailand: Abuses and exploitation of migrant workers exposed." http://action.amnesty.org.au/news/comments/179/.

Anders, Gerhard. 2005. "Good governance as technology: Towards an ethnography of the Bretton Woods institutions." In Mosse and Lewis 2005, 37–60.

Anderson, Bridget. 2000. *Doing the dirty work? The global politics of domestic labour.* London: Zed Books.

———. 2007a. "Battles of time: The relation between global and labour mobilities." Working Paper 55, Centre on Migration, Policy and Society, University of Oxford.

———. 2007b. "Motherhood, apple pie and slavery: Reflections on trafficking debates." Working Paper 48, Centre on Migration, Policy and Society, University of Oxford.

———. 2008a. "Review essay: Sex, slaves and stereotypes." Centre for Migration, Policy and Society, University of Oxford.

———. 2008b. "A very private business: Exploring the demand for migrant domestic workers." *European Journal of Women's Studies* 14 (3): 247–264.

Anderson, Bridget, and Julia O'Connell Davidson. 2003. *Is trafficking in human beings demand driven? A multi-country pilot study.* Geneva: IOM (International Organization for Migration).

———. 2004. *Trafficking—a demand led problem? Part I: Review of evidence and debates.* Stockholm: Save the Children Sweden.

Aphornsuvan, Thanet. 1998. "Slavery and modernity: Freedom in the making of modern Siam." In *Asian freedoms: The idea of freedom in East and Southeast Asia,* ed. David Kelly and Anthony Reid, 161–186. New York: Cambridge University.

Appadurai, Arjun. 1986. "Introduction: Commodities and the politics of value." In *The social life of things: Commodities and cultural perspective,* ed. Arjun Appadurai, 3–63. New York: Cambridge University Press.

———. 1996. *Modernity at large: Cultural dimensions of globalization.* Minneapolis: University of Minnesota Press.

ARCM (Asian Research Center for Migration) and FHI (Family Health International). 2005. *Cross border migration between Thailand and Lao PDR: A qualitative assessment of Lao migration and its contribution to HIV vulnerability.* Bangkok: Institute for Asian Studies, Chulalongkorn University.

ARCPPT (Asia Regional Cooperation to Prevent People Trafficking). 2002. *Asia Regional Cooperation to Prevent People Trafficking: Project design document.* Vol. 1. ARCPPT.

———. 2004. *Identification and treatment of victims of trafficking.* ACIL and AusAID.

———. 2006 [2003]. *Gender, human trafficking, and the criminal justice system in the Lao PDR.* Vientiane: ARCPPT.

Asian Migrant Centre. 2002. *Migration: Needs, issues, and responses in the greater Mekong subregion.* Hong Kong: Clearcut Publishing and Printing.

Askew, Marc. 1999. "Strangers and lovers: Thai women sex workers and Western men in the 'pleasure space' of Bangkok." In *Converging interests: Traders, travellers, and tourists in Southeast Asia,* ed. Jill Forshee, Christina Fink, and Sandra Cate, 109–148. Berkeley: University of California.

———. 2002. *Bangkok, place, practice and representation.* London: Routledge.

———. 2006. "Sex and the sacred: Sojourners and visitors in the making of the southern Thai borderland." In *Centering the margin: Agency and narrative in Southeast Asian borderlands,* ed. Alexander Horstmann and Reed L. Wadley, 177–206. New York: Berghahn Books.

Askew, Marc, William S. Logan, and Colin Long. 2007. *Vientiane: Transformations of a Lao landscape.* London: Routledge.

AusAID. 2002. *Asia Regional Cooperation to Prevent People Trafficking: Project Design Document.* Vol. 1.

Aye, Nwe Nwe. 2002. "Can we outsmart traffickers?" *Step by Step: UN Inter-Agency Project Newsletter,* no. 8, 3, 7.

Bales, Kevin. 2005. *Understanding global slavery: A reader*. Berkeley: University of California Press.

Bangkok Post. 2006. "Not the kind of fame we crave." 25 April.

————. 2007. "Inhuman trafficking." http://archives.mybangkokpost.com/bkkarchives/frontstore/news_detail.html?aid=207605.

Barth, Fredrik. 1981. *Process and form in social life*. Vol. 1. London: Routledge and Kegan Paul.

————. 1993. *Balinese worlds*. Chicago: University of Chicago Press.

BBC World. 2007. *Teenage North Korean defectors freed*. http://news.bbc.co.uk/2/hi/asia-pacific/6590629.stm.

Beare, Margaret E. 1999. "Illegal migration: Personal tragedies, social problems, or national security threats?" In Williams 1999, 11–41.

Berger, Herve. 2001. "SURAC—the two for one committee." *Step by Step: UN Inter-Agency Project Newsletter*, 2nd Quarter, 4–5.

Berman, Jacqueline. 2003. "(Un)popular strangers and crises (un)bounded: Discourses of sex-trafficking, the European political community and the panicked state of the modern state." *Journal of International Relations* 9 (1): 37–86.

Bhattacharyya, Gargi. 2005. *Traffick: The illicit movement of people and things*. London: Pluto Press.

Bishop, Ryan, and Lillian S. Robinson. 1998. *Night market: Sexual cultures and the Thai economic miracle*. New York: Routledge.

Bourdieu, Pierre. 1977 [1972]. *Outline of a theory of practice*. Cambridge: Cambridge University Press.

————. 1984. *Distinction: A social critique of the judgement of taste*. London: Routledge and Kegan Paul.

————. 1998. *Practical reason: On the theory of action*. Cambridge, UK: Polity.

————. 2003. "Participant objectivation." *Journal of the Royal Anthropology Institute* 9:281–294.

Braithwaite, John. 2000. "The new regulatory state and the transformation of criminology." *British Journal of Criminology* 40:222–238.

Brettell, Caroline B., and James F. Hollifield. 2000. "Introduction: Migration theory; Talking across disciplines." In *Migration theory: Talking across disciplines*, ed. Caroline B. Brettell and James F. Hollifield, 1–26. New York and London: Routledge.

Brigg, Morgan. 2002. "Post-development, Foucault and the colonisation metaphor." *Third World Quarterly* 23 (3): 421–436.

Brown, Christopher Leslie. 2006. *Moral capital: Foundations of British abolitionism*. Chapel Hill: University of North Carolina Press.

Burchell, Graham, Colin Gordon, and Peter M. Miller, eds. 1991. *The Foucault effect: Studies in governmentality; With two lectures by and an interview with Michel Foucault*. London: Harvester Wheatsheaf.

Caldwell, Gillian, Steve Galster, Jyothi Kanics, and Nadia Steinzor. 1999.

"Capitalizing on transition economies: The role of the Russian mafia in trafficking women for forced prostitution." In Williams 1999, 42–73.

Callon, Michel. 1998. "Introduction: The embeddedness of economic markets in economics." In Callon et al. 1998, 1–57.

Callon, Michel, Colin Gordon, and Peter M. Miller, eds. 1998. *The laws of the markets*. Oxford: Blackwell.

Caouette, Therese M. 1998. *Needs assessment of cross-border trafficking in women and children—the Mekong sub-region*. Bangkok: UN Working Group on Trafficking in the Mekong Sub-region.

Carné, Louis de. 2000. *Travels on the Mekong Cambodia, Laos and Yunnan: The political and trade report of the Mekong Exploration Commission (June 1866–June 1868)*. Bangkok: White Lotus Press.

Carrier, James G. 1997. *Meanings of the market: The free market in Western culture*. Oxford: Berg.

Carrier, James G., and Daniel Miller. 1998. *Virtualism: A new political economy*. Oxford: Berg.

Chamberlain, James, R. 2006. *Preventing the trafficking of women and children and promoting safe migration in the Greater Mekong Sub-region*. Asian Development Bank.

Chantavanich, Supang. 2008. "Human trafficking: Migrate to die." *Bangkok Post*, 19 April.

Chanthavysouk, Khamsavath. 2006. "Export of labour: A contribution to Lao development." Technical background paper prepared for the third National Human Development Report. Vientiane: Lao National Statistics Centre (NSC).

Chapin, Jessica. 2003. "Reflections from the bridge." In *Ethnography at the border*, ed. Pablo Vila, 1–22. Minneapolis: University of Minnesota Press.

Chapkis, Wendy. 2003. "Trafficking, migration, and the law: Protecting innocents, punishing immigrants." *Gender and Society* 17 (6): 923–937.

Chapman, Malcolm, and Peter J. Buckley. 1997. "Markets, transaction costs, economists and social anthropologists." In *Meanings of the market: The free market in Western culture*, ed. James G. Carrier, 225–250. Oxford: Berg.

Clifford, James. 1997. *Routes: Travel and translation in the late twentieth century*. Cambridge: Harvard University Press.

Cochoy, Franck. 1998. "Another discipline for the market economy: Marketing as a performative knowledge and know-how for capitalism." In Callon et al. 1998, 194–221.

Cohen, Erik. 1986. "Lovelorn *farangs*: The correspondence between men and Thai girls." *Anthropological Quarterly* 59 (3): 115–127.

Cohen, Paul, and Gehan Wijeyewardene. 1984. "Introduction to spirit cults and the position of women in northern Thailand." *Mankind* 14 (4): 249–262.

COMMIT (Coordinated Mekong Ministerial Initiative against Trafficking). 2004. *Country paper: Lao PDR*. United Nations Inter-Agency Project on Human Trafficking in the Greater Mekong Sub-region (UNIAP).

"Community action with a difference." 2002. *Step by Step: UN Inter-Agency Project Newsletter*, 3rd Quarter, no. 8, 1.

Cowan, Jane K., Marie-Bénédicte Dembour, and Richard A. Wilson, eds. 2001. *Culture and rights: Anthropological perspectives*. Cambridge: Cambridge University Press.

Creighton, Millie R. 1990. "Revisiting shame and guilt cultures: A forty-year pilgrimage." *Ethos* 18 (3): 279–307.

Darwin, Muhadjir, Anna Marie Wattie, and Susi Yuarsi, eds. 2003. *Living on the edges: Cross-border mobility and sexual exploitation in the greater Southeast Asia-sub-region*. Yogyakarta: Center for Population and Policy Studies, Gadjah Mada University.

Davidson, Julia O'Connell. 1998. *Prostitution, power, and freedom*. Ann Arbor: University of Michigan Press.

———. 2002. "The rights and wrongs of prostitution." *Hypatia* 17 (2): 84–98.

———. 2003. "'Sleeping with the enemy'? Some problems with feminist abolitionist calls to penalise those who buy commercial sex." *Social Policy and Society* 2 (1): 55–63.

———. 2004. "'Child sex tourism': An anomalous form of movement?" *Journal of Contemporary European Studies* 12 (1): 31–46.

———. 2006. "Men, middlemen, and migrants: The demand side of 'sex trafficking.'" *Eurozine*. http://www.eurozine.com/articles/2006-07-27 -davidson-en.html.

Davies, John. 2008. "How to use a trafficked woman: The alliance between political and criminal trafficking organisations." *Recherches Sociologiques et Anthropologiques* 1:114–131.

Davis, David Brion. 1966. *The Problem of slavery in Western culture*. Ithaca, NY: Cornell University Press.

Davis, Jerry Allen, director. 2008. *The Shanghai hotel* (film). Cornucopia Productions.

Day, Tony, and Craig J. Reynolds. 2000. "Cosmologies, truth regimes, and the state in Southeast Asia." *Modern Asian Studies* 34 (1): 1–55.

de Certeau, Michel. 1988. *The practice of everyday life*. Berkeley: University of California Press.

"Demand for virgins brings girls into Cambodian sex trade at young age." 2007. *International Herald Tribune*, 18 September. http://www.crin.org/ violence/search/closeup.asp?infoID=14917.

Derks, A. 2008. *Khmer women on the move*. Honolulu: University of Hawai'i Press.

Derrida, Jacques. 2001. *On cosmopolitanism and forgiveness*. London: Routledge.

Ditmore, Melissa. 2005. "Trafficking in lives: How ideology shapes policy." In Kempadoo et al. 2005, 107–126.

Doezema, Jo. 2000. "Loose women or lost women? The re-emergence of the myth of white slavery in contemporary discourses of trafficking in women." *Gender Issues* (Winter): 23–50.

———. 2007. "Who gets to choose? Coercion, consent, and the UN trafficking protocol." *Gender and Development* 10 (1): 20–27.

Donnan, Hastings, and Thomas M. Wilson. 1999. *Borders: Frontiers of identity, nations and state.* Oxford: Berg.

Doussantousse, Serge, and Bea Keovonghit. 2006. *Migration of children and youth from Savannakhet Province, Laos to Thailand: A research study.* Vientiane: World Vision Lao PDR.

Duffield, Mark R. 2001. *Global governance and the new wars: The merging of development and security.* London: Zed Books.

Duguay, Christian, director. 2005. *Human trafficking* (film). Muse Entertainment Enterprises.

Dupont, Alan. 1999. "Transnational crime, drugs, and security in east Asia." *Asian Survey* 39 (3): 433–455.

ECOSOC (United Nations Economic and Social Council). 2002. *Recommended principles and guidelines on human rights and human trafficking.* Geneva.

Edelman, Marc, and Angelique Haugerud. 2005. "Introduction: The anthropology of development and globalization." In *The anthropology of development and globalization,* ed. Marc Edelman and Angelique Haugerud, 1–74. Oxford: Blackwell.

Embree, John F. 1969 [1950]. "Thailand—a loosely structured social system." In Evers 1969 [1950], 3–15.

Emirbayer, Mustafa, and Ann Mische. 1998. "What is agency?" *American Journal of Sociology* 103 (4): 962–1023.

Emners, Ralph. 2003. "ASEAN and the securitization of transnational crime in Southeast Asia." *Pacific Review* 16 (3): 419–438.

England, Robert J. K. 1998. "The art of levitation: Reflections of a UN resident coordinator." Unpublished discussion paper. Bangkok.

———. 2001. "Corralling cats: Management in the UN environment." Unpublished discussion paper.

Eriksen, Thomas Hylland, Ellen Bal, and Oscar Salemink, eds. 2010. *A world of insecurity: Anthropological perspectives on human security.* London: Pluto Press.

Escobar, Arturo. 1994. *Encountering development: The making and unmaking of the third world.* Princeton, NJ: Princeton University Press.

Evans, Grant. 1998. *The politics of ritual and remembrance: Laos since 1975.* Honolulu: University of Hawai'i Press.

———. 2002. *A short history of Laos: The land in between.* Chiang Mai, Thailand: Silkworm Books.

———. 2004. *Laos: Situation analysis and trend assessment.* Independent analysis commissioned by United Nations High Commissioner for Refugees, Protection Information Section (DIP). Writenet.

———. 2007. Review of *Vientiane: Transformations of a Lao landscape,* by Marc Askew, William S. Logan, and Colin Long. *Contemporary Southeast Asia* 29 (3): 533–534.

Evers, Hans-Dieter, ed. 1969 [1950]. *Loosely structured social systems: Thailand in comparative perspective.* New Haven, CT: Yale University.

Featherstone, Mike, ed. 1990. *Global culture: Nationalism, globalization and modernity.* London: Sage.

Feeny, David. 1989. "Decline of property rights in man in Thailand, 1800–1913." *Journal of Economic History* 49 (2): 285–296.

Feingold, David. 1997. "The hell of good intentions: Some preliminary thoughts on opium in the political ecology of the trade in girls and women." In *Where China meets Southeast Asia: Social and cultural change in the border regions,* ed. Grant Evans, Chris Sutton, and Kuah Khun Eng, 183–203. Singapore: Institute of Southeast Asian Studies.

———. 1998. "Sex, drugs and the IMF: Some implications of 'structural readjustment' for the trade in heroin, girls and women in the Upper Mekong region." *Refuge* 17 (5): 4–10.

———, director. 2002. *Trading women: The trade in drugs and the trade in women* (film). Ophidian Research Institute.

Ferguson, James. 1990. *The anti-politics machine: "Development," depoliticization, and bureaucratic power in Lesotho.* New York: Cambridge University Press.

———. 2005. "Seeing like an oil company: Space, security, and global capital in neoliberal Africa." *American Anthropologist* 107 (3): 377–382.

Fine, Ben. 2002. *The world of consumption: The material and cultural revisited.* London: Routledge.

Fordham, Graham. 1998. "Northern Thai male culture and the assessment of HIV risk: Toward a new approach." *Crossroads* 12 (1): 77–164.

———. 2004. *A new look at Thai AIDS: Perspectives from the margin.* Oxford: Berghahn Books.

Foucault, Michel. 1975. *Discipline and punish: The birth of the prison.* 2nd ed. New York: Vintage Books.

———. 1980. *The history of sexuality.* Vol. 1, *An introduction.* New York: Vintage Books.

———. 1981. "The order of discourse." In *Untying the text: A post-structuralist reader,* ed. Robert Young, 48–78. Boston: Routledge.

———. 1982. "The subject and power." *Critical Inquiry* 8 (4): 777–795.

———. 1991. "Governmentality." In Burchell et al. 1991, 87–104.

Frederick, John. 2005. "The myth of Nepal-to-India sex trafficking: Its creation, its maintenance, and its influence on anti-trafficking interventions." In Kempadoo et al. 2005, 127–147.

Gallagher, Anne. 2001. "Human rights and the new UN protocols on trafficking and migrant smuggling: A preliminary analysis." *Human Rights Quarterly* 23:975–1004.

———. 2006a. "Recent legal developments in the field of human trafficking: A critical review of the 2005 European Convention and related instruments." *European Journal of Migration and Law* 8:163–189.

———. 2006b. "A shadow report on human trafficking in Lao PDR: The US approach vs. international law." *Asian and Pacific Migration Journal* 15 (4): 525–552.

Gallagher, Anne, and Elaine Pearson. 2010. "The high cost of freedom: A legal and policy analysis of shelter detention for victims of trafficking." *Human Rights Quarterly* 32 (1): 73–114.

Garland, David. 2001. *The culture of control: Crime and social order in contemporary society*. Oxford: Oxford University Press.

Gellner, Ernst. 1996. "Ernest Gellner's reply: 'Do nations have navels?'" *Nations and Nationalism* 2 (3): 366–370.

Giddens, Anthony. 1984. *The constitution of society: Outline of the theory of structuration*. Cambridge, UK: Polity Press.

———. 1990. *The consequences of modernity*. Stanford, CA: Stanford University Press.

———. 1991. *Modernity and self-identity: Self and society in the late modern age*. Stanford, CA: Stanford University Press.

———. 1994. "Living in a post-traditional society." In *Reflexive modernization: Politics, tradition and aesthetics in the modern social order*, ed. Ulirch Beck, Anthony Giddens, and Scott Lash, 56–109. Cambridge, UK: Polity Press.

Giddens, Anthony, and Will Hutton. 2001. *On the edge: Living with global capitalism*. London: Vintage.

Ginzburg, Oren. 2002a. *Building projects on assumptions*. Bangkok: UN Inter-Agency Project on Trafficking in Women and Children in the Mekong Sub-region (UNIAP).

———. 2002b. *Combating trafficking at community level: Cambodia trip report, February 4–26*. Bangkok: UN Inter-Agency Project on Trafficking in Women and Children in the Mekong Sub-region (UNIAP).

———. 2004. *Reintegration of victims of trafficking: Defining success and developing indicators; Cambodia, Laos, Myanmar, Vietnam*. Bangkok: IOM (International Organization for Migration).

Girling, John L. S. 1981. *Thailand: Society and politics*. Ithaca, NY: Cornell University Press.

Global Alliance against Traffic in Women. N.d. "FAQ: Understanding trafficking in persons." Accessed 24 May 2010. http://www.gaatw.org/index.php?option=com_content&view=article&id=454:understanding-trafficking&catid=158:faq.

Goffman, Erving. 1981 [1959]. *The presentation of self in everyday life.* Harmondsworth, UK: Penguin.

Goldman, Michael. 2001. "The birth of a discipline: Producing authoritative green knowledge, World Bank–style." *Ethnography* 2 (2): 191–217.

Goss, Jon D., and Bruce Lindquist. 1995. "Conceptualizing international labor migration: A structuration perspective." *International Migration Review* 29 (2): 317–351.

Gotehus, Aslaug. 2006. *Crossing the river: Perceptions of "human trafficking" among villagers in Bokeo Province, northern Laos.* Master's thesis, Ås: Norwegian University of Life Sciences.

Gould, Jeremy. 2005. "Timing, scale and style: Capacity as governmentality in Tanzania." In Mosse and Lewis 2005, 61–84.

Government of Lao PDR (People's Democratic Republic) and Government of the Kingdom of Thailand. 2002. "MOU between the Government of Lao People's Democratic Republic and the Government of the Kingdom of Thailand on labour co-operation."

———. 2005. "Memorandum of understanding between the Government of the Lao People's Republic and the Government of the Kingdom of Thailand on cooperation to combat trafficking in persons, especially women and children."

Graycar, Adam. 1999. "Trafficking in human beings." Paper presented at the International Conference on Migration, Culture and Crime, Israel, 7 July. Available from Australian Institute of Criminology, Canberra.

Gregory, Chris. 2009. "Whatever happened to economic anthropology?" *Australian Journal of Anthropology* 20 (3): 285–300.

Grossman, Sanford J., and Joseph E. Stiglitz. 1980. "On the impossibility of informationally efficient markets." *American Economic Review* 70 (3): 393–408.

Guilmoto, Christophe Z., and Frederic Sandron. 2001. "The internal dynamics of migration networks in developing countries." *Population* 13 (2): 135–164.

Hamilton, Annette. 1997. "Primal dream: Masculinism, sin, and salvation in Thailand's sex trade." In Manderson and Jolly 1997, 145–165.

Hanks, L. M. 1977. "The corporation and the entourage: A comparison of Thai and American social organization." In Schmidt et al. 1977, 161–167.

Hanks, William F. 2005. "Pierre Bourdieu and the practices of language." *Annual Review of Anthropology* 34:67–83.

Hannerz, Ulf. 1997. *Flows, boundaries and hybrids: Keywords in transnational anthropology.* Stockholm: Stockholm University.

————. 2003. "Being there . . . and there . . . and there! Reflections on multi-site ethnography." *Ethnography* 4 (2): 201–216.

Hantrakul, Sukanya. 1988. "Prostitution in Thailand." In *Development and displacement: Women in Southeast Asia*, ed. Glen Chandler, Norma Sullivan, and Jan Branson, 115–136. Melbourne: Monash University.

Haughton, James. 2006. *Situational analysis of human trafficking in the Lao PDR: With emphasis on Savannakhet.* Vientiane: World Vision Lao PDR.

Hettne, B. 2009. *Thinking about development.* New York: Zed Books.

High, Holly. 2004. "'Black' skin 'white' skin: Riches and beauty in Lao women's bodies." *Yunnan Project Bulletin* (June): 7–9.

Huda, Sigma. 1999. *Trafficking and prostitution in Bangladesh: Contradictions in law and practice.* Coalition against Trafficking in Women. http://www.uri.edu/artsci/wms/hughes/mhvbang.htm.

Hughes, Donna. 2000. "The 'Natasha' trade: The transnational shadow market of trafficking in women." *Journal of International Affairs* 53 (2): 625–651.

————. 2002. "The demand: The driving force of sex trafficking." Paper presented at the conference "The Human Rights Challenge of Globalization in Asia-Pacific-U.S.: The trafficking in persons, especially women and children," Honolulu, Hawai'i, 13–15 November.

————. 2004. *Best practices to address the demand side of sex trafficking.* http://www.uri.edu/artsci/wms/hughes/demand_sex_trafficking.pdf.

————. 2005. *The demand for victims of sex trafficking.* http://www.uri.edu/artsci/wms/hughes/demand_for_victims.pdf.

Huguet, Jerrold W., and Varamon Ramangkura. 2007. *The long road home: Analysis of regional and national processes for the return and reintegration of victims of trafficking in the greater Mekong sub-region.* Bangkok: IOM (International Organization for Migration).

Huijsmans, Roy. 2007. "Approaches to Lao Minors Working in Thailand." *Juth Pakai: Perspectives on Lao Development* 8:18–33.

HumanTrafficking.org. 2006a. "Help comes to Laotian trafficking victims." http://www.humantrafficking.org/updates/391.

————. 2006b. "Human trafficking mars a generation in Lao PDR." http://www.humantrafficking.org/updates/420.

————. 2006c. "Lao Workers in Thailand Legalized." http://www.humantrafficking.org/updates/341.

ILO (International Labour Organization). 1998. *Forced labour in Myanmar (Burma): Report of the Commission of Inquiry appointed under article 26 of the Constitution of the International Labour Organization to examine the observance by Myanmar of the Forced Labour Convention, 1930 (No. 29).* Geneva: ILO.

————. 2003. *Labour migration survey in Khammuane, Savannakhet and Champasack.* Vientiane: Ministry of Labour and Social Welfare, Lao PDR, and ILO.

———. 2006. *Demand side of human trafficking in Asia: Empirical findings.* Geneva.

ILO-IPEC (International Labour Organization, International Programme on the Elimination of Child Labour). 2002. *Micro-finance interventions to combat the worst forms of child labour, including trafficking.* Technical Intervention Area Summary Notes, TIA-3. Bangkok.

IOM (International Organization for Migration). 2004a. *From Lao PDR to Thailand and home again: The repatriation of trafficking victims and other exploited women and girl workers; A study of 124 cases.* Bangkok.

———. 2004b. *Revisiting the human trafficking paradigm: The Bangladesh experience.* Part 1, *Trafficking of adults.* Geneva.

Ireson-Doolittle, Carol, and Geraldine Moreno-Black. 2004. *The Lao: Gender, power, and livelihood.* Boulder, CO: Westview.

Jackson, Peter J., and Nerida M. Cook, eds. *Genders and sexualities in modern Thailand.* Chiang Mai, Thailand: Silkworm Books.

Jeffrey, Leslie Ann. 2002. *Sex and borders: Gender, national identity, and prostitution policy in Thailand.* Honolulu: University of Hawai'i Press.

Kapferer, Bruce. 2006. "Anthropology and the dialectic of enlightenment: A discourse on the definition and ideals of a threatened discipline." *Australian Journal of Anthropology* 18 (1): 72–94.

Kapur, Ratna. 2005. "Cross-border movements and the law: Renegotiating the boundaries of difference." In Kempadoo et al. 2005, 25–41.

Keefer, Colonel Sandra L. 2006. *Human trafficking and the impact on national security for the United States.* Carlisle Barracks, PA: US Army War College.

Kempadoo, Kamala. 2005. "Introduction: From moral panic to global justice; Changing perspectives on trafficking." In Kempadoo et al. 2005, vii–xxxiv.

Kempadoo, Kamala, Jyoti Sanghera, and Bandana Pattanaik, eds. 2005. *Trafficking and prostitution reconsidered: New perspectives on migration, sex work, and human rights.* London: Paradigm.

Keyes, Charles F. 1984. "Mother or mistress but never a monk: Buddhist notions of female gender in rural Thailand." *American Ethnologist* 11 (2): 223–241.

King, Anthony. 2000. "Thinking with Bourdieu against Bourdieu: A 'practical' critique of the habitus." *Sociological Theory* 18 (3): 417–433.

Kirsch, Thomas A. 1969. "Loose structure: Theory or description." In Evers 1969 [1950], 39–60.

———. 1996. "Buddhism, sex roles, and the Thai economy." In *Women of Southeast Asia,* ed. Penny Van Esterik, 13–32. De Kalb: Northern Illinois University.

Kleinman, Arthur, and Erin Fitz-Henry. 2007. "The experiential basis of subjectivity: How individuals change in the context of societal transformation." In *Subjectivity: Ethnographic investigations*, ed. João Biehl, Byron Good, and Arthur Kleinman, 52–65. Berkeley: University of California Press.

Kongrut, Anchalee, and Wimol Nukaew. 2008. "No human trafficking here." *Bangkok Post*, 22 April. http://www.bangkokpost.com/topstories/topstories.php?id=127231.

Kopytoff, Igor. 1982. "Slavery." *Annual Review of Anthropology* 11:207–230.

———. 1986. "The cultural biography of things: Commoditization as process." In *The social life of things: Commodities and cultural perspective*, ed. Arjun Appadurai, 64–91. New York: Cambridge University Press.

Kwong, Peter. 1997. *Forbidden workers: Illegal Chinese immigrants and American labor*. New York: New Press.

Lande, Carl H. 1977. "Networks and groups in Southeast Asia: Some observations on the group theory of politics." In Schmidt et al. 1977, 75–98.

Lao National Tourism Administration. 2006. *Guide 2006*. Vientiane.

Lao PDR (People's Democratic Republic). 2004. *National Growth and Poverty Eradication Strategy (NGPES)*. Vientiane: Government of Laos.

Leidholdt, Dorchen A. 2004. "Demand and the debate." Coalition against Trafficking in Women. http://action.web.ca/home/catw/readingroom.shtml?x=53793.

Levett, Connie. 2007. "Thailand backs down over Hmong refugees." *Sydney Morning Herald*, 1 February.

Lindquist, Johan A. 2009. *The anxieties of mobility: Migration and tourism in the Indonesian borderlands*. Honolulu: University of Hawai'i Press.

Löfgren, Orvar. 2002. "The nationalization of anxiety: A history of border crossings." In *The postnational self: Belonging and identity*, ed. Ulf Hedetoft and Mette Hjort, 250–274. Minneapolis and London: University of Minnesota Press.

Long, Lynellyn D. 2004. "Anthropological perspectives on the trafficking of women for sexual exploitation." *International Migration* 42 (1): 5–31.

Lyttleton, Chris. 1994. "The good people of Isan: Commercial sex in northeast Thailand." *Australian Journal of Anthropology* 5 (3): 257–279.

———. 1999a. "Any port in a storm: Coming to terms with HIV in Lao PDR." *Culture, Health and Sexuality* 1 (2): 115–130.

———. 1999b. "Changing the rules: Shifting bounds of adolescent sexuality in northeast Thailand." In Jackson and Cook 1999, 28–42.

———. 2000. *Endangered relations: Negotiating sex and AIDS in Thailand*. Amsterdam: Harwood Academic.

———. 2008. *Build it and they will come: Lessons for mitigating exploitation, HIV and other diseases from the construction of Lao Route 3*. Asian Development Bank (ADB) Study Series: HIV and infrastructure in the GMS—Technical Report 2. Manila: ADB.

Lyttleton, Chris, and Amorntip Amarapibal. 2002. "Sister cities and easy passage: HIV, mobility and economies of desire in a Thai/Lao border zone." *Social Science and Medicine* 54:505–518.

Lyttleton, Chris, Paul Cohen, Houmphanh Rattanavong, Bouakham Thong-khamhane, and Sourivanh Sisaengrat. 2004. *Watermelons, bars and trucks: Dangerous intersections in northwest Lao PDR; An ethnographic study of social change and health vulnerability along the road through Muang Sing and Muang Long.* Vientiane: Institute for Cultural Research of Laos; Macquarie University.

Manderson, Lenore. 1997. "Parables of imperialism and fantasies of the exotic: Western representations of Thailand—place and sex." In Manderson and Jolly 1997, 123–144.

Manderson, Lenore, and Margaret Jolly, eds. 1997. *Sites of desire, economies of pleasure: Sexualities in Asia and the Pacific.* Chicago: University of Chicago Press.

Marcus, George E. 1995. "Ethnography in/of the world system: The emergence of multi-sited ethnography." *Annual Review of Anthropology* 24:95–117.

Marshall, Phil. 2001. "Globalization, migration and trafficking: Some thoughts from the Southeast Asian region." Paper presented at the Workshop on the Impact of Globalization on the Full Enjoyment of Economic, Social and Cultural Rights and the Right to Development in Kuala Lumpur, 8–10 May. UN Inter-Agency Project on Trafficking in Women and Children in the Mekong Sub-region, Occasional Paper 1.

———. 2003. "Opinion piece: Labour exploitation and a bunch of red herrings." *Step by Step: UN Inter-Agency Project Newsletter*, no. 10, 4–5.

Marshall, Phil, and Susu Thatun. 2005. "Miles away: The trouble with prevention in the greater Mekong sub-region." In Kempadoo et al. 2005, 43–63.

Massey, Douglas S. 1998. "Contemporary theories on international migration." In *Worlds in motion: Understanding migration at the end of the millennium*, ed. Douglas S. Massey, 244–277. Oxford: Clarendon Press.

McLachlan, Dee, director. 2007. *The jammed* (film). Arclight Films.

Miller, John. 2005. "A modern slave trade." http://www.soc.iastate.edu/sapp/SlaveTrade4.pdf.

Mills, Mary Beth. 1995. "Attack of the widow ghosts: Gender, death, and modernity in northeast Thailand." In *Bewitching women, pious men: Gender and body politics in Southeast Asia*, ed. Aihwa Ong and Michael G. Peletz, 244–273. Berkeley: University of California Press.

———. 1997. "Contesting the margins of modernity: Women, migration and consumption." *American Ethnologist* 24 (1): 37–61.

———. 1999. *Thai women in the global labor force.* New Brunswick, NJ: Rutgers University Press.

———. 2005. "Engendering discourses of displacement: Contesting mobility and marginality in rural Thailand." *Ethnography* 6 (3): 385–419.

Molland, Sverre. 2005. "Human trafficking and poverty reduction: Two sides of the same coin?" *Juth Pakai: Perspectives on Lao Development* 4:27–37.

———. 2010a. "The perfect business: Human trafficking and Lao–Thai cross-border migration." *Development and Change* 41 (5): 831–855.

———. 2010b. "The value of bodies: Deception, helping and profiteering in human trafficking along the Thai-Lao border." *Asian Studies Review* 34 (2): 211–229.

———. 2011. "The trafficking of scarce elite commodities: Social change and commodification of virginity along the Mekong." *Asia Pacific Journal of Anthropology* 12 (2): 129–145.

Montgomery, Heather. 2001a. "Imposing rights? A case study of child prostitution in Thailand." In Cowan et al. 2001, 80–101.

———. 2001b. *Modern Babylon: Prostituting children in Thailand*. New York: Berghahn Books.

Moodysson, Lukas, director. 2002. *Lilya 4-Ever* (film). Newmarket Films.

Mosse, David. 2004. "Is good policy unimplementable? Reflections on the ethnography of aid policy and practice." *Development and Change* 35 (4): 639–671.

———. 2005. "Global governance and the ethnography of international aid." In Mosse and Lewis 2005, 1–36.

Mosse, David, and David Lewis, eds. 2005. *The aid effect: Giving and governing in international development*. London: Pluto Press.

Muecke, Marjorie A. 1992. "Mother sold food, daughter sells her body: The cultural continuity of prostitution." *Social Science and Medicine* 35 (7): 891–901.

Mulder, J. A. Niels. 1969. "Origin, development, and use of the concept of 'loose structure' in the literature about Thailand: An evaluation." In Evers 1969 [1950], 16–38.

Munck, Ronaldo. 2008. "Globalisation, governance and migration: an introduction." *Third World Quarterly* 29, no. 7: 1227–1246.

Murray Li, Tanya. 2007. *The will to improve: Governmentality, development, and the practice of politics*. London: Duke University Press.

Muttarak, Raya. 2004. "Domestic service in Thailand: Reflection of conflicts in gender, class and ethnicity." *Journal of Southeast Asian Studies* 35 (3): 503–529.

Nation. 1993. "Ranong brothel raids net 148 Burmese girls." 16 July.

———. 2004. "Thailand unveils war on human trafficking." 6 August. http://www.burmanet.org/news/2004/08/06/the-nation-thailand-unveils-war-on-human-trafficking/.

———. 2006. "Thailand, Laos agree to end refugee problem." 21 August.

National Assembly of the Lao PDR. 2004. *Law on the development and protection of women*. Vientiane.

Ngaosyvathn, Mayoury. 1993. *Lao women: Yesterday and today*. Vientiane: State Publishing Enterprise.

Nordstrom, Carolyn. 2007. *Global outlaws: Crime, money, and power in the contemporary world*. Berkeley: University of California Press.

O'Connor, Lucy. 2006. *"People trafficking" baseline awareness survey in three provinces, Lao PDR*. Vientiane: International Labour Organization (ILO).

OHCHR (Office of the United Nations High Commissioner for Human Rights). 2008. Introduction to "Special Rapporteur on trafficking in persons, especially in women and children: Introduction." http://www2 .ohchr.org/english/issues/trafficking/index.htm.

Olivier de Sardan, Jean-Pierre. 2005. *Anthropology and development: Understanding contemporary social change*. New York: Zed Books.

Ortner, Sherry B. 1978. "The virgin and the state." *Feminist Studies* 4 (3): 19–35.

———. 1981. "Gender and sexuality in hierarchical societies: The case of Polynesia and some comparative implications." In *Sexual meanings: The cultural construction of gender and sexuality*, ed. Sherry B. Ortner and Harriet Whitehead, 359–409. Cambridge: Cambridge University Press.

———. 1984. "Theory in anthropology since the sixties." *Comparative Studies in Society and History* 26 (1): 126–166.

———. 1995. "Resistance and the problem of ethnographic refusal." *Comparative Studies in Society and History* 37 (1): 173–193.

Outshoorn, Joyce. 2005. "The political debates on prostitution and trafficking of women." *Social Politics: International Studies in Gender, State and Society* 12 (1): 141–155.

Parliament of the Commonwealth of Australia. 2004. *Inquiry into the trafficking of women for sexual servitude*. Canberra: Parliament of the Commonwealth of Australia.

Patterson, Horace Orlando. 1982. *Slavery and social death: A comparative study*. Cambridge: Harvard University Press.

Pearson, Elaine. 2005. *The Mekong challenge: Human trafficking; Redefining demand; Destination factors in the trafficking of children and young women in the Mekong sub-region*. Bangkok: International Labour Organization (ILO).

Pessar, Patricia R., and Sarah J. Mahler. 2001. "Gender and transnational migration." Paper presented at the conference "Transnational Migration: Comparative Perspectives," Princeton University, 30 June–1 July.

Phetsiriseng, Inthasone. 2001. *Preliminary assessment on trafficking of children and women for labour exploitation in Lao PDR*. Vientiane: International Labour Organization (ILO).

Phillips, Herbert P. 1974. *Thai peasant personality: The patterning of interpersonal behavior in the village of Bang Chan*. Berkeley: University of California Press.

Pholsena, Vatthana. 2006. *Post-war Laos: The politics of culture, history and identity*. Singapore: Silkworm Books.

Phongpaichit, Pasuk. 1982. *From peasant girls to Bangkok masseuses*. Women, Work, and Development Series. Geneva: International Labour Office (ILO).

———. 1999. "Trafficking in people in Thailand." In Williams 1999, 74–104.

Phouthonesy, Ekaphone. 2007a. "Garment factories face labour shortage." *Vientiane Times*. http://www.vientianetimes.org.la/FreeContent/FreeContent _Garment.htm.

———. 2007b. "The high cost of unemployment." *Vientiane Times*, 2 April.

———. 2007c. "Passports not helpful: Labourers." *Vientiane Times*, 8 June.

Pieke, Frank N., and Xiang Biao. 2007. *Legality and labour: Chinese migration, neoliberalism and the state in the UK and China*. Oxford: University of Oxford.

Pieke, Frank N., Pal Nyiri, Mette Thunø, and Antonella Ceccagno. 2004. *Transnational Chinese: Fujianese migrants in Europe*. Stanford, CA: Stanford University Press.

Pongkhao, Somsack. 2007. "Trafficking victim repatriated with brain injuries." *Vientiane Times*. http://www.vientianetimes.org.la/FreeContent/ FreeContent_T.htm.

PSI (Population Services International). 2005. *Tracking results continuously (TRaC) survey: Female sex workers in the Lao PDR*. Washington, DC: PSI.

Punyodyana, Boonsanong. 1969. "Social structure, social system, and two levels of analysis: A Thai view." In Evers 1969 [1950], 77–105.

Rabibhadana, Akin. 1969. *The organization of Thai society in the early Bangkok period, 1782–1873*. Ithaca, NY: Cornell University Press.

Rehbein, Boike. 2007. *Globalization, culture and society in Laos*. London: Routledge.

Reid, Anthony. 1983. "Introduction: Slavery and bondage in Southeast Asian history." In *Slavery, bondage and dependency in Southeast Asia*, ed. Anthony Reid, 1–43. St. Lucia: University of Queensland Press.

Rigg, Jonathan. 2005. *Living with transition in Laos: Market integration in Southeast Asia*. New York: Routledge.

———. 2006. "Moving lives: Migration and livelihoods in the Lao PDR." *Population, Space and Place* 13:163–178.

Rigg, Jonathan, Bounthong Bouahom, and Linkham Douangsavanh. 2004. "Money, morals, and markets: Evolving rural labour markets in Thailand and the Lao PDR." *Environment and Planning* 36:983–998.

Rigg, Jonathan, and Randi Jerndal. 1999. "From buffer state to crossroads state: Spaces of human activity and integration in the Lao PDR." In *Laos: Culture and society*, ed. Grant Evans, 35–60. Chiang Mai, Thailand: Silkworm Books.

Robinson, Lillian S., and Ryan Bishop. 1999. "Genealogies of exotic desire: The Thai night market in the Western imagination." In Jackson and Cook 1999, 191–205.

Rosaldo, Renato. 1989. *Culture and truth: The remaking of social analysis.* Boston: Beacon Press.

Rubin, Gayle. 1975. "The traffic in women: Notes on the 'political economy' of sex." In *Towards an anthropology of women,* ed. Rayna R. Reiter, 157–210. New York: Monthly Review Press.

Ruggiero, Vincenzo. 1997. "Trafficking in human beings: Slaves in contemporary Europe." *International Journal of the Sociology of Law* 25:231–244.

Sahlins, Marshall. 1976. *Culture and practical reason.* Chicago: University of Chicago Press.

Salt, John. 2000. "Trafficking and human smuggling: A European perspective." Special issue, *International Migration* 38 (3): 31–56.

Salt, John, and Jeremy Stein. 1997. "Migration as a business: The case of trafficking." *International Migration* 35 (4): 467–494.

Santoni, Ronald E. 1995. *Bad faith, good faith, and authenticity in Sartre's early philosophy.* Philadelphia: Temple University Press.

Sartre, Jean-Paul. 1957. *Being and nothingness: An essay on phenomenological ontology.* London: Methuen.

Scheper-Hughes, Nancy. 1992a. *Death without weeping: The violence of everyday life in Brazil.* Berkeley: University of California Press.

———. 1992b. "Hungry bodies, medicine, and the state: Toward a critical psychological anthropology." In *New directions in psychological anthropology,* ed. Theodore Schwartz, Geoffrey M. White, and Catherine A. Lutz, 221–247. Cambridge: Cambridge University Press.

Schloenhardt, Andreas. 1999. "The business of migration: Organised crime and illegal migration in Australia and the Asia-Pacific region." *Adelaide Law Review* 21:81–114.

Schmidt, Steffen W., James C. Scott, Carl Lande, and Laura Guasti, eds. 1977. *Friends, followers, and factions.* Berkeley: University of California Press.

Scott, James C. 1976. *The moral economy of the peasant: Rebellion and subsistence in Southeast Asia.* New Haven, CT: Yale University Press.

———. 1977. "Patron-client politics and political change in Southeast Asia." In Schmidt et al. 1977, 123–146.

———. 1986. *Weapons of the weak: Everyday forms of peasant resistance.* London: Yale University Press.

———. 1998a. "Freedom and freehold: Space, people and state simplification in Southeast Asia." In *Asian freedoms: The idea of freedom in East and Southeast Asia,* ed. David Kelly and Anthony Reid, 37–64. Cambridge: Cambridge University Press.

———. 1998b. *Seeing like a state: How certain schemes to improve the human condition have failed.* New Haven, CT: Yale University Press.

Scott, James C., and Benedict J. Kerkvliet. 1977. "How traditional rural patrons lose legitimacy: A theory with special reference to Southeast Asia." In Schmidt et al. 1977, 439–458.

Seabrook, Jeremy. 1996. *Travels in the skin trade: Tourism and the sex industry.* London: Pluto Press.

Sene-Asa, Oloth. 2007. *The transition of garment factory girls into prostitution in Laos.* Geneva: Institute Universitaire d'Études du Développement.

Shangera, Jyoti. 2005. "Unpacking the trafficking discourse." In Kempadoo et al. 2005, 3–24.

Silverman, Vicki. 2003. "Trading women: Filmmaker shatters myths about human trafficking." Washington File, Bureau of International Information Programs, U.S. Department of State, 11 September. http://www.america.gov/st/washfile-english/2003/September/20030911115501namrevlisv0.2781031.html.

Singer, Linda. 1993. *Erotic welfare: Sexual theory and politics in the age of epidemic.* New York: Routledge.

Sirisackda, Anousone, director. 2006. *Lessons of life* (film). Lao Art Media, Lao National Television, and UNICEF.

Sobieszczyk, Teresa. 2000. "Pathways abroad: Gender and international migration recruitment choices in northern Thailand." *Asian and Pacific Migration Journal* 9 (4): 391–428.

State Planning Committee and National Statistical Centre. 1997. *Results from the population census 1995.* Vientiane: National Statistical Centre.

Steinfatt, Thomas, Simon Baker, and Allan Beesey. 2002. *Measuring the number of trafficked women in Cambodia: 2002; Part I of a series.* Honolulu: Globalization Research Center, University of Hawai'i at Mānoa.

Storvik, Kaia. 2006. "Norge er et fristed for menneskehandel." http://www.dagsavisen.no/innenriks/article256899.ece.

Stratton, Jon. 1996. *The desirable body: Cultural fetishism and the erotics of consumption.* Manchester, UK: Manchester University Press.

Stuart-Fox, Martin. 1997. *A history of Laos.* Melbourne: Cambridge University Press.

———. 2005. *Politics and reform in the Lao People's Democratic Republic.* Perth: Murdoch University.

———. 2006. "The political culture of corruption in the Lao PDR." *Asian Studies Review* 30:59–75.

Sullivan, Barbara. 2003. "Feminism and new international law." *International Feminist Journal of Politics* 5 (1): 67–91.

Tambiah, Stanley Jeyaraja. 1976. *World conqueror and world renouncer: A study of Buddhism and polity in Thailand against a historical background.* Cambridge: Cambridge University Press.

Taylor, Lisa Rende. 2005. "Dangerous trade-offs: The behavioural ecology of child labor and prostitution in rural northern Thailand." *Current Anthropology* 46 (3): 411–431.

Terwiel, B. 1983. "Bondage and slavery in early nineteenth century Siam." In *Slavery, bondage and dependency in Southeast Asia,* ed. Jonathan Rigg, 118–137. St. Lucia: University of Queensland Press.

Thomas, Frederic, and Florence Pasnik. 2002. *Surveys on the behaviors and attitudes of tourists and foreign clients with sex-abused children and young women, Kingdom of Cambodia 2001–2002.* Phnom Penh: Association Internationale pour le Développement, le Tourisme et la Santé.

Tsing, Anna Lowenhaupt. 2000. "The global situation." *Cultural Anthropology* 15 (3): 327–360.

Turner, V. W. 1967. *The forest of symbols: Aspects of Ndembu ritual.* Ithaca, NY: Cornell University Press.

Turton, Andrew. 1980. "Asian and African systems of slavery." In *Asian and African systems of slavery,* ed. James L. Watson, 251–292. Oxford: Blackwell.

Tyldum, Guri, and Anette Brunovskis. 2005. "Describing the unobserved: Methodological challenges in empirical studies on human trafficking." *International Migration* 43 (1): 17–34.

UN (United Nations). 2000. *Protocol to prevent, suppress and punish trafficking in persons, especially women and children, supplementing the United Nations Convention against Transnational Organized Crime.* New York.

———. 2001. *United Nations Convention against Transnational Organized Crime.* New York: UN General Assembly.

UNDP (United Nations Development Programme) and NSC (Committee for Planning and Investment, National Statistics Centre). 2006. *International trade and human development, Lao PDR.* National Human Development Report. Vientiane.

UNESCAP (United National Economic and Social Commission for Asia and the Pacific). 2001. "Key statistics of population and households in Nong Khai." Bangkok.

UNIAP (United Nations Inter-Agency Project on Human Trafficking in the Greater Mekong Sub-region). 2003. *UNIAP proposal for phase II—19 Feb.* Bangkok.

———. 2006. "About human trafficking." http://www.no-trafficking.org/.

———. 2008a. *SIREN human trafficking data sheet.* Vientiane.

———. 2008b. *Statistical methods for estimating numbers of trafficking victims.* Strategic Information Response Network (SIREN), UNIAP, Phase III. Bangkok.

———. 2008c. *The state of counter-trafficking: A tool for donors.* Strategic Information Response Network (SIREN), UNIAP, Phase III. Bangkok.

UNIAP and Ministry of Labour and Social Welfare, Lao PDR. 2001. *Trafficking in women and children in the Lao PDR: Initial observations.* Vientiane.

UNIAP, UNICEF Laos, and Ministry of Labour and Social Welfare, Lao PDR. 2004. *TRACE: Trafficking from Community to Exploitation*. Vientiane.

UNIAP and UNIFEM (United Nations Development Fund for Women). N.d. *Trafficking in persons: A gender and rights perspective*. Bangkok.

UNICEF (United Nations Children's Fund) and Ministry of Labour and Social Welfare, Lao PDR. 2001. *How I got here: Commercial sexual exploitation of children in the Lao PDR*. Vientiane.

———. 2004. *Broken promises shattered dreams: A profile of child trafficking in the Lao PDR*. Vientiane.

UNODC (United Nations Office on Drugs and Crime). 2002. *Results of a pilot survey of forty selected organized criminal groups in sixteen countries*. UNODC.

———. 2006a. *Assistance for the implementation of the ECOWAS plan of action against trafficking in persons: Training manual*. New York: United Nations.

———. 2006b. *Toolkit to combat trafficking in persons: Global Programme against Trafficking in Human Beings*. New York: United Nations.

———. 2006c. *Trafficking in persons: Global patterns*. UNODC.

———. 2009. *Global report on trafficking in persons*. UNODC.

US GAO (United States Government Accountability Office). 2006. *Human trafficking: Better data, strategy, and reporting needed to enhance U.S. anti-trafficking efforts abroad*. GAO-06-825. Washington, DC.

US State Department. 2006. *Trafficking in persons report*. US State Department Publication 11335, Office of the Under Secretary for Global Affairs.

———. 2007. *Trafficking in persons report*. US State Department Publication 11407, Office of the Under Secretary for Democracy and Global Affairs and Bureau of Public Affairs.

———. 2008. *Guidelines for anti-trafficking-in-persons project proposals through the Office to Monitor and Combat Trafficking in Persons (G/TIP)*.

Vallee, Julie, Marc Souris, Florence Fournet, Audrey Bochaton, Virginie Mobillion, Karine Peyronnie, and Gerard Salem. 2007. "Sampling in health geography: Reconciling geographical objectives and probabilistic methods; An example of a health survey in Vientiane (Lao PDR)." *Emerging Themes in Epidemiology* 4 (6): 1–23.

Van Esterik, Penny. 1992. "Thai prostitution and the medical gaze." In *Gender and development in Southeast Asia: Proceedings of the twentieth meetings of the Canadian Council for Southeast Asian Studies, York University, October 18–20, 1991*, ed. Penny Van Esterik and John Van Esterik, 133–150. Montreal: Canadian Asian Studies Association, McGill University.

———. 1996. "Nurturance and reciprocity in Thai studies." In *State power and culture*, ed. E. P. Durrenberger, 22–46. New Haven, CT: Yale University Southeast Asia Studies.

———. 2000. *Materializing Thailand*. Oxford and New York: Berg.

van Schendel, Willem, and Itty Abraham, eds. 2005. *Illicit flows and crimi-*

nal things: States, borders, and the other side of globalization. Indianapolis: Indiana University Press.

van Ufford, Philip Quarles. 1993. "Knowledge and ignorance in the practices of development policy." In *An anthropological critique of development: The growth of ignorance*, ed. M. Hobart, 135–159. London: Routledge.

Väyrynen, Raimo. 2003. *Illegal immigration, human trafficking, and organized crime.* World Institute for Development Economics Research of the United Nations University.

Vientiane Times. 2006. "Lao government steps up effort to combat human trafficking." 23 August.

———. 2007a. "Human trafficking action plan takes shape." http://www.vientianetimes.org.la/FreeContent/Current_Human.htm.

———. 2007b. "Lao man seeks fortune in Thailand." http://www.vientianetimes.org.la/Previous_229/Feature/Feature_lao.htm.

———. 2007c. "Report reveals causes of human trafficking." http://www.vientianetimes.org.la/Previous_224/Feature/Feature_human.htm.

———. 2007d. "Thai govt to repatriate all Lao Hmong by 2008." http://www.vientianetimes.org.la/Previous_224/Current/Current_thai.htm.

Vila, Pablo. 2003. "Introduction: Border ethnographies." In *Ethnography at the border*, ed. Pablo Vila, ix–xxxv. Minneapolis: University of Minnesota Press.

Walker, Andrew. 1999. *The legend of the golden boat: Regulation, trade and traders in the borderlands of Laos, Thailand, Burma and China.* Surrey, England: Curzon Press.

———. 2009. *Tai lands and Thailand: Community and the state in Southeast Asia.* Copenhagen: NIAS Press.

Warning, Christina. 2003. *Jumping on the UN–human rights treaties bandwagon.* Australian National University. http://www.aseanfocus.com/asiananalysis/article.cfm?articleID=680.

Weitzer, Ronald. 2005. "Flawed theory and method in studies of prostitution." *Violence against Women* 11 (7): 934–949.

———. 2007. "The social construction of sex trafficking: Ideology and institutionalization of a moral crusade." *Politics and Society* 35:447–475.

Westerfjell, Torunn P. 2002. "Lilja 4 ever." NRK. http://www.nrk.no/nyheter/kultur/2156627.html.

Wheaton, Elizabeth, Edward J. Schauer, and Thomas V. Galli. 2010. "Economics of human trafficking." Special issue, *International Migration* 48 (4): 114–141.

Whittaker, Andrea. 1999. "Women and capitalist transformation in a northeastern Thai village." In Jackson and Cook 1999, 43–62.

Wille, Christina. 2001. *Thailand–Lao People's Democratic Republic and Thailand-Myanmar border areas: Trafficking in children into the worst forms of child labour; A rapid assessment.* Geneva: ILO-IPEC (International

Labour Organization, International Programme on the Elimination of Child Labour).

Wilson, Ara. 2004. *The intimate economies of Bangkok: Tomboys, tycoons, and Avon ladies in the global city.* Berkeley: University of California Press.

Wolff, Ismail. 2006. "Resettlement hopes feed traffickers." *ThaiDay*, 23 August. http://www.manager.co.th/IHT/ViewNews.aspx?NewsID =9490000107114.

Wolff, Jackson M., and Louise Donnan. 1970. "Prostitution in Laos: A sociological study." *International Journal of Anthropology and the Social Sciences* 34:178–192.

Wong, Diana. 2005. "The rumor of trafficking." In van Schendel and Abraham 2005, 69–100.

Woodiwiss, Michael. 2000. "Organized crime—The dumbing of discourse." In *The British Criminology Conference: Selected Proceedings*, vol. 3, *Papers from the British Society of Criminology Conference, Liverpool, 1999*, ed. George Mair and Roger Tarling. British Society of Criminology.

Yambi, Olivia. 2006. "Opening remarks: COMMIT strategic planning and prioritization meeting." Vientiane: United Nations.

Yang, Li, director. 2007. *Blind mountain* (film). China.

Yates, David, director. 2006. *Sex traffic* (film). United Kingdom.

Zelizer, Viviana A. 1998. "The proliferation of social currencies." In Callon et al. 1998, 58–68.

Zhang, Sheldon, and Ko-Lin Chin. 2002. "Enter the dragon: Inside Chinese smuggling organizations." *Criminology* 40 (4): 737–767.

Zimmerman, Cathy. 2003. *WHO ethical and safety recommendations for interviewing trafficked women.* Geneva: World Health Organization.

Index

About the Author

Sverre Molland is a social anthropologist with ten years of program and research experience in the Mekong region. He has published extensively on development aid and mobility in relation to discourses of human trafficking in mainland Southeast Asia. Dr. Molland teaches anthropology and development studies at the Australian National University and has previously worked as a project adviser for a regional anti-trafficking project implemented by the United Nations.

OTHER VOLUMES IN THE SERIES

Production Notes for
MOLLAND/THE PERFECT BUSINESS?

Cover design by Mardee Melton.

Series design by Richard Hendel.
Composition by Josie Herr with text and display in Goudy.

Printing and binding by Sheridan Books, Inc.

Printed on 60 lb. House White Text, 444 ppi.